The History and Use
OF
Hymns and Hymn-Tunes

The History and Use

OF

Hymns and Hymn-Tunes

BY THE

REV. DAVID R. BREED, D. D.

PROFESSOR IN THE WESTERN THEOLOGICAL
SEMINARY

CHICAGO   NEW YORK   TORONTO

FLEMING H. REVELL COMPANY

LONDON   EDINBURGH

MCMIII

CHICAGO: 63 WASHINGTON STREET
NEW YORK: 158 FIFTH AVENUE
TORONTO: 27 RICHMOND STREET, W.
LONDON: 21 PATERNOSTER SQUARE
EDINBURGH: 30 ST. MARY STREET

PREFACE

This book is the outgrowth of my own needs, as a teacher of practical theology. I desired a text-book from which my students might obtain a comprehensive knowledge of the history and use of sacred song, without being burdened with those technical details which a beginner has neither the time to master nor the ability to understand. I also desired a book in which the study of hymns and of tunes was combined.

No such book was at hand, and for several years I was compelled to refer my classes to various authors, some in hymnology, others in church music; supplementing their studies with explanatory lectures. This, however, became more and more unsatisfactory, and I therefore determined to supply my own needs. In so doing I hoped to supply also the needs of others and to furnish many besides theological students with an acceptable and useful guide to a large and increasingly interesting subject.

I have therefore included extended notice only of authors and composers of the first rank, or whose work bears some vital relation to the development of the hymn or of the hymn-tune. The volume is intended to be first of all a text-book, though I hope it may serve other useful purposes and be greatly blessed of Him whose praises we sing to those who would sing them "in a nobler, sweeter song."

v

My special thanks are due to the Rev. Louis F. Benson, D.D., and Professor Edward Dickinson for the use of copy-righted material. I am also under great obligations to my colleague, Professor Charles N. Boyd, instructor in church music in the Western Theological Seminary, for his kind revision of Part II. on hymn-tunes.

DAVID R. BREED.

CONTENTS

PART I: HYMNS

vii

Contents

PART I.—HYMNS

CHAPTER I

ANCIENT HYMNS

Sacred song seems to be the instinctive utterance of the human soul. Poetry and music are as old as the race, and they have been employed from the first in the service of religion. The sacred song of savage nations receives but rude expression. With the growth of intelligence and of language it becomes more elaborate and refined. Hymns in praise of the gods are therefore found among the most ancient specimens of literature.

It is said that the reputation of Homer was created by the number and beauty of his hymns, and many of them still remain in his poems.

The Greeks who followed him imitated his example. The Greek poets were hymn-writers. The Muses themselves were supposed to be chiefly engaged in the service of divine praise, and he who invoked them was expected to partake of the same occupation. At certain of the Greek games rewards were offered for the best hymns, and the young were stimulated to memorize them. So important was this considered to the maintenance of religion that we find the Emperor Julian, in his attempt to re-establish heathenism, urging the return to this custom, and arguing that the old Greek's hymns were the product of inspiration, similar to that which the Christians claimed for the Psalms of David.

It is quite clear from all this that while the Greek mythology contributed nothing to the Christian religion, the poetical development of Greek song had much to do with the form into which the early Greek hymns of the Christian church were subsequently cast.

But the Greeks were not alone in their devotion to sacred song. It prevailed among all the cultivated nations of antiquity. The singing of hymns was the largest part of the old Egyptian ritual. Four times a day—at sunrise, noon, sunset, and night—the priests regularly chanted the praises of their divinities, and it is not unlikely that the poetical genius of Moses himself was so cultivated, in the providence of God, that it might be consecrated to the worship of the One True God.

HEBREW HYMNS

Among the Hebrews the record of the use of sacred song begins with the beginning of their national life, though there is evidence that it had been long employed by their ancestors. The fugitives from Egyptian bondage had scarcely crossed the Red Sea when Moses and Miriam provided for the expression of their praise.   (Exodus xv.)

> "I will sing unto the LORD, for he hath triumphed gloriously;
> "The horse and his rider hath he thrown into the sea.
> "The LORD is my strength and song,
> "And he is become my salvation:
> "This is my God, and I will praise him;
> "My father's God, and I will exalt him.
> "The LORD is a man of war;
> "The LORD is his name," etc., etc.

It is evident that this is not the work of a novice; neither is it the expression of those to whom sacred song is an unpracticed art; for, making all proper allowance for the influence of inspiration, its human elements are indicative of thorough culture in this particular department of literature.

It was probably sung antiphonally; Moses and the men upon the one side, answered by Miriam and the women on the other side. It is thus the oldest specimen of choral song in all literature, and it is one of the finest. Scholars have united to give it most unqualified praise. It served also to some extent as a model for succeeding generations. Its various expressions are repeated in subsequent Scripture, and it fixed not only the Jewish form of divine praise, but also formulated the Jewish conception of their divine Deliverer as "A Man of War."

From this time Hebrew song is distinguished from that of all other nations, in that it was employed almost exclusively in the worship of Jehovah. The poetry of other nations covers a wide range of subjects; but not so the poetry of Israel. It seems to have been regarded as almost sacred in itself, and therefore it might not be prostituted to unworthy uses. For this reason, because its aim was so high, and guided by divine inspiration, the poetry of the Hebrews attained a rank incomparably beyond that of any other people; and this in spite of what might seem defects to the ordinary student of classic poetry. It has a form of its own—a form made manifest to the average reader of the Bible in its recent revisions.

It is not metrical; it cannot be "scanned"; yet it is poetical to the last degree, and by its peculiar structure admirably lends itself, as we find to-day, to lyrical purposes.   Indeed, when it is cast into meter it not only loses its distinctive literary quality, but is also shackled to a musical style to which it is not adapted and which impairs its quality.

In the progress of Hebrew history song was added to song until a rich and varied repertoire was gathered, which succeeding generations have found inexhaustible.   In the reign of David, and stimulated by his own example, a new impetus was given to the composition and rendering of sacred song.   The worship of the tabernacle was greatly enriched.   The service of song was distinctly organized on a hitherto unparalleled scale.   A great choir of some four thousand musicians and vocalists was gathered and trained; great religious musical festivals were organized, and systematic praise became a permanent feature of Hebrew worship.   These musicians were recruited from the Levites.   Asaph was the instrumental leader; Chenaniah the vocal leader.   There were three grand divisions: the Kothathites under Heman, the Gershonites under Asaph, and the Merarites under Ethan.   (See I Chronicles xv. and xvi.)   These men were also composers as well as performers, and a number of psalms are attributed to them as authors.

The provisions of David were extended under Solomon to the services of the Temple, and its choral music was probably the most magnificent which has ever been employed in the worship of God.

From this time sacred music was regularly taught in the Jewish schools and the people generally became proficients. By and by when they were transported to distant Babylon the reputation of their melodies excited the interest of their captors, who urged them to sing for them the songs of Zion. But the request was declined. Their inhospitable surroundings, their alien audiences, and their own pitiable condition conspired to hush the minstrelsy of Israel, and for a long generation their harps were left unstrung and their songs unsung. But upon the return from captivity both the composition and the practice of sacred song were resumed. It was continued in all the synagogues of the Dispersion and the old words to the old tunes resounded from the River Euphrates to the Pillars of Hercules.

In the time of Christ the ritual of the Temple was elaborated to a degree exceeded only in the days of Solomon. A large choir of Levites, assisted by some, selected for their special accomplishments, from those who had intermarried with Levitical families, led the praise of the worshipers. This choir was composed in the main of men and boys, but female singers were occasionally introduced. The psalms to be sung upon the several occasions were distinctly specified, one for each day of the week as follows: for the first day, Psalm xxiv.; for the second, Ps. xlviii.; for the third, Ps. lxxxii.; for the fourth, Ps. xciv.; for the fifth, Ps. lxxxi.; for the sixth, Ps. xciii.; for the seventh, Ps. xcii.; and others were indicated for festivals and similar special times. It all culminated on the last day of the Feast of Tabernacles, that "Great Day of the Feast," the day of the "Great Hosannah," the choir leading the multitudes in chanting Psalm lxxxii., while at intervals the priests blew their trumpets and the people bowed in solemn worship.

Such were the songs in which Jesus was trained; such the songs in which he joined with his disciples. The "hymn" which they sung at the conclusion of the Paschal Supper was probably the second portion of the *Hallel* (Ps. cxv. to cxviii.), or Ps. cxxxvi., which stands near the conclusion of the more modern ritual.

EARLY CHRISTIAN HYMNS

After the ascension of the Redeemer the members of the infant church continued for some time to use the songs of Jewish origin. But very soon they became possessed also of songs of their own, distinctively Christian. Some of these were the direct product of inspiration; others, if not inspired, were invested with peculiar sacredness.

There are eight of these most ancient Christian hymns, as follows:

1. The *Gloria in Excelcis;* called "*The Greater Doxology*" to distinguish it from the one which follows. It was also called the "Angelic Hymn" because its opening words are taken from the Angel's song at Bethlehem. Its authorship is not known, but it may be traced back to the early years of the second century. Its English form is:

CHAPTER I

ANCIENT HYMNS

Sacred song seems to be the instinctive utterance of the human soul. Poetry and music are as old as the race, and they have been employed from the first in the service of religion. The sacred song of savage nations receives but rude expression. With the growth of intelligence and of language it becomes more elaborate and refined. Hymns in praise of the gods are therefore found among the most ancient specimens of literature.

It is said that the reputation of Homer was created by the number and beauty of his hymns, and many of them still remain in his poems.

The Greeks who followed him imitated his example. The Greek poets were hymn-writers. The Muses themselves were supposed to be chiefly engaged in the service of divine praise, and he who invoked them was expected to partake of the same occupation. At certain of the Greek games rewards were offered for the best hymns, and the young were stimulated to memorize them. So important was this considered to the maintenance of religion that we find the Emperor Julian, in his attempt to re-establish heathenism, urging the return to this custom, and arguing that the old Greek's hymns were the product of inspiration, similar to that which the Christians claimed for the Psalms of David.

It is quite clear from all this that while the Greek mythology contributed nothing to the Christian religion, the poetical development of Greek song had much to do with the form into which the early Greek hymns of the Christian church were subsequently cast.

But the Greeks were not alone in their devotion to sacred song. It prevailed among all the cultivated nations of antiquity. The singing of hymns was the largest part of the old Egyptian ritual. Four times a day—at sunrise, noon, sunset, and night—the priests regularly chanted the praises of their divinities, and it is not unlikely that the poetical genius of Moses himself was so cultivated, in the providence of God, that it might be consecrated to the worship of the One True God.

HEBREW HYMNS

Among the Hebrews the record of the use of sacred song begins with the beginning of their national life, though there is evidence that it had been long employed by their ancestors. The fugitives from Egyptian bondage had scarcely crossed the Red Sea when Moses and Miriam provided for the expression of their praise.   (Exodus xv.)

> "I will sing unto the LORD, for he hath triumphed gloriously;
> "The horse and his rider hath he thrown into the sea.
> "The LORD is my strength and song,
> "And he is become my salvation:
> "This is my God, and I will praise him;
> "My father's God, and I will exalt him.
> "The LORD is a man of war;
> "The LORD is his name," etc., etc.

"Glory be to God on high and on earth peace, good will toward men. We praise thee, we bless thee, we worship thee, we glorify thee, we give thanks to thee for thy great glory, O Lord God, Heavenly King, God the Father Almighty. O Lord the Only-begotten Son, Jesus Christ; O Lord God, Lamb of God, Son of the Father, that takest away the sins of the world, have mercy upon us. Thou that takest away the sins of the world, have mercy upon us. Thou that takest away the sins of the world, receive our prayer. Thou that sittest at the right hand of God the Father, have mercy upon us. For thou only art holy; Thou only art the Lord; Thou only, O Christ, with the Holy Ghost, art most high in the glory of God the Father. Amen."

2. The *Gloria Patri;* called the "*Lesser Doxology.*" The first portion of this song, "Glory be to the Father and to the Son and to the Holy Ghost," was from the earliest times the common doxology of Christendom. Its closing portion was added by the Western Church after the rise of the Arian controversy: "As it was in the beginning, is now, and ever shall be world without end. Amen."

3. The "*Ter Sanctus.*" This is based on the "thrice holy" of Isaiah vi. 3 and Rev. iv. 8. It was introduced by various prefaces, as in the Episcopal Prayer-book, but always concluding "Therefore, with angels and archangels, and with all the company of heaven, we laud and magnify thy glorious Name, evermore praising thee and saying, Holy, Holy, Holy Lord God of hosts; heaven and earth are full of thy glory; Glory be to thee, O Lord, Most High. Amen." It was therefore called the *Cherubical Hymn*.

4. The *Hallelujah*. This was the response of the people to the call to praise. For many centuries it was used in its Hebrew form. In the liturgy of

the Episcopal Church it now appears as "Praise ye the Lord," by the officiating priest; with the response of the worshipers "The Lord's name be praised."

5. The *Benedicite*. This "Song of the Three Hebrew Children," taken from the Apocrapha, is a paraphrase of the forty-eighth Psalm. It may be found in the Episcopal Prayer-book, where it is used interchangeably with the *Te Deum*.

6. The *Nunc Dimittis*. So called from the Latin Vulgate's rendering of the aged Simeon's words (Luke ii. 29), and because it was generally sung in the evening worship, the *Evening Hymn*.

7. The *Magnificat*. The song of the Virgin Mary, so named from the Vulgate of the opening words. (Luke i. 46.)

8. The *Te Deum*, or *Te Deum Laudamus*, so called from its opening words. The authorship of this celebrated hymn is unknown. It is certainly of very ancient origin. The Latin version is doubtless based on a very early Greek original. The English version is familiar to all worshiping Christians, as its use obtains in all denominations throughout the world. The opening lines of the Latin version are subjoined.

"Te Deum laudamus, te Dominum confitemur.
"Te æternum patrem omnis terra veneratur.
"Tibi omnes angeli, tibi cœli et universæ potestates.
"Tibi Cherubim et Seraphim inaccessibili voce proclamant.
"Sanctus, Sanctus, Sanctus Dominus Deus Sabaoth."

To these may also be added another hymn from the Gospel by Luke, thus including all the advent songs recorded in his book. This is the *Benedictus*, the

song of the aged priest Zacharias on the birth of his
son John.   (Luke i. 68.)

Such doubtless was the character, and such perhaps were the very words of the hymns to which
Pliny refers in his letter to the Emperor Trajan, about
110 A.D., in which he testifies that the Christians
offered praise to Christ as God.   His letter at least
indicates that at the opening of the second century
the Christian Church was using in its worship hymns
other than those of Jewish origin.

As time passed on the number of these Christian
hymns multiplied.   We learn from Eusebius that in
the first half of the third century there was a profu-
sion of sacred song, very little of which now remains.
The only entire hymn belonging to this period, which
has come down to us, is that attributed to Clemens of
Alexandria, about 220 A.D., though he himself
attributes it to an earlier author.

Titus Flavius Clemens was a convert from pagan-
ism.   Ordained a presbyter he became the successor
of Pantænus in the catechetical school of Alexandria.
Origen was one of his pupils.   The English translation of his hymn below is by the Rev. Henry Martyn
Dexter, D.D., editor of *The Congregationalist*,
Boston.

> "Shepherd of tender youth,
>   Guiding in love and truth
>   Through devious ways;
>   Christ our triumphant King,
>   We come thy name to sing;
>   Hither our children bring
>   To shout thy praise.

"Thou art our holy Lord,
The all-subduing Word,
  Healer of strife:
Thou didst thyself abase,
That from sin's deep disgrace
Thou mightest save our race,
  And give us life.

"Thou art the great High Priest;
Thou hast prepared the feast
  Of heavenly love;
While in our mortal pain
None calls on thee in vain;
Help thou dost not disdain,
  Help from above.

"Ever be thou our guide,
Our shepherd and our pride,
  Our staff and song:
Jesus, thou Christ of God,
By thy perennial word
Lead us where thou hast trod,
  Make our faith strong.

"So now, and till we die,
Sound we thy praises high,
  And joyful sing:
Infants, and the glad throng
Who to thy Church belong,
Unite to swell the song
  To Christ our King."

CHAPTER II

GREEK AND LATIN HYMNS

The first systematic attempts in Christian hymnody were the outgrowth of orthodox opposition to heresy. The oldest distinctive hymn-writers were Gnostics, and following them the Arians, who sought to propagate their errors, as Luther long after sought to propagate the truths of his reform, through sacred song.

This began in the second century, when Bardesanes, of the Syrian Church, wrote hymns in imitation of the psalms, but with Gnostic additions. He was followed by Valentinus of Alexandria and by others, until the songs of the heretics had received wide circulation.

So far as we can find, however, no concerted attempt was made to counteract this influence until the early years of the fourth century. When, under Constantine, Christianity became the religion of the state, the songs employed in public worship assumed new and greater importance as a part of the liturgy of the church; then it was that the leaders of the orthodox party adopted distinct measures for the introduction of a suitable body of Christian hymns. The hymns of Arius and of the Gnostics were not only the more numerous, but also the more popular, inasmuch as they inculcated practical graces and duties, while the orthodox hymns were few in number and consisted chiefly of dogmatic formulas. But a new era in hymnology was now at hand, in which the great Greek hymns, in large variety, were to be given to the church.

The herald of this important movement however was not a Greek, but a Syrian. He is known in history as Ephrem (or Ephraim) Syrus. He was born at Nisibis in northern Mesopotamia, A.D. 307, and died at Edessa, 373. He was the most distinguished father of the Syrian Church, and a voluminous writer on theological and kindred subjects. His zeal for the faith was doubtless heightened by his attendance upon the Council of Nicæa, A.D. 325, when he was only eighteen years old, and thence until his death he was the champion of orthodoxy. His hymns were written in the same meters as those of the Gnostics, evidently to advance his purpose, and exercised a mighty influence.

The great hymnic era was thereby introduced and a large number of hymnographers followed him in both Syriac and Greek. So far, however, as known to the writer, there is no translation of any of his hymns in the collections now in use.

GREEK HYMNS

The next great name of this era, and the first of its Greek hymnographers, is Gregorius Nazianzenus (St. Gregory Nazianzen). He was born in the town whose name is affixed to his own, in Cappadocia, A.D. 325. His father was a bishop, and he himself

became one.   He is reckoned as one of the greatest
of the Greek fathers.   His life was full of adventure.
His education, began in Cappadocia, was continued in
Alexandria and Athens, continuing for ten years in
the latter place, where he was a fellow-student of
Julian the Apostate.   After serving as his father's
coadjutor he was made bishop of Constantinople
(A.D. 379), where he spent two years.   The closing
years of his life were passed in retirement, during
which most of his hymns were written.

The following verses from the translation of one
of Gregory's finest hymns is from "Songs and Hymns
of Earliest Greek Christian Poets," by the Rev.
Allen W. Chatfield of England.   One may derive
from it a good idea of his fine culture, his elevated
style, and his devout orthodoxy.

> "O thou the One supreme o'er all!
>   For by what other name
>   May we upon thy greatness call
>   Or celebrate thy fame?
>
> "How, unapproached, shall mind of man
>   Descry thy dazzling throne?
>   And pierce and find thee out, and scan
>   Where thou dost dwell alone.
>
> "Unuttered thou! all uttered things
>   Have had their birth from thee;
>   The one unknown, from thee the springs
>   Of all we know and see.
>
> "And lo! all things abide in thee,
>   And through the complex whole
>   Thou spread'st thine own divinity,
>   Thyself of all the goal."

The formative period in Greek Church poetry continued, after Gregory, until about 650 A.D. It was at its height for the two following centuries, until the year 850. Then followed the period of decline and decay, ending with the fall of Constantinople, in 1453. The hymns of the various poets who flourished during these periods are best known to the worshipers of the present day in the translations of the Rev. John Mason Neale, D.D., whose important services will be noted hereafter. Those below may be taken as illustrations, in chronological order. They may be found at length in many hymn-books.

1. Anatolius. A hymn-writer of the seventh or eighth century, of whom very little is known apart from his hymns. He is not to be confounded with St. Anatolius, bishop of Constantinople, who died 458.

"Fierce was the billow, dark was the night," and

"The day is past and over."

2. St. Andrew of Jerusalem, died 732. There is little of note attached to his name except his influence on Greek hymnody.

"Christian, dost thou see them?"

3. St. Cosmas, the Melodist, died about 760. He early retired with his foster-brother, St. John of Damascus, to the monastery of St. Sabas in the Kedron Valley, from which issued much of the best literature of the ancient Greek Church.

"Christ is born, tell forth his fame."

4. St. John of Damascus, died about 780. He is esteemed the greatest of all the Greek hymn-writers.

"The day of resurrection."

5. St. Stephen, nephew of St. John, died 794. He was also an inmate of St. Sabas, where he was placed by his uncle when he was only ten years of age and where he lived for fifty years. Doubtless he would be voted to-day the most beloved of all the Greek hymn-writers, were they judged by their translations.

"Art thou weary, art thou languid?"

6. St. Joseph, the hymnographer, about 840. His life was passed in Constantinople. He wrote more hymns than any other of his class.

"Let the church new anthems raise."

LATIN HYMNS

It is an interesting fact that the production of Latin hymns was stimulated at the first by the same influences which developed the Greek hymnody. Hilary of Poitiers, banished to Phrygia by Constantius, was incited by the singing of the Arians, which he there heard, to write similar songs for the propagation of the orthodox faith. The date of his birth, in the city whose name he bears, is not certainly known. He became its bishop about 350. His learning, zeal, and courage were all remarkable. He defended Athanasius in the council of Beziers, and even ventured to publicly rebuke Constantius himself, declaring him to be the antichrist. For this he was compelled to go into exile. Restored to liberty at the command of Julian, he traveled extensively throughout Europe in defense of Catholic truth. His enemies at last commanded sufficient influence to compel his final retirement to his own city, where he died 367.

The poetical work of Hilary was adopted by Ambrose, bishop of Milan, who, because not only of his great work in hymnody, but also in church music, is called the father of Latin church song. He died in 397.

After Ambrose comes Prudentius, who has been called "The first Christian poet." He was born near Saragossa, in Spain, about 348. His conversion occurred late in life when he was fifty-seven years of age. Up to that time he had been engaged in various secular pursuits, which he now abandoned for the service of the church. He died about 413. It will thus be seen that the earliest Latin hymn-writers and the earliest Greek ones were contemporaries.

From this time the number of Latin hymns continued to increase and their quality to improve until the eleventh and twelfth centuries—the golden age of Latin hymnody. Thence there is decadence until the fourteenth century, and with the fifteenth the era of Latin hymnody is closed.

The Latin hymns not only surpass the Greek in number, but also in quality. The special characteristic of the Greek hymn is its objectiveness. The Greek poet contemplated Revelation in itself, and found his delight therein. He seldom regarded himself. His themes were the divine perfections, the divine out-goings, or the divine incarnation in Christ. With the Latin poet it was otherwise. He was more of a mystic. While not oblivious to the high themes which engaged the Greek mind, he added a tender subjectiveness and engaged himself with the personal appropriation of divine redemption. The varied experiences of the disciple of Jesus furnished him with subjects, and in consequence his work has continued to commend itself to the heart of Christendom.

Greek hymnody has in it very little of value for the ordinary worshiper of the present day, and what value it has grows less and less. But Latin hymnody has in it very much of value, and value that is ever on the increase. Let this be borne in mind as we proceed.

Another distinctive feature of the Latin hymnody should also be remarked—its absolute departure from the form of the classic models of poetry, in the substitution of accent for quantity and in the addition of rhyme. The change was not effected at once. The early hymn-writers clung to the classic meters, but as Archbishop Trench remarks, in his "Sacred Latin Poetry," "a true instinct must have told the church at once, or after a very few trials, that these were not the forms which she required. A struggle, therefore, commenced from the first, between the old heathen form and the new Christian spirit. The new wine went on fermenting in the old bottles till it burst them asunder; but not to be spilt and lost in the process, but to be gathered into nobler chalices." The result was the varied form of the evangelical song, the form which it still retains, the graceful alliance of poetry and religion, the very climax of refined literature. This we owe to the great hymn-writers of the Latin Church.

The so-called Seven Great Hymns of the Latin Church are: (1) *Laus Patriæ Cælestis*, by Bernard of Cluny; (2) *Veni Sancte Spiritus*, by Hermannus Contractus, according to Duffield, though generally attributed to King Robert II. of France; (3) *Veni Creator Spiritus*, authorship very uncertain, probably Rabanus Maurus, bishop of Mainz, (4) *Dies Iræ*, by

Thomas of Celano; (5) *Stabat Mater;* and (6) *Mater Speciosa*, by Jacobus de Benedictis; (7) *Vexilla Regis*, by Fortunatus.

Some of these hymns are truly "catholic." They are cherished and sung by all Christian denominations the world over. They will be further considered below. Others, such as the *Stabat Mater* and *Mater Speciosa*, are too decidedly Roman to receive any recognition by Protestants.

THE TWO BERNARDS

We are particularly concerned, however, with those Latin hymn-writers whose legacies have been treasured by the church at large, and whose words are sung to-day by all worshiping congregations in devout homage to God and sincere gratitude to their authors.

Judged by this standard Bernard of Cluny holds beyond all question the highest place. Very little is known concerning him. He was born in Morlaix in Brittany of English parents. His monastic life was probably included between the years 1122 and 1156. He wrote but one poem—like so many other great hymn-writers. This is generally known by the title given above, *Laus Patriæ Cœlestis*, but this was not his own title. It was affixed by Archbishop Trench to the selected one hundred lines with which the church is most familiar. The original poem contains nearly three thousand lines, and is entitled *De Contemptu Mundi*. It is a lamentation over the wickedness of the world—a veritable jeremiad. Very naturally, however, the author turns from his "con-

tempt of the world" to sing the "praise of the celestial
fatherland," and thus was produced that wonderful
passage which has evoked the praises of Christendom
for its author and voices the praises of Christendom
to its God.

The poem is written in a most peculiar meter,
almost impossible to reproduce in English and make
good sense. Translators have been obliged to take
some liberties with it, altering somewhat its expressions, but preserving its spirit. Its opening lines are

"Hora novissima, tempora pessima sunt, vigilemus!
"Ecce minaciter, imminet arbiter, ille supremus."

This has been carefully rendered,

"These are the latter times,
"These are not better times,
"Let us stand waiting!
"Lo, how with awfulness,
"He first in lawfulness
"Comes arbitrating."

This is very faithful to the original, but it is wretched
English poetry. So it is with the entire poem, when
the translator attempts a literal version.

That portion of the poem known as *Laus Patriæ
Cælestis* begins with the lines

"Hic breve vivitur, hic breve plangitur, hic breve fletur;
"Non breve vivere, non breve plangere retribuetur;
"O retributio! stat brevis actio vita perennis;
"O retributio! Cœlica mansio stat lue plenis;
"Quid datur et quibus? Æther egentibus et cruce dignis,
"Sidera vermibus, optima sontibus, astra malignis."

There is marvelous beauty of diction and marvelous
pathos in this for those who can read it with the
understanding. The English rendering by Dr.

Neale departs from its phraseology, but appeals with all the beauty and pathos of the original to our deepest hearts.

"Brief life is here our portion;
    Brief sorrow, short-lived care;
The life that knows no ending,
    The tearless life, is there:
Oh, happy retribution!
    Short toil, eternal rest;
For mortals, and for sinners,
    A mansion with the blest!"

The hymn known as *Jerusalem the Golden* is taken from this same portion of the poem.   In the Latin it begins:

"Urbs Syon aurea, patria lactea, cive decora,
"Omne cor obrius, omnibus obstruis, et cor et ora.
"Nescio, nescio quæ jubilatio lux tibi qualis,
"Quam socialia guadia, gloria quam specialis;
"Laude studens ea tollere, mens mea victa fatiscit;
"O bona gloria, vincor; in omnia laus tua vicit."

Dr. Neale's translation is as follows:

"Jerusalem the golden,
    With milk and honey blest!
Beneath thy contemplation
    Sink heart and voice oppressed:
I know not, oh, I know not,
    What social joys are there,
What radiancy of glory,
    What light beyond compare.

"They stand, those halls of Zion,
    All jubilant with song,
And bright with many an angel,
    And all the martyr throng;
The Prince is ever in them,
    The daylight is serene;
The pastures of the blessed
    Are decked in glorious sheen.

"There is the throne of David;
   And there, from care released,
The song of them that triumph,
   The shout of them that feast;
And they who, with their Leader,
   Have conquered in the fight
For ever and for ever
   Are clad in robes of white."

As there is no question with regard to the first of all the Latin hymn-writers, judged by our standard, so also there is no question with regard to the second. And the second is not far behind the first, while together the two form a class of which they are the only members.

The second place belongs to Bernard of Clairvaux. In marked contrast to Bernard of Cluny, the details of his life are fully known. He was born near Dijon in Burgundy, of a noble family, in 1091; became the first abbot of Clairvaux in 1115; died in 1153. He was the most notable figure of his times, and his words and works made a deep and lasting impression not only upon his own age, but upon all succeeding ages. He is best known by his founding of a religious order, his discomfiture of Abelard, his preaching of the second Crusade. But these, important as they were, were but a small part of his great and varied labors. Archbishop Trench well says: "Probably no man during his lifetime ever exercised a *personal* influence in Christendom equal to his; the stayer of popular commotions, the queller of heresies, the umpire between princes and kings, the counselor of popes." No student of the church should fail to read his life in one of the many forms in which it has been presented.

The hymn of Bernard which is dearest to the heart of the modern church is that entitled "De Nomine Jesu," though more generally known by its first line. It originally consisted of fifty stanzas of four lines each, the first two stanzas being

"Jesu, dulcis memoria
    Dans vera cordi gaudia
    Sed super mel et omnia
    Ejus dulcis præsentia.

"Nil canitur suavius,
    Nil auditur jucundius,
    Nil cogitatur dulcius
    Quam Jesus Dei Filius."

Long before this hymn was rendered into English it was one of the favorite songs of devoted souls. The knights who kept guard over the holy sepulchre at Jerusalem sang it in their bivouacs. It has been translated again and again, and it will continue to invite the labor of the hymn-writers of the future. It is most acceptable to-day in the version of the Rev. Edward Caswall.

"Jesus, the very thought of thee
    With sweetness fills my breast;
But sweeter far thy face to see
    And in thy presence rest.

"Nor voice can sing, nor heart can frame,
    Nor can the memory find
A sweeter sound than thy blest name,
    O Saviour of mankind!

"O Hope of every contrite heart!
    O Joy of all the meek!
To those who fall how kind thou art!
    How good to those who seek!

"But what to those who find?   Ah! this,
 Nor tongue nor pen can show;
 The love of Jesus, what it is,
 None but his loved ones know.

"Jesus, our only joy be thou,
 As thou our prize wilt be;
 Jesus, be thou our glory now,
 And through eternity."

Duffield says of this, "It is supremely fine in spirit
and expression."   And Robinson says, "One might
call this poem the finest in the world and be within
the limits of all extravagance."

Another portion of the same hymn is given in
Caswall's translation,

"O Jesus! King most wonderful."

Dr. Ray Palmer also has added to his own reputation
and to that of Bernard in another translation, beginning

"Jesus, thou joy of loving hearts."

But our indebtedness to Bernard does not rest with
this single poem.   Scarcely inferior to it is his *Salve
caput cruentatem*.   This is the second part of a
hymn entitled "Oratio Rhythmica ad Christum a
Cruce Pendentem," in seven portions, in which the
author addresses various members of the body of the
Saviour as he hangs upon the cross.

The second portion is "Ad Faciem."

"Salve caput cruentatum,
 Totum spinis coronatum,
 Conquassatum, vulneratum
 Arundine verberatum
     Facie sputis illita."

The translation of this hymn comes to us through

the German in a most interesting manner.   First we have Paul Gerhardt's "O Haupt voll Blut und Wunden," then by the translation of the German hymn the beautiful English lines of the Rev. Dr. James W. Alexander:

"O sacred Head, now wounded,
    With grief and shame weighed down,
Now scornfully surrounded
    With thorns, thine only crown;
O sacred Head, what glory,
    What bliss, till now was thine!
Yet, though despised and gory,
    I joy to call thee mine.

"What thou, my Lord, hast suffered
    Was all for sinners' gain;
Mine, mine was the transgression,
    But thine the deadly pain;
Lo, here I fall, my Saviour!
    'Tis I deserved thy place;
Look on me with thy favor,
    Vouchsafe to me thy grace.

"What language shall I borrow,
    To thank thee, dearest Friend,
For this, thy dying sorrow,
    Thy pity without end?
Lord, make me thine forever,
    Nor let me faithless prove:
Oh let me never, never,
    Abuse such dying love.

"Be near when I am dying,
    Oh, show thy cross to me!
And for my succor flying,
    Come, Lord, and set me free!
These eyes, new faith receiving,
    From Jesus shall not move;
For he who dies believing,
    Dies safely through thy love."

Has not the biographer of Bernard well said, "They canonized him in 1174; but it is better to have written a song for all saints than to be found in any breviary."

THOMAS OF CELANO

We have spoken in these notices of "our standard," that is, the usage of Protestant worship. But we ought not to close this account of the great Latin hymns without special reference to that splendid poem which has been praised beyond all of its class, the *Dies Iræ*. Its author was Thomas of Celano, a Franciscan monk. Its opening verses are as follows:

"Dies iræ, dies illa
Solvet sæclum in favilla,
Teste David cum Sibylla.

"Quantus tremor est futurus,
Quando Judex est venturus,
Cuncta stricte discussurus.

"Tuba, mirum spargens sonum
Per sepulchra regionum,
Coget omnes ante thronum.

"Mors stupedit et natura,
Quum resurget creatura,
Judicanti responsura.

"Liber scriptus proferetui,
In quo totum continetur,
De quo mundus judicetur."

Dr. Robinson, in his "Annotations," says of this hymn, "It stands pre-eminent not only because of the grandeur of the theme, but also from the perfection of its form and rhythm," and quotes from an English critic, "The meter so grandly devised, fitted to bring

out the noblest powers of the Latin language, the
solemn effect of the triple rhyme—like blow following
blow of the hammer on the anvil—the majestic, una-
dorned plainness of the style—these merits, with many
more, have given the 'Dies Iræ' a foremost place
among the masterpieces of sacred song.'' The translation of this hymn has been attempted again and
again; about one hundred and sixty times in English.

The one below is Dean Stanley's version of Part I.

"Day of wrath, oh, dreadful day,
    When this world shall pass away,
    And the heavens together roll,
    Shriv'ling like a parchéd scroll,
    Long foretold by saint and sage,
    David's harp, and Sibyl's page.

"Day of terror, day of doom,
    When the Judge at last shall come;
    Through the deep and silent gloom,
    Shrouding every human tomb,
    Shall the Archangel's trumpet tone
    Summon all before the throne.

"Then shall nature stand aghast,
    Death himself be overcast;
    Then, at her Creator's call,
    Near and distant, great and small,
    Shall the whole creation rise
    Waiting for the great assize.

'Then the writing shall be read
    Which shall judge the quick and dead;
    Then the Lord of all our race
    Shall appoint to each his place;
    Every wrong shall be set right,
    Every secret brought to light.''

Some other important Latin hymns will be discussed
hereafter under the names of their English translators.

CHAPTER III

GERMAN HYMNS

The German hymns outnumber those in any other language, the evangelical singers alone having produced about eighty thousand.

The Germans have always been a music-loving people. It is not that they simply enjoy listening to the singing of others, but they particularly enjoy singing themselves. Germany is the very home of choral music to this day, and the large majority of musicians throughout Europe and North America are of German origin.

We find therefore that from the earliest times the hymn was the natural expression of German religion. Many of the so-called Latin hymns, indeed, are Latin only in language; their authors were Germans. And when congregational singing was generally abandoned by the Roman Church, the people of Germany were still permitted a part in public praise—their musical instincts could not be wholly repressed. But the part was so small that the people determined that if they could not sing inside the churches they would at least sing outside of them. There were sacred poets who translated the old Latin hymns into the vernacular and added original ones and these were heartily sung at festivals, on pilgrimages, and similar occasions.

These have not descended in any number to our

generation for several reasons.   In the days of papal
Germany they were discountenanced and subsequently
Protestant Germany discarded them.   Still there
were some hymns, written by those among whom the
Protestant spirit was already kindling, which continued to exercise their influence, and were preserved in
the Reformation.   Chief among the hymn-writers of
this period was Heinrich of Laufenburg, a monk of
the monastery of the Knights of St. John at Strass-
burg, which he entered in 1445.   Most of his hymns,
like the others of his day, were written in praise of
the Virgin or other saints, but some were evangelical
in form and spirit.   They were generally accommo-
dations of secular ballads, transformed by the substitution of religious terms.   Here is a verse of one
founded on a popular song, entitled "Innsbruck, I
must forsake thee":

> "O world, I must forsake thee,
> And far away betake me
> To seek my native shore;
> So long I've dwelt in sadness
> I wish not now for gladness
> Earth's joys for me are o'er."

Heinrich's sentiment was exceeding sweet and tender.
It would be hard to find a lovelier cradle-song than
his, beginning

> "Ah, Jesu Christ, my Lord most dear,
> As thou wast once an infant here,
> So give this little child, I pray,
> Thy grace and blessings day by day.
> Ah Jesu, Lord divine,
> Guard me this babe of mine."

The followers of John Huss, Bohemians and Moravians, gave special attention to popular praise. In 1504 Lucas of Prague, the Bohemian bishop, collected four hundred of the best German hymns, printed and published them. This is worthy of particular note, since this is the first example of a hymn-book provided for congregational use.

LUTHER

With the Reformation we come to a most important era in the development of hymnody, and chiefly through the indomitable faith, the untiring labor, and the prophetic foresight of the great Luther. He who gave to the people in their own tongue the Bible and the catechism, gave them also the hymn-book, as one has well said, "So that God might speak directly to them in his Word and that they might directly answer him in their songs."

The great reformer is also the greatest of German hymnists. He began to write hymns in 1523, and continued to do so for twenty years, yet with such a high regard for quality, rather than quantity, that he averaged only one a year.

His first German hymn-book appeared in 1524. It contained only eight hymns, four of them by Luther. He published in all about twenty-one originals, about the same number of translations from the Latin, and a few modifications of earlier German hymns. The effect of this work in the spread of the Reformation is too well known to require mention. "The whole people," they said, "is singing itself into this Lutheran doctrine."

Luther's greatest hymn is his *Ein Feste Burg*, so much so that it is generally known by pre-eminence as "Luther's Hymn"—as though it was his only one. He drew his inspiration for it from the 46th Psalm: "God is our refuge and strength, a very present help in trouble." The date of its composition is uncertain. It was soon known, however, to the whole body of Protestants, and inspired them with such courage that Heine has well called it "The Marseillaise of the Reformation." It has been translated into English a number of times. Three of these translations are found in our various hymn-books, one by Miss Winkworth, one by Thomas Carlyle, one by Dr. Hedge. The last is gradually displacing the others, proving the most acceptable version. The translator, the Rev. Frederick Henry Hedge, D.D., was born 1805, in Cambridge, Massachusetts. He graduated at Harvard University, and was settled over a Unitarian church at Bangor, Maine.

What gives to this hymn peculiar interest and power to-day is that it is always sung to the tune probably composed by Luther; both words and music are his own.

> "A mighty fortress is our God,
>   A bulwark never failing;
>   Our Helper he, amid the flood
>   Of mortal ills prevailing.
> For still our ancient foe
> Doth seek to work his woe;
> His craft and power are great,
> And armed with cruel hate,
>   On earth is not his equal.

> "Did we in our own strength confide,
>   Our striving would be losing;
> Were not the right man on our side,
>   The man of God's own choosing.
> Dost ask who that may be?
> Christ Jesus, it is he;
> Lord Sabaoth is his name,
> From age to age the same,
>   And he must win the battle.

> "And though this world, with devils filled,
>   Should threaten to undo us;
> We will not fear, for God hath willed
>   His truth to triumph through us.
> Let goods and kindred go,
> This mortal life also:
> The body they may kill:
> God's truth abideth still,
>   His kingdom is for ever."

A number of Luther's hymns may be found in most collections. We need not quote them. Perhaps that which ranks next to "Ein Feste Burg" in popular estimation, is his *Gelobet seist Du, Jesus Christ*. The English translation first appeared in the "Sabbath Hymn-book," Andover, 1858. No name was attached to it, and its author has not since been discovered. Its diction is so free and flowing, and the English idiom is so carefully followed, especially in the beautiful antithesis with which the hymn abounds, that one would not suspect a foreign original. Yet it is only the translation of a translation; for Luther himself obtained it by the free rendering of an old Latin hymn of the ninth century.

> "All praise to thee, eternal Lord,
>   Clothed in a garb of flesh and blood;

Choosing a manger for thy throne,
While worlds on worlds are thine alone!

"Once did the skies before thee bow;
A virgin's arms contain thee now;
Angels, who did in thee rejoice,
Now listen for thine infant voice.

"A little child, thou art our guest,
That weary ones in thee may rest;
Forlorn and lowly is thy birth,
That we may rise to heaven from earth.

"Thou comest in the darksome night
To make us children of the light;
To make us, in the realms divine,
Like thine own angels round thee shine.

"All this for us thy love hath done:
By this to thee our love is won;
For this we tune our cheerful lays,
And shout our thanks in ceaseless praise."

CO-LABORERS OF LUTHER

In the publication of his hymn-books Luther enlisted the co-operation of a number of friends, and some of their productions became as popular as his own. Justus Jonas, his colleague at the University of Wittenberg, gave special attention to the versification of the psalms, selecting for his purpose those which had a special application for the trying times in which he lived. Some of them remind us of Luther's own hymn and show the influence of his example. Here is Jonas's rendering of the opening verses of Psalm cxxiv., "If it had not been the Lord who was on our side," etc.

"If God were not upon our side
   When foes around us rage,
Were not himself our help and guide
   When bitter war they wage,
Were he not Israel's mighty shield
To whom their utmost crafts must yield
   We surely must have perished."

Another co-laborer of Luther, also a professor at Wittenberg, was Paul Eber, whose hymnody is a delightful counterpart to the more rugged and martial melodies of his confrères. Eber's music is tender, consoling. He brings to the persecuted Protestants not so much courage and stimulus as comfort and peace—lines like these:

"Then this our comfort is alone
   That we may meet before thy throne
And cry, O faithful God, to thee
For refuge from our misery."

He wrote a number of songs for the dying, such as this:

"I fall asleep in Jesus' arms,
   Sin washed away, hushed all alarms,
For his dear blood, his righteousness,
My jewels are, my glorious dress,
   Wherein before my God I stand
When I shall reach the heavenly land."

These hymns were the support of the Protestants during the trials of the "Thirty Years' War," which began in 1618 and ended with the Peace of Westphalia, 1648. The most celebrated of all German hymns, after Luther's, belongs to this distressing period. It is associated with the name of Gustavus Adolphus and is known as his "Battle Hymn," and again as his "Swan Song," because his army sang it

on the eve of the battle of Lützen, in which he conquered, but was mortally wounded.   It was the product, however, of the Rev. Johann Michael Altenburg,
who composed it when he received the news of the
preceding battle, in which Gustavus was signally
victorious—the battle of Leipzig, September 17, 1631.
The original is known as "Verzage nicht, du Häuflein
Klein"; the translation is by Miss Winkworth:

"Fear not, O little flock, the foe
    Who madly seeks your overthrow;
        Dread not his rage and power;
    What though your courage sometimes faints,
    His seeming triumph o'er God's saints
        Lasts but a little hour.

"Be of good cheer; your cause belongs
    To him who can avenge your wrongs;
        Leave it to him, our Lord!
    Though hidden yet from mortal eyes,
    He sees the Gideon that shall rise
        To save us and his word.

"As true as God's own word is true,
    Not earth nor hell with all their crew
        Against us shall prevail;
    A jest and by-word are they grown;
    God is with us, we are his own,
        Our victory cannot fail.

"Amen, Lord Jesus, grant our prayer!
    Great Captain, now thine arm make bare,
        Fight for us once again!
    So shall thy saints and martyrs raise
    A mighty chorus to thy praise,
        World without end: Amen!"

The same period is very rich in similar compositions.   Among the more notable are the following:

Martin Rinkart, author of "Nun danket alle Gott," about 1644. This has been called the "Te Deum" of Germany. Rinkart was both preacher and soldier, and performed such conspicuous deeds of valor as to be called "Savior of his Country." The translation is by Miss Winkworth. The tune to which it is generally sung is by Johann Crüger, one of the best composers of German choral music, as we shall note hereafter.

"Now thank we all our God,
    With heart, and hands, and voices,
Who wondrous things hath done,
    In whom the world rejoices;
Who from our mother's arms
    Hath blessed us on our way
With countless gifts of love,
    And still is ours to-day.

"Oh, may this bounteous God
    Through all our life be near us,
With ever joyful hearts
    And blesséd peace to cheer us;
To keep us in his grace,
    And guide us when perplexed,
And free us from all ills
    In this world and the next.

PAUL GERHARDT

Paul Gerhardt, next to Luther, is the greatest of all German hymn-writers (1606-1676). We have already mentioned his name in connection with the translation of one of the hymns of Bernard of Clairvaux. Gerhardt was born near Wittenberg, and was educated in its university. Ordained to the ministry, he preached for a time in Berlin. But his life was a

troubled one.   In his early years, amidst the horrors
of the Thirty Years' War, he was cast about from
place to place.   He was not settled permanently any-
where until he was forty-four years of age, nor
married until he was forty-eight.   He endured great
affliction in the long illness and death of his wife and
in the loss of four out of five of his children.   Finally
he was dispossessed of his position, and retired to a
humble parish at Lübben, where he labored for seven
years among a rude, unsympathetic people, and
where he died.   The words attached to his portrait
at Lübben are an apt commentary on his career:
"Theologus in cribo Satanæ versatus," a reference
to Luke xxii. 31, "Simon, Simon, behold Satan hath
desired to have you that he may sift you as wheat."

But it has ever been out of just such experiences
as he endured that the Saviour brings most valuable
instruction and tender consolation for souls ignorant
or distressed.   The German hymn received at Gerhardt's hands a refinement which had hitherto been
lacking.   His poems are truly "songs of the heart."
He imports into the objective realities, with which
the Reformation had been so vitally concerned, that
subjective tone which marks the transition to the
modern style of hymnody.   The frequent use of the
personal pronoun "I" is the exponent of his work,
and thereby the individual soul is brought face to face
with its God.   A large number of his hymns have
been translated into English, and are now in use.
One of the most beautiful is *Ist Gott für mich, so
trete*, translated by Miss Winkworth:

"Since Jesus is my friend,
   And I to him belong,
It matters not what foes intend,
   However fierce and strong.

"He whispers in my breast
   Sweet words of holy cheer,
How they who seek in God their rest
   Shall ever find him near;

"How God hath built above
   A city fair and new,
Where eye and heart shall see and prove
   What faith has counted true.

"My heart for gladness springs;
   It cannot more be sad;
For very joy it smiles and sings—
   Sees naught but sunshine glad.

"The sun that lights mine eyes
   Is Christ, the Lord I love;
I sing for joy of that which lies
   Stored up for me above."

Others well known to all worshipers are those beginning

"Give to the winds thy fears,"

and

"All my heart this night rejoices."

And so the great work in German hymnody continued. It was the resultant of a mighty outpouring of divine grace, by reason of which it swelled into immense volume and rose to transcendent height. Hymn-books and hymn-writers multiplied and the continent was flooded with sacred melody. The quality indeed, as well as the quantity, had its ebb and flow. There were fluctuations in literary merit and doctrinal fidelity.   But upon the whole the movement was fraught with unspeakable blessing.

Count von Zinzendorf

We shall mention, however, but two other German hymn-writers.   Not that the rest are unworthy of notice, but that their hymns are not so generally used by English-speaking worshipers.   Nicholaus Ludwig, Count von Zinzendorf was born at Dresden, May 26, 1700.   He was educated at the University of Wittenberg; was licensed to preach in 1734; was consecrated bishop of the Moravian Brethren's Unity at Berlin, May 10, 1737; died at Herrnhut, May 9, 1760.   He was a man of great gifts and profound influence.   He did so much for the community over which he presided that he is called its "Second Founder."   During a period of banishment from Saxony he spent several years in America, principally in Pennsylvania, where the fruit of his work still abides.   He wrote more than two thousand hymns, most of which were fugitive.   He is criticised as "caring more for quantity than for quality"; but quality certainly is not lacking in some of his poems. They reflect the deep devotion of their author, whose motto was "I have but one passion, and that is He, only He."   It is not easy to say which is his best hymn.   The one that is most sung perhaps is "Jesu geh, voran."   Two translations of this hymn, very similar in language and structure, are in use, one by the Rev. Arthur T. Russell, and the other by Miss Jane Borthwick.   The latter reads:

"Jesus, still lead on,
   Till our rest be won;
And although the way be cheerless;
We will follow, calm and fearless;
   Guide us by thy hand
   To our Fatherland.

"If the way be drear,
   If the foe be near,
Let not faithless fears o'ertake us,
Let not faith and hope forsake us;
   For, through many a foe,
   To our home we go.

"When we seek relief
   From a long-felt grief,
When temptations come, alluring,
Make us patient and enduring;
   Show us that bright shore
   Where we weep no more.

"Jesus, still lead on,
   Till our rest be won;
Heavenly Leader, still direct us,
Still support, console, protect us,
   Till we safely stand
   In our Fatherland.

Other hymns by Count Zinzendorf in common use are:

"Glory to God whose witness train,"

translation by John Wesley; and

"Jesus thy blood and righteousness,"

also translated by Wesley.

CARL JOHANN SPITTA

Rev. Carl Johann Spitta, D.D., is considered the greatest German hymn-writer of the nineteenth century. He was born at Hanover, August 1, 1801.

His father died when he was only four years of age,
and his mother, discouraged by the feebleness of his
constitution, abandoned the idea of training him for a
profession and apprenticed him to a watch-maker.
But it was soon discovered that he was not fitted for
such work, and he was permitted to prepare for the
ministry. He was educated at the University of
Göttingen, ordained December 10, 1828, and settled as pastor at various places. He died September
28, 1859.

The poetic instinct manifested itself in Spitta in
early childhood. He composed verses when he was
only eight years old. After his conversion he wrote
to a friend, "In the manner in which I formerly sang,
I sing no more. To the Lord I consecrate my life
and my love and likewise my song. He gave to me
song and melody. I give it back to him."

Many of Spitta's songs have been rendered into
English. The most familiar is "O Jesu meine
Sonne," translated by Richard Massie:

> "I know no life divided,
>   O Lord of life, from thee:
> In thee is life provided
>   For all mankind and me;
> I know no death, O Jesus,
>   Because I live in thee;
> Thy death it is that frees us
>   From death eternally.
>
> "I fear no tribulation,
>   Since, whatsoe'er it be
> It makes no separation
>   Between my Lord and me.

If thou, my God and Teacher,
  Vouchsafe to be my own,
Though poor, I shall be richer
  Than monarch on his throne.

"If, while on earth I wander,
  My heart is right and blest,
Ah, what shall I be yonder,
  In perfect peace and rest?
Oh, blesséd thought! in dying
  We go to meet the Lord,
Where there shall be no sighing,
  A kingdom our reward.

CHAPTER IV

PSALMODY

The term "psalmody" is applied to that body of sacred song which is composed of metrical versions of the psalms, wherein they are adapted to modern methods of singing. It generally includes, also, similar paraphrases of other portions of Scripture.

The subject is an immensely large one of itself, and its literature most extensive. Julian, in his *Dictionary of Hymnology*, gives a list of three hundred and twenty-six separate publications, of substantially the entire Psalter, in English alone; besides about one hundred and twenty minor versifications. To these must be added, before exhausting the catalogue, similar attempts in other languages and also the vast number of songs ranking simply as "hymns," but virtually belonging to psalmody. We are compelled by our limits to treat only of the most important versions, as they are known to-day, specially those in the English language.

Clement Marot

Psalmody, in its modern sense, began with Clement Marot of France, court-poet to King Francis I. The time and circumstances should be carefully noted. Francis reigned from 1515 to 1547. These years cover the most momentous events in modern history,

the Reformation, the rise of Spanish ascendency under
Charles V., and all else that was associated there-
with.   Marot was writing his psalms while Francis
and Charles were engaged in bitter warfare over their
respective claims to the control of Italy, while Luther
was stirring all Christendom with his attacks upon the
papacy, while the Huguenots were struggling for the
control of France, while Cardinal Wolsey was running
his eccentric but influential course in England.   It is
not strange that such work as his in psalmody in such
an age should have been productive of permanent
results.

Marot became *valet de chambre* to Marguerite de
Valois at the age of twenty-one.   Her influence over
him was so great that he espoused the Huguenot faith,
though his religion does not seem to have become
particularly vital.   His character is variously represented by Catholic and Huguenot.   He was certainly
a gay, witty, and volatile soul, and his poems are for
the most part short pieces—ballads, epigrams, and
the like.   Yet he suffered again and again for his
Protestant principles, though we are tempted to
believe it was chiefly because his Protestantism was
so largely displayed in his satires upon the Roman
clergy, even though these alternate with expressions
of simple, unaffected faith.   King Francis seems to
have promoted him in his own persistent attempt
to use anything or anybody who would serve his
cause against the emperor.   But even Charles V.
subsequently admired his gifts and richly rewarded
him for his work.

We do not know when Marot began to versify the psalms.   Thirty of them were in circulation, in manuscript form, in 1537, and became the fashion of the hour.   The king and his court sang them to ballad tunes, and from France they spread to adjoining countries.   Their subsequent publication, in 1542, brought upon Marot the persecution of the Roman authorities and he fled to Geneva.   Thence his psalmody spread through the Protestant world, and set the example for the host of versifiers who followed.

The Genevan Psalter

In 1543 was published at Geneva a remarkable historic volume known as *The Genevan Psalter*, the permanent influence of which may be attested by reference to any modern hymn-book.   Marot died in 1544; his psalter was enlarged and revised by Beza at the request of Calvin, and much which was objectionable, in its gayety, classical allusions, and references to the members of the French court, was removed.   This psalter passed into a second edition in 1554; and into a third in 1562, when the work was completed by the versification of all the psalms. Marot's name is still attached to it, as appears in the title, "*Les Pseaumes mis en rime francoise par Clement Marot et Theodore de Bèze.*"

The success and influence of this work were most remarkable.   It was largely adopted among all the French-speaking people and was used to a considerable extent even by the Catholics.   Francis I. cherished it upon his deathbed. Charles II. used one of its numbers as a hunting-song! The Huguenots everywhere were acquainted with it, and their Catholic enemies disguised their identity at times by singing its melodies. Very touching stories are related of its use on the battle-field, and in the sad times following the Revocation of the Edict of Nantes. At least one thousand editions of it were issued, and its influence extended throughout the Protestant world.

It was translated into many languages, including Dutch, German, Italian, Spanish, Bohemian, Polish, Latin, and even Hebrew. In England several translations appeared, and a number of the versions that succeeded it in Great Britain followed its form and expression in many particulars. Take it for all in all, it is doubtful if any book of praise—the original Psalms alone excepted—has ever had so important a mission or exercised so great an influence.

English Psalmody

Great Britain received the continental treasures of psalmody with her adoption of the doctrines of the Reformation. Marot's influence seems to have been immediately felt in England, for in 1538 Myles Coverdale, bishop of Exeter, published a metrical version of thirteen psalms, entitled "Goastly Psalmes and Spirituall Songes drawn out of the Holy Scripture." This was the beginning of English psalmody; but it had no decided influence.

The first important work in psalmody in Great Britain was that of George Buchanan, 1548. Buchanan was the greatest of all the British psalmists, and for many years the most distinguished, though now the least known. This is because his translation was in Latin.

Buchanan was tutor to the Earl of Moray, the natural son of James V. Having embraced Protestantism and written in its defense, his life was endangered and he fled to Portugal. But he was apprehended and cast into prison. During his confinement he occupied his time with the composition which made him famous. It subsequently passed through a number of editions, and has received unqualified praise from the best authorities. At that time Latin was still a living language, and Buchanan's psalms were studied with great pleasure by many scholars. They are said to have even stimulated the genius of Isaac Watts. It may be very interesting to the student to observe a single example. The following is Buchanan's rendering of Psalm xxiii.:

> "Quid frustra rabidi me petitis canes?
>   Livor propositum cur premis improbum?
>   Sicut pastor ovem, me dominus regit;
>   Nil decrit penitus mihi.

> "Per campi vividis mitia pabula,
>   Que veris teneri pingit amœnitas,
>   Nunc pascor placide; nunc saturum latus
>   Fessus molliter explico.

> "Puræ rivus aquæ leniter astrepens
>   Membris restituit robora lanquidis,
>   Et blando recreat somite spiritus
>   Solis sub space torrida.

"Saltus quum peteret meus vaga devios,
    Errorum teneras illecebras sequens,
    Retraxit miserans denero me bonus
        Pastor justitiæ in viam.

"Nec si per trepidas luctifica manu
    Intentet tenebras mors mihi vulnera,
    Formidem duce te pergere; me pledo
        Securum facies tuo.

"Tu mensas epulio accumulas, merum
    Tu plenis pateris sufficis, et caput
    Unguento exhiliras conficit æmulos,
        Dum spectant, dolor anxius.

"Me nunquam bonitas destituet tua
    Prosususque bonis perpetuo favor;
    Et non sollicitæ longa domi tuæ
        Vitæ tempora transfigam."

The movement in English psalmody virtually originated with Thomas Sternhold, "groom" to Henry VIII.—not a stable-boy, however, as might be imagined, but an important officer in charge of the royal wardrobe. Sternhold's first attempts were made for his own "godly solace" and sung by him to his own organ. Afterwards he increased the number with the design of furnishing the people with sacred ballads which might displace the ungodly songs in common use. These songs were heard by the young King Edward and were repeated in his presence. The first edition published was dedicated to him, but its date cannot be determined. It contained nineteen psalms. The second edition, published in 1549, contained thirty-seven.

At this time Sternhold associated with himself another poet, John Hopkins, of whose personal history little is known, except that he was educated at Oxford and settled as a minister at Suffolk.

The third edition of the psalter, with additions by Hopkins, appeared in 1551.

And now the scene changes to Geneva, and the direct influence of Marot on English psalmody begins to be positively exercised. "Bloody Mary," daughter of Henry VIII. and Catherine of Aragon, comes to the English throne (1553), and her attempts to restore the Catholic faith are associated with the persecution of the Protestants, even to the burning of bishops, clergymen, and people. A number of refugees seek safety on the continent, and a religious congregation of English and Scotch Protestants is organized at Frankfort-on-the-Main. John Knox is chosen pastor. But the Episcopalian and Dissenting brethren do not get on well together, and Knox, with his adherents, retires to Geneva, 1555. Here a distinct church is formed and a "Book of Order" published, and to complete it, the psalms of Sternhold and Hopkins are adopted—though with considerable alteration, and others are added. This was in 1556.

To this Anglo-Genevan psalter several psalms and tunes in use to-day may be traced, notably "Old Hundred," both the tune, as we know it, and the words beginning,

"All people that on earth do dwell."

Other editions of the Genevan psalter followed.

In 1563 appeared the most important of all the

English works of this kind up to this date. The entire one hundred and fifty psalms were now versified and appeared in a book entitled " *The whole Boke of Psalms, collected into English metre by Thomas Sternhold, J. Hopkins, and others; confirmed with the Ebrue, with apt notes to sing them withal. Faithfully perused and allowed, according to the order appointed in the Queenes Majesties injunctions, very mete to be used by all sorts of people privately for their solace and comfort, laying apart all ungodly songs and ballades, which tend only to the nourishment of vice and corrupting of youth. Imprinted at London by John Day, dwelling over Aldersgate benethe Saint Martins. Cum gratia et privilegia Regie Majestatis per septennium an 1563.*

This book contained, in addition to psalms, other metrical versions, the Creed, the Ten Commandments, the Lord's Prayer, the "Veni Creator," "Venite," "Te Deum," and a number of other ancient hymns with some modern originals. This work was known in subsequent times as the "Old Version." It was in use in England for about one hundred years, or until the Restoration.

Scotch Psalmody

Meanwhile the Scotch psalmody was developing along lines of its own. The Scotch Church adopted eighty-seven of the psalms in the Anglo-Genevan collection, selected and altered forty-two from Sternhold and Hopkins, and added twenty-one of its own. Its psalter was completed December, 1564, and the

General Assembly ordered its use by all its ministers.
Thereafter for forty years no further attention was
given to the matter.   In 1600 King James I. pro-
posed to the Assembly the revision of its psalm-book,
and undertook to conduct the work himself.   He
addressed himself to the task and had proceeded as
far as the thirty-fifth psalm when his work was interrupted by his death.   His labors were, however, continued by William Alexander, afterwards Earl of
Stirling, who presented to the people the version in
which the king had had so large a part, and which
was consequently known as the "Royal Psalter."
This was in 1630.   Charles I., the successor of
James I., in his desire to fasten Episcopacy upon the
Scotch, attempted to substitute this psalter for the
one in use.   In 1636 a revised edition appeared,
bound up with a liturgy prepared by the Scotch bishops.   This he thrust upon Scotland, with the order
that no other psalm-book should be used in the land,
and prohibiting the printing or importing of any other.
But the indignant Scotch simply characterized it as
"The Masse in English," and would have none of it.

Nevertheless, the work had its influence.   Many
of the loyal sons of the Scotch Church felt and expressed the desire for something better than they
were using, and this finally culminated in the production of the celebrated "Rous' Version."   Francis
Rous was a Presbyterian by conviction and a lawyer
by profession.   He attained to great celebrity apart
from his attempts at sacred poetry.   He was several
times a member of Parliament during the reigns of

James and Charles I. He represented Truro in the
Long Parliament, and took sides against the king and
bishops. He was appointed a member of the Westminster Assembly of Divines, occupied the position
of provost of Eton College, and held other important
offices. During the twelve years previous to 1640,
when Parliament was not permitted to assemble, he
occupied much time in turning the psalms into meter.
When, therefore, the Westminster Assembly was
called, and undertook as part of its business the selection of a psalter, Rous became the successful com-
petitor. The consequence was that Rous' Version
came into very general use in England. The Scotch
spent seven years in amending and revising it, and
then universally adopted it. The version as finally
adopted and published, in 1650, became the psalter
of the psalm-singing churches of the English tongue
for two hundred years. It is still in use in Scotland
and in those American churches known as "Coven-
anters."

Rous' Version at the time of its publication was
in many respects the best metrical translation of the
Psalms ever published. Its close adherence to the
original text, however, was inseparable from that
grace of English diction which is so large a part of
poetic merit. It cannot be reconciled with the best
modern taste, and many illustrations might be given
of its defects if it were necessary. It is also written
almost exclusively in the common meter, and therefore limited in the range of tunes to which its parts
may be sung. Yet it contains many single verses

and some entire psalms upon which later attempts have scarcely improved. We may smile at such a torture of the English as this:

> "The na-ti-ons of Ca-na-an,
> By his Almighty hand,
> Before his face he did expel
> Out of their native land."

But we should be slow to criticise the time-honored lines:

> "The Lord's my Shepherd, I'll not want,
> He makes me down to lie
> In pastures green; he leadeth me
> The quiet waters by."

TATE AND BRADY

We now return to England for the next important development in psalmody. The "Old Version" is now to be displaced by the "New Version," though it has held the field for one hundred and fifty years. This "New Version" was the work of Nahum Tate and Nicholas Brady. It was published in London in 1696. The authors were Irishmen. Tate was the son of a clergyman in Dublin; was educated at Trinity College; was stimulated in his literary work by the poet Dryden; published a number of poetical works; and became poet laureate. Brady was born at Bandon, studied at Oxford and Trinity, and became a prebendary of Cork. He published several volumes of sermons and some poetical works, including a translation of Virgil's Ænid.

Tate and Brady's psalter had no intrinsic merits to recommend it. It was no special improvement upon that of Sternhold and Hopkins. Its general adoption was due to royal and commercial influence. It received the special indorsement of King William III., and the copyright was vested in the Stationers' Company, through whose exclusive control it was, so to speak, put upon the market. And yet this version had a certain literary flavor which contributed to its popularity. It has been accused indeed, by Keble for example, of sacrificing fidelity to the original to literary form. Before long it had supplanted the "Old Version" throughout the entire English (that is, the Episcopal) Church. Additions and changes were made in subsequent editions and certain hymns added. From England it passed over to America. In 1789 it was adopted entire by the Protestant Episcopal Church in the United States, and bound up with the prayer-book. The general convention of this church at subsequent periods added about two hundred hymns to the psalms—the number of psalms decreasing as the number of hymns increased until the latter were used much the more generally.

The development of psalmody in England reaches its climax with Dr. Isaac Watts' "Imitation of the Psalms of David in the language of the New Testament" (1707), a notice of which appears under its author's name. (See Chapter VI.)

AMERICAN PSALMODY

It is an exceedingly interesting fact that the first book printed on the American continent was a psalm-book. This was at first known as "The Bay Psalm-

ist," and afterwards as "The New England Version."
It was an entirely independent and original production.

Previous to the appearance of the "Bay Psalmist"
the colonists had employed what was known as the
"Ainsworth Version." This was the book of the
Puritan refugees in Holland, published eight years
before the departure of the Pilgrims in 1620, and
taken by them to the New World. This was the
book they used when

> "Amid the storm they sang,
>   And the stars heard and the sea;
>   And the sounding aisles of the dim woods rang
>   With the anthem of the free."

This is the book to which Longfellow refers in his
"Courtship of Miles Standish," when John Alden

"Heard as he drew near the door the musical voice of Priscilla."

But by and by a new translation was demanded, and
in 1636 a committee was appointed by the Congregational churches to undertake the work. Thereupon
the version was made by Thomas Welde of Roxbury,
Richard Mather of Dorchester, and John Eliot, the
apostle to the Indians. The book was printed by
President Dunster of Harvard College on a press sent
out from Holland as a present from sympathizing
friends and the novel work was completed.

The "Bay Psalmist" passed through a number of
editions unaltered for about one hundred years, and
met with favor even in the mother country. In Scotland it was printed and bound up with the Bible, and
thence imported again into the American colonies.
It was almost universally adopted by the New Eng-

land congregations, though in many of them the old Ainsworth Version was tardily and reluctantly abandoned.

The Bay Psalmist has been followed in America by other attempts at versification, which we cannot consider in detail. The most notable are the following: Dr. Cotton Mather's "Psalterium Americanum," in blank verse, 1778; Joel Barlow's revision of the Psalms of Watts, 1785; Dr. Timothy Dwight's revision of Watts, as itself revised, 1800, by a committee of the Presbyterian Assembly. From this book we have derived the well-known rendering of Psalm cxxxvii.:

> "I love thy kingdom, Lord,
>   The house of thine abode,
> The church our blest Redeemer saved
>   With his own precious blood."

Of the psalm-books now in use it is not necessary to speak. They may be easily acquired and studied by any one desiring to do so. It is a most interesting fact, however, that at the time of this writing a joint committee from nine different religious bodies of the United States and Canada is busily engaged upon the preparation of a new psalter which will in time be offered to the co-operating churches. It is the very earnest desire of many, among whom the writer is included, that the labors of this committee may be productive of a psalter which shall prove acceptable to all evangelical denominations and serve to unite them the more closely as respects their forms of divine praise. It is a very large and serious question

whether the displacement of psalmody by hymnody
has not been extreme, and whether it may not be to
the improvement of public worship and of the spiritual life to return more closely to former customs and
give the "Psalter" the place which it ought to hold
in relation to the "Hymnal," a place original and
supreme.

A completely satisfactory judgment of the merits
of the various versions of the psalms cannot be formed
except by extended comparison, because the selection
of a single psalm or even of several might do considerable injustice to the remaining ones.   Yet it will be
at least an interesting illustration of their respective
styles to add a selection from several of the more
celebrated versions.   The following is the first psalm
as it appears in the versions indicated.   It will be
found to furnish ample variety of treatment and to
some extent exhibit the peculiarity of the authors as
already noted:

STERNHOLD AND HOPKINS

"The man is blest that hath not lent
    To wicked men his ear,
Nor led his life as sinners do,
    Nor sat in scorner's chair.

"But in the law of God the Lord
    Doth set his whole delight,
And in the same doth exercise
    Himself both day and night.

"He shall be like a tree that is
    Planted the rivers nigh,
Which in due season bringeth forth
    Its fruit abundantly.

"Whose leaf shall never fade nor fail,
   But flourishing shall stand,
E'en so all things shall prosper well
   That this man takes in hand.

"As for ungodly men, with them
   It shall be nothing so,
But as the chaff which by the wind
   Is driven to and fro.

"Therefore the wicked men shall not
   In judgment stand upright,
Nor in assembly of the just
   Shall sinners come in sight.

"For why? the way of godly men
   Unto the Lord is known,
Whereas, the way of wicked men
   Shall be quite overthrown."

ROUS

"That man hath perfect blessedness
   Who walketh not astray
In counsel of ungodly men
   Nor stands in sinners' way;
Nor sitteth in the scorner's chair;
   But placeth his delight
Upon God's law, and meditates
   On his law, day and night.

"He shall be like a tree that grows
   Near planted by a river,
Which in his season yields his fruit
   And his leaf fadeth never;
And all he doth shall prosper well.
   The wicked are not so,
But they are like unto the chaff
   Which wind drives to and fro.

"In judgment therefore shall not stand
　　Such as ungodly are,
Nor in th' assembly of the just
　　Shall wicked men appear,
Because the way of godly men
　　Unto the Lord is known;
Whereas the way of wicked men
　　Shall quite be overthrown."

TATE AND BRADY

"How blest is he who ne'er consents
　　By ill advice to walk,
Nor stands in sinners' ways nor sits
　　Where men profanely talk;
But makes the perfect law of God
　　His business and delight;
Devoutly reads therein by day
　　And meditates by night.

"Like some fair tree, which fed by streams
　　With timely fruit does bend,
He still shall flourish, and success
　　All his designs attend.
Ungodly men and their attempts
　　No lasting root shall find;
Untimely blasted and dispersed
　　Like chaff before the wind.

"Their guilt shall strike the wicked dumb
　　Before their judge's face;
No formal hypocrite shall then
　　Amongst the saints have place
For God approves the just man's ways,
　　To happiness they tend,
But sinners and the paths they tread
　　Shall both in ruin end."

AINSWORTH

"O blessed man that doth not in
    The wicked's counsel walk;
Nor stand in sinners' ways, nor sit
    In seat of scornful folk.

"But setteth in Jehovah's law
    His pleasureful delight;
And in his law doth meditate
    By day and eke by night.

"And he shall be like as a tree
    By water-brooks planted;
Which in his time shall give his fruit
    His leaf eke shall not fade.

"And whatsoever he shall do,
    It prosp'rously shall thrive;
Not so the wicked, but as chaff
    Which wind away doth drive.

"Therefore the wicked shall not in
    The judgment stand upright;
And in th' assembly of the just
    Not any sinful wight.

"For of the just Jehovah he
    Acknowledgeth the way;
And way of the ungracious
    Shall utterly decay."

CHAPTER V

ENGLISH HYMNOLOGY. PERIODS

Poetry is the index of its age. It surpasses all other forms of literature in reflecting the character of the times in which it is produced. But beyond all other poetry the songs of a people are the most expressive of their state; in them is the quintessence of their sentiments and aspirations. It follows, therefore, that in religious song we reach the very climax of characteristic literature, because it voices the deepest feelings of the soul. Neither David nor David's times can be so well known from the Books of Samuel as from David's psalms. The first is but external history; the last is the record of the heart. The hopes and fears and trials and successes of the great singer of Israel are reflected in his poetry. It is even so in the case of our English hymnody. It bears the impress of its age. And so the character of its hymns varies from time to time, with the varying features of outward life. The hymns produced at one time are not reproduced thereafter. We may truly say they could not be. The peculiar form of faith or activity presented in one century is not presented in another, because it does not exist. Some other form presses for utterance and the character of the hymnody is altered.

For similar reasons many hymns produced in one

age are rejected by the next, because they do not meet its conditions and its needs. But meanwhile some are retained, cherished, and sung, because they answer the abiding yearnings of the soul, and these become the permanent heritage of the worshiping people of God. This will all be fully illustrated in the study of English Hymnology to which we now proceed.

We distinguish three periods in English Hymnology, as follows: (1) The First Period, Doctrinal and Didactic, 1650 to 1780; (2) The Second Period, Missionary and Evangelistic, 1780 to 1850; (3) The Third Period, Experimental and Devotional, 1850 to the present time. We describe each in order in this chapter and subsequently consider the work of their great representatives.

FIRST PERIOD—1650–1780
Doctrinal and Didactic

These were troubled times in both state and church. Society in all its forms was very unsettled. Bitter controversy, violent factions, forcible overturnings of existing order, the clash of arms and opinions were the characteristic features of the civilized world. Europe and America were kept in a state of continual ferment, and worse than all, the English-speaking peoples were at war among themselves.

1. Consider the condition in the state: what was it when our first great English hymn-writers were penning their songs?

The year 1650 finds Europe terrible distressed and

devastated by the Thirty Years' War. It is only two years since the Peace of Westphalia was concluded. It finds France under the heel of a Roman cardinal, where Richelieu had brought it, and Mazarin directing the government in triumphant disregard of nobles and people. It finds Cromwell at the head of the commonwealth, which he has already governed for a year, and over which he is to preside for nearly nine years longer. Charles the First has just been beheaded, and Cromwell is moving against a rebellion in Ireland in behalf of young Charles, son of the executed king. In this same year it will be suppressed with terrible severity, and Charles will escape in disguise to Normandy.

In America there is in 1650 the distress of the colonists, with which the reader is doubtless familiar. Already apprehensive for their liberties, they looked with dismay upon the troubled state of the mother country and hesitated in expression of their sentiments and sympathies lest either through the commonwealth or the monarchy they should be despoiled. Harassed on all sides by their savage foes, the New England colonies entered into a defensive league, from which Rhode Island was excluded. The Dutch and English are in conflict throughout the middle colonies, the English expelling the Dutch from Connecticut, and within a few years to obtain possession also of New Amsterdam, which will henceforth be known as New York. Such in brief is the political condition of the English world at the opening of our period.

A mere sketch must suffice to trace its events to its close. It covers one hundred and thirty years. It is one of the most turbulent periods that Europe has ever seen. It is foreshadowed in the "Year of Wonders" (1665), five years after the restoration of the monarchy under Charles II. The terrible events of this single year are prophetic of the century that follows: the great plague in London which carried to the grave a hundred thousand of its citizens; the great fire following, in which almost the entire city was consumed. These were swiftly followed by the two wars with Holland (1667, 1672), and by the English Revolution (1685), the coming of William and Mary, the flight of James II., and the final triumph of Protestantism. Then comes the war of the "Grand Alliance" (1689 to 1697), in which France was shorn of her great power. The eighteenth century opens with the war of the "Spanish Succession," in which almost all Europe combines again, in opposition to France and Spain, and the great Duke of Marlborough of England and the almost equally great Eugene of Savoy direct the forces of the allies. Ere long comes Frederick the Great of Prussia with his wars (1740–1786); the campaigns against the Pretender in Scotland (1745, 1746); the French and Indian wars in America (1744–1763); the American Revolution (1775–1783); and in France the dreadful echoes of a storm upon the horizon soon to break in the fury of the French Revolution.

2. The condition of the state during this period is reflected in the condition of the church. Indeed, to a

very great degree, the first was occasioned by the second. The conflict of religious opinions and the jealousies of religious parties issued in political complications and the strife of nations. The alliance of the church with the state was the explanation—the two were identified. The wars were therefore religious wars. The parties to them were not so much race against race as faith against faith; not so much France and Spain against England and her allies as Catholic against Protestant.

But bad as this was, it was not the worst; for the various divisions of Protestantism were arrayed against each other with almost equal virulence. The story of the commonwealth in England is not simply that of commoner against the crown; but that of Independency against Presbytery, and of both against Episcopacy. Even the followers of Cromwell were called "Roundheads" from the religious custom of cutting the hair closely, rather than permitting it to fall in tresses on the shoulders. And so while the Puritans joined Cromwell the Presbyterians favored the king and the restoration was ultimately accomplished through the combined influence of Presbyterians and Episcopalians. But ere long the character of the conflict changed, and then changed again. In 1673 all Dissenters were excluded from office by act of Parliament, and very soon all Protestants of every name were put in peril by Romish intrigue. James II. initiated one of the most trying periods in English history (1685–1688). Oblivious to his own solemn promise to defend the Church of England, he adopted the most cruel measures to extinguish religious liberty and coerce the people into the old religion. The notorious Jeffreys and Claverhouse appear, the "Bloody Assizes" begin, and a terrible persecution follows, terminated only by the coming of William and Mary.

It is impossible within our space to recount or even refer to all the significant events of those distracted times; we may merely indicate their character. The history to the close of the period is traced in connection with such things as these: the Revocation of the Edict of Nantes (1685); the low state of religion in the English church occasioning the rise of Methodism (1729); then the fierce disputes between Arminians and Calvinists, in which devoted Christian laborers parted in passion and were permanently estranged from each other; and to crown all, the coming of the most influential infidels that the modern church has encountered, such as Hume (d. 1776), Voltaire (d. 1778), Gibbon (d. 1794), and others. Such was the age which persecuted Baxter for nine long years, until his health failed under his sufferings, and kept Bunyan in jail for twelve years simply because he would preach the gospel in his own way to his own people.

Yet it is in just such times that poetry reaches its supreme height and draws prose also after it. The "Saint's Rest" and the "Pilgrim's Progress" are joined with sacred songs, in which the heart swells with sweetest melody. The loftiest themes then invite the attention of the sacred bard, the profoundest experiences are expressed in stirring tones, and the English language contains no hymns which equal those of this period.   There is intensity and feeling in them. Doctrine is set forth with emphasis; faith in God expressed with deep conviction.   Many hymns indeed appear which are an argument rather than an aspiration.   Partisan theology sometimes displaces evangelical truth.   But by and by these blemishes will be corrected, excrescences will fall away, or even the entire imperfect portions will be rejected, and that which remains after these eliminations will furnish the church a body of versified praise incomparable, enduring.

Second Period—1780–1850
Missionary and Evangelistic

As we pass from the first period into the second we enter a new atmosphere, almost a new world. Protestantism has become dominant in those countries in which it is henceforth to characterize the life of the people; the mutual animosities of Protestant denominations begin to be allayed and Protestant England has become the chief power in Europe.   There will be revolutions and wars indeed during the period, but in a different sphere of action, with a different motive and a different outcome.   And what is more to our present purpose, the English-speaking peoples, with the exception of the comparatively unimportant war of 1812, will be at peace with themselves. There will be no violent civil disturbances in Great Britain like those from which her people suffered in the preceding period.   The religious concerns of

Protestant Christendom will be disentangled from
political complications, spiritual forces will have a
correspondingly larger growth and wider influence,
and all this will find glowing expression in the hymnody of the age.

1. The period is opened with the French Revolution (1789-1794), with which we are accustomed to
associate all that is lawless and brutal.   It was not so
much, however, the expression of blind and purposeless
malice as an inevitable upheaval of repressed society,
a volcanic eruption in which the pent-up fury of a
people who had long suffered the irresponsible injustice, immorality, and cruelty of its monarchs was
poured forth.   Its effects were salutary.   It buried
beneath its scoria the last remnants of feudalism and
absolutism and furnished a new, rich soil for the
growth of political and religious rights.

Then came the Napoleonic wars, depopulating
France, disturbing all other nations, and turning
Europe into a charnel-house.   But even these were
not without their good effects.   For though Napoleon
was a royalist upon principle, a democrat in no true
sense of the word, it was not without meaning that he
called himself, not the emperor of France, but the
emperor of the French.   He gathered about him the
ablest men in all departments of knowledge, he brought
much order out of chaos, he gave Europe the best
code of laws it had ever had, and he was tolerant of
all religions.   So, royalist though he was, his sense of
royalty was not that of his predecessors, and in the
change of dynasty which he effected, hereditary abso-

lutism received a check from which it was never to recover.

England, of course, was deeply concerned with all that transpired upon the Continent. Her people suffered in the continental wars. The draft upon her resources was enormous. But in her triumphs the cause of the Protestant faith was advanced. Trafalgar (1805) gave her the sovereignty of the seas; Waterloo (1815) confirmed her supremacy upon the land. Meanwhile in her prolonged internal peace reforms of various kinds were quietly but surely effected—even the political disabilities of Roman Catholics were removed—a great era of scientific invention was ushered in, and the blessed Victorian age began. Our hymns relate none of the external events of this period, but they are fully indicative of its character.

2. The period begins with the year 1780. The state of the Protestant Church at the time was most deplorable. Vital religion was at its lowest ebb. The influence of the great infidels of the last period was at its height, and upon both sides of the Atlantic outspoken skepticism characterized the enemies of the Cross and apathy its friends. But for just this reason there were those in whom the Spirit of God was stirring. They called mightily upon God for help and the answer soon came in one of the most remarkable religious movements the world has ever known. The movement—like the hymns which it evoked—was twofold, evangelistic and missionary. The Great Revival of 1800 and the birth of modern missions were coincident. In England the missionary element

was the first to take definite shape, and in America
the evangelistic; but England soon shared very largely
in the evangelistic as America did in the missionary.

The first of the great modern missionary societies,
the English Baptist, was organized October 2, 1792,
chiefly through the efforts of William Carey. The
first great English missionary hymn was written by
one of the members of this society, Benjamin Beddome. Seven years later (1799) the English Church
Missionary Society was formed, and from its devoted
Bishop Heber came the greatest of missionary hymns.
The American Board was organized 1810, and with
it virtually begins all American hymnology. Other
societies followed in swift succession, and soon the
entire Protestant Church presented the sublime spec-
tacle of the Body of Christ girding itself anew for the
conquest of the world.

The Great Revival of 1800 began in America, and
its more apparent effects were largely confined to this
continent; but its influence extended to Great Britain
also. In it modern evangelism was born, as modern
missions in the corresponding movement abroad. It
is not easy to mark the exact initial point of this great
awakening. It was distinctly noted as early as 1797
in the central portion of the country, particularly Ken-
tucky. Thence it spread from state to state, and
from church to church, until in 1800 it had covered
the whole land.

Religious interest continued at its height for several
years and then declined; but only to rise again and
again—successive tidal waves of spiritual influence.

Thus the whole religious aspect of America and to some extent of Great Britain was altered. Christianity was no longer a subject of contempt, but of interest and admiration. Its representatives came the more to the front, its principles of love were widely exhibited, and every department of life felt the power of its teachings and examples. No better illustration of this can be found than in the abolition of the slave-trade, 1807, followed in 1833 by the absolute and voluntary abandonment of the system of slavery throughout the dominions of Great Britain.

The church had ceased to contend with itself and extended its sympathies to the whole lost world. It summoned all its energies to save the heathen at home and the heathen abroad. Its expanded hopes and enlarged efforts found expression in its songs. Surely it is a new atmosphere—almost a new world.

THIRD PERIOD—1850——
Devotional and Experimental

Little need be said concerning the third and last period. Its events are sufficiently familiar to the average student. In hymnody it is distinctly a period of decadence, a decadence which has continued to become more pronounced until the present day. This is not because religion is losing its hold upon the minds of men or because its practical effects upon the life are diminishing. The contrary is emphatically true. The reason of the decadence is found in the absence of a fresh impulse. Great poetry does not continue with the continuance of hopes, struggles, and

successes; no more do great hymns.   The further the
stimulating cause retires into the past, the more does
the spirit of song subside.   Therefore our later hymns
are of the sentimental kind, and no writer is found the
equal of some of the past periods.

Christian experience is expressed in exquisite measures; but there are no clarion notes, no trumpet calls
—these have already been sounded and there remain
only their echoes.   Not that our present hymnody is
not elevating and useful.   It is eminently so, because
like that which went before, it suits and characterizes
its own age.   One of its singular characteristics is the
multiplication of female hymnists—a far greater proportion than in any preceding time.   This, too, is in
keeping with the character of the age.   It is pre-
eminently the woman's age; she is more prominently
connected with the work of the church than she has
ever been.   So she has become its chief singer.   One
single name, that of Fanny Crosby, is appended to
over three thousand hymns.   But the men are otherwise engaged.   Very few attempt to write hymns.
And so we wait for a fresh outpouring of the Holy
Spirit, involving some new struggle with the powers
of darkness, some new development of spiritual life
which shall stir the heart of Christendom and evoke
again its noblest melodies.

CHAPTER VI

THE BEST HYMNS

Before passing to the examination of the hymns themselves we should endeavor to fix upon a standard by which they may be judged and their comparative rank determined.

It is generally conceded that this standard cannot be such as is applied to other classes of literature. Hymnody is unique. It is employed for one specific purpose and must be judged by rules of its own. So while it is admitted that the canons of literary criticism may have due weight, and while room is given for the expression of competent authority, the final arbiter must be Christian usage. What the church generally adopts must be a good hymn, and the hymns that are most generally adopted must be the best hymns.

It then becomes our duty to determine the qualities possessed by such hymns, and conclude that the degree to which a hymn exhibits these qualities it is entitled to take rank.

But even so, it is necessary to exercise a judicious care. How shall we determine Christian usage? What testimony shall we receive? In short, what sort of use establishes usage?

Manifestly a song that aspires to be a hymn does not fulfil the conditions simply because of its mere popularity. It may be sung far and wide, in various gatherings, caught up by the multitude, and even whistled by the boys in the street. This does not place it in the rank of the great hymns. It must certainly conform to at least four conditions before it can be said to be adopted.

1. It must obtain a hold upon the great Christian community. It must not be partisan or sectional, else it is not "adopted."

2. Its hold must be permanent. If its spirit accords with but a single juncture or a single generation, if its sentiment suits but a single age, it is not adopted.

3. It must find a place in the solemn and stated worship of the great congregation. If it is used only in the camp-meeting, the Sunday school, or some similar portion of worship, it cannot be said to be adopted.

4. It must be embodied in some authorized body of sacred song, put forth or sanctioned by some recognized organization of Christians. If it never emerges from the publication of some irresponsible person or firm, it cannot be called "adopted." Such principles have been accepted by those who have sought to determine usage as a standard by which to judge our hymns.

Several systematic and learned attempts have been made in this direction, the most notable of which are the following:

1. *Anglican Hymnology.** The subtitle of this

---

*Anglican Hymnology, by Rev. James King, M.A. London, Hatchards, Piccadilly, 1885.

book is, *"Being an account of the 325 standard hymns of the highest merit, according to the verdict of the whole Anglican Church."*

As to the method pursued the author says he "collected and collated with much labor fifty-two representative hymnals used in the Church of England at home and abroad. These included hymnals of the Scottish Episcopal, American, and Colonial churches in communion with the Anglican." "The fifty-two were regarded as a committee, each member of which could, as it were, give one vote for each approved hymn." "Two thousand of our best known hymns have thus been tested, and those that have obtained most marks have been selected and classified on the following principle": Hymns receiving thirty votes and upwards, *First Rank;* hymns receiving twenty votes and upwards, *Second Rank;* hymns receiving fifteen votes and upwards, *Third Rank;* hymns receiving less than fifteen votes regarded as not generally approved.

In this examination not a single hymn received the votes of all the hymnals! So that not one is great by unanimous consent. The author also admits that some hymns may not have obtained votes enough to be enrolled in a high rank because of their too recent date. It takes from twenty to fifty years for some hymns to win their way to favor.

According to the collation of this author the first-rank hymns are one hundred and five in number. Four of these stand at the head of the list, greatly distinguished in that they obtain fifty-one votes—

within one vote of unanimity. They are therefore frequently referred to as *The Great Four*. They are the following, though the actual order need not be preserved, as all obtained the same number of votes.

1. All Praise to thee, my God, this night.—Bp. Ken.
2. Hark! the Herald Angels Sing.—C. Wesley.
*3. Lo! He comes with clouds descending.
    Cennick-Wesley.
4. Rock of Ages, cleft for me.—Toplady.

Six other hymns received forty-nine votes ana are here added:

5. Abide with me; fast falls the eventide.—Lyte.
6. Awake my soul and with the sun.—Bp. Ken.
7. Jerusalem the golden.—Bernard-Neale.
8. Jesus, Lover of my soul.—C. Wesley.
9. Sun of my soul, thou Saviour dear.—Keble.
10. When I survey the wondrous cross.—Watts.

2. *The National Hymn-Book.*† This is an attempt similar to that of the *Anglican Hymnology*, but applied to America. The author selects the hymnaries of the following denominations: Baptists, Congregationalists, Episcopalians, Lutherans, Methodists, Presbyterians, and Reformed and some others—thirty in all. From these a hymn-book is compiled. The author, however, includes no hymn, whatever its merits, not found in the hymnal of the Protestant Episcopal Church.

This is somewhat more catholic in method than that pursued in the *Anglican Hymnology*, but its use-

*As to authorship of this hymn, see page 124.
†The National Hymn-Book of the American Churches. Edited by Robert Ellis Thompson, S.T.D. Philadelphia, John D. Wattles, 1893.

fulness for our purposes is destroyed by its peculiar limitation. The standard is virtually the hymnal of the Episcopal Church, with other hymnals corroborating.

III. *The Best Church Hymns.** The author of this book has collated one hundred and seven hymn-books, among which are included those of the two authors above. He then takes eighty per cent as the proportion of books in which a hymn must be found to attain the first rank. This gives him thirty-two hymns which may be called "the best church hymns." This makes an invaluable little book—incomparably the best of its kind extant. The work has been done in the spirit of broadest charity, with no evidence of sectarianism of any kind, and the results embody the judgment of our common Protestantism. The author, however, expresses the same caution as that of the *Anglican Hymnology*, that there may be certain first-rank hymns not included in the list simply because they have not as yet had time to find their way into the collections. These thirty-two, however, are not likely to be superseded. The list is as follows, the number of votes for each following. For purposes of comparison the rank of each hymn, also according to the *Anglican Hymnology*, is placed after the author's name:†

1. Rock of Ages, cleft for me (106).   Toplady.   A.H. 4.
2. When I survey the wondrous cross (104).   Watts.   A.H. 10.
3. Jesus, Lover of my soul (104).   Wesley.   A.H. 8.

*The Best Church Hymns, by the Rev. Louis F. Benson, D.D.   Philadelphia, The Westminster Press, 1898.
†Copyright list.   Used by permission.

4. All praise to Thee, my God, this night (103). Ken. A.H. 1.
5. Jesus, I my cross have taken (103). Lyte. A.H. 287.
6. Sun of my soul, Thou Saviour dear (103). Keble. A.H. 9.
7. Awake, my soul, and with the sun (101). Ken. A.H. 6.
8. Hark! the herald angels sing (101). Wesley. A.H. 2.
9. Abide with me: fast falls the eventide (101). Lyte. A.H. 5.
10. Jerusalem, my happy home (101). Montgomery. A.H. 16.
11. How sweet the Name of Jesus sounds (101).
     Newton. A.H. 15.
12. Nearer, my God, to Thee (100). Adams. A.H. 13.
13. From Greenland's icy mountains (100). Heber. A.H. 17.
14. Our God, our Help in ages past (100). Watts. A.H. 19.
15. Jerusalem the golden (99). Bernard-Neale. A.H. 7.
16. Lo! He comes with clouds descending (94).
     Cennick-Wesley. A.H. 3.
17. Jesus shall reign where'er the sun (94). Watts. A.H. 40.
18. Glorious things of thee are spoken (93). Newton. A.H. 31.
19. Hark the glad sound! the Saviour comes (92).
     Doddridge. A. H. 14.
20. Come, let us join our cheerful songs (92). Watts. A.H. 30.
21. All hail the power of Jesus' Name (92). Perronet. A.H. 46.
22. Hail to the Lord's Anointed (91). Montgomery. A.H. 26.
23. O worship the King (91). Grant. A.H. 32.
24. Christ the Lord is risen to-day (90). Wesley. A.H. 37.
25. Guide me, O Thou Great Jehovah (90). Williams. A.H. 58.
26. Just as I am, without one plea (90). Elliott. A.H. 64.
27. God moves in a mysterious way (90). Cowper. A.H. 49.
28. Jesus, the very thought of Thee (89).
     Bernard-Caswall. A.H. 59.
29. Children of the heavenly King (87). Cennick. A.H. 55.
30. There is a land of pure delight (87). Watts. A.H. 70.
31. Thou whose almighty word (86). Marriott. A.H. 29.
32. Brief life is here our portion (86). Bernard-Neale. A.H. 22.

While the numbers do not exactly coincide they show a remarkable degree of correspondence. The only surprising disagreement is with regard to Lyte's hymn, "Jesus, I my cross have taken," which is 5 in Dr. Benson's list, and only 287 in Mr. King's, being there assigned to the "third rank." But it will be observed that in the two lists there are seven hymns common to the first ten, fifteen common to the first twenty, and twenty common to the entire list of thirty-two.

Here, then, we have something upon which we can depend and by which we may be safely guided. We shall therefore recur to these lists as we pursue our studies of the separate hymns in the succeeding chapters.

We now inquire, What are the qualities possessed by these hymns which have secured their general adoption? The answers to this question as given by Mr. King and Dr. Benson are in substantial agreement. Mr. King states them as follows: (1) Terse in thought and expression; (2) Scriptural in phraseology; (3) Catholic in doctrine; (4) Clothed in poetic language. Dr. Benson finds the following, prefaced with a remark concerning the catholicity of the church's judgment, in that the writers represent so many different religious bodies: (1) Lyrical quality; (2) Literary excellence; (3) Liturgical propriety; (4) Reverence; (5) Spiritual reality.

Admitting the propriety of these conclusions, we are persuaded that for the purposes of this volume a somewhat different arrangement must be made.

The qualities of the best hymns must be so stated as to be both inclusive and exclusive, and therefore it does not fulfil all our conditions to note simply certain features of those hymns which have been generally adopted by the church.

The standard must be expressed in terms which shall as certainly rule out objectionable verses as it rules in acceptable ones. The following may then be given as the indispensable qualities of a true hymn.

1. *It must be Scriptural, both in sentiment and expression.* Beyond all question this is chief. The hymn must be absolutely true to Scripture. Nor is it enough that its thought is not a violation of Scripture truth; the very form in which that thought is cast must be just as true to the Scripture as the thought itself. Otherwise we cannot be safeguarded in the offering of divine praise.

The abstract truth of Scripture is one thing; the spirit of Scripture—its tone and temper—is quite another. But both must be present in a correct transcription of Scriptural thought. The naked truth may be preserved while its spirit is violated; and on the other hand, its spirit may be presented while the statement of the truth is inaccurate. We cannot certainly save ourselves from both errors except by insisting on fidelity in both sentiment and expression.

"Spiritual reality" is imperative; but it is not enough. Some poems that aspire to be hymns, possess it, that are nevertheless trivial, misanthropic, uncharitable, or even vulgar. It is a very solemn responsibility which he accepts who undertakes to voice the praise of the Almighty and it is an almost equally solemn one which he assumes who invites others to engage in it. No one should ever venture to do either who does not keep close to the Word of God.

It is not necessary, perhaps, to paraphrase consecutive verses of Scripture, as has been done in the versions of the Psalms, but nothing should be called a hymn, and nothing should ever be sung in our assemblies, which is not virtually a paraphrase—and that a very faithful one — of Scripture passages, whether they are immediately connected in the Holy Word or not.

If, now, we apply this rule to the hymns adopted in the usage of the church, we will find that it obtains. Take the first great hymn as an example, "Rock of Ages" is a Scriptural thought in Scriptural form. How often is Jehovah called a Rock!   But in Isaiah xxvi. 4, where the King James version reads "In the Lord Jehovah is everlasting strength," the margin has "the Lord Jehovah is the Rock of Ages." The Revised Version has "the Lord Jehovah is an everlasting rock" with "A Rock of Ages" in the margin. Toplady, then, exhibited scholarship, poetry, and profound devotion in seizing the expression as the theme of his song, and all Christendom has responded. But as we proceed with the lines of his hymn we can verify them in like manner and the student is urged to apply the rule to other hymns.

Our psalm-singing brethren are right in general principles, though we may deny their limited application; and these principles should contain the first great, inviolable element whereby the true hymn shall be determined.

2. *The true hymn must be devotional.* In this is included profound reverence and "liturgical propriety." Some other things are also included in the term. True devotion contemplates God in the various relations which he sustains towards his earthly creatures. The true hymn must therefore have a motion Godward. It is not exactly necessary that God should be directly addressed—indeed, the express form of address may be otherwise—but God must be uppermost in the thought even if not particularly conspicuous in the expression. The true hymn must tend towards God; bring him to mind; exalt his name and seek his glory. Those which are simply introspective, didactic, dogmatic, sentimental, egotistical, and the like, are not hymns. The Pharisee's utterances in the Temple, when he went up thither with the Publican, did not contain a single element of prayer. Some so-called hymns are like it—they do not contain a single element of praise.

Devotion is also worshipful. A hymn must contain nothing inconsistent with this, nothing that may not properly be uttered in approaching the Infinite, Adorable God. Those which are coarse, irreverent, trifling, or calculated to form an unworthy image in the mind should be severely excluded from our worship.

Let the student test the adopted hymns by this rule. "Jerusalem, my happy home," does not address God in a single stanza, but is adjudged a true hymn—its motion is distinctly Godward—the Saviour is set forth as the center and attraction of the place.   The same characteristic will be found in some others; all are grave and dignified; all express the adoration of the worshiper in reverential strains.

3. *The true hymn must be lyrical.*   This means much more than that it may be set to music.   The question should be asked, Is it improved by being set to music?   If not, it is not a lyric.   There must be, indeed, an interaction between the words and the music that is harmonious and reciprocal.   The tune must be a help to the hymn and the hymn a help to the tune, else either tune or hymn is at fault—perhaps both.

The true lyric does not receive its best interpretation until it is sung; so that it is not enough to say, "It may be sung"—it *must* be sung.   It is not well interpreted until it is sung.   It does not express all its meaning nor exert all its power.   We should rigidly reject, therefore, anything claiming to be hymn which is better said than sung.   If a fine elocutionist can give it greater influence in declaiming it than a fine vocalist by singing it, it ought not to be called a hymn.

Apply this rule to the hymns adopted by the Church.   It certainly applies to a very striking degree.   Look again over the list of first lines given above; recall the tunes to which so many have been irrevocably wedded and their lyrical qualities will certainly appear.

These three rules are deemed sufficient.   It does not appear that any other qualities are imperative.

Poetic language certainly adds to the merit of a hymn, but it is not indispensable. Some of the great hymns are not particularly great as poetry. Even Bishop Ken's Morning Hymn, ranking sixth in *Anglican Hymnology* and seventh in *The Best Church Hymns*, is not very far removed above good prose. But it is not thereby degraded in rank. At all events, if we take these three qualities, Scriptural, devotional, lyrical, as exhibited in the hymns generally adopted by the Church at large, we have a test sufficiently critical and comprehensive to apply to all poetic aspirants for hymnic honors.

With them, therefore, we proceed to our examination of the separate compositions.

CHAPTER VII

HYMNS OF THE FIRST PERIOD. I

In our account of the hymn-writers of the three periods in English Hymnology we shall give particular attention only to those of the first rank, as determined by usage.

BISHOP KEN.—1637–1711

The Reverend Thomas Ken, D.D., was born at Berkhampstead, Hertfordshire, July, 1637, and died at Longleat, Somersetshire, March 19, 1711. It will be observed that his life covers that troubled period in English history distinguished by the Commonwealth and the Restoration.

His preparatory education was received at the Winchester school, where his name is still to be seen cut into one of the stone pillars. He was graduated from Oxford, and after filling a number of positions, was appointed chaplain to Charles II., 1682. Two years later he was made bishop of Bath and Wells. His advancement was not due to sycophancy. On the contrary, he was fearless in his rebuke of royal immorality, like another John the Baptist. While serving at Winchester the king visited the place and desired his residence as a temporary dwelling for some of the worthless characters of his train. "Not for the king's kingdom," was the heroic clergyman's

94

reply, and his very courage and fidelity to his trust so aroused the king's admiration as to lead to his preferment. James II. continued him in place, but with William and Mary began his years of humiliation and suffering. He was deprived of his honors by the new dynasty, reconciled under Queen Anne, but recognized only as a private member of the Church of England, with a pension of two hundred pounds per year. His fourteen years of trial were then followed by a season of comparative comfort, until his peaceful end. He himself compared his career to that of another displaced bishop of old, Gregory of Nazianzus, and posterity has approved his comparison. They were much alike, both in gifts and experiences.

Bishop Ken wrote many hymns. It was his earnest desire that the saints of God might continue to praise God in words of his own composing, and his desire has been remarkably fulfilled.

Only two of his songs are in common use, but they are very widely sung, and the doxology in long meter which was appended to his "Evening Hymn" is sung by more Christians the world over than any other single English verse in existence.

The "Anglican Hymnology" ranks his "Evening Hymn" with the four masterpieces of English praise —the others being "Rock of Ages," by Toplady, and "Hark! the herald angels sing" and "Lo! He comes with clouds descending," both by Wesley, the last having been altered by him from the original by Cennick.

His "Evening Hymn" is as follows:

"Glory to thee, my God, this night,
For all the blessings of the light;
Keep me, oh, keep me, King of kings!
Beneath thine own almighty wings.

"Forgive me, Lord, for thy dear Son,
The ill which I this day have done;
That with the world, myself, and thee,
I, ere I sleep, at peace may be.

"Teach me to live that I may dread
The grave as little as my bed:
Teach me to die, that so I may
Rise glorious at the judgment day.

"Oh, let my soul on thee repose,
And may sweet sleep mine eyelids close!
Sleep, which shall me more vigorous make
To serve my God when I awake.

"Praise God, from whom all blessings flow;
Praise him, all creatures here below;
Praise him above, ye heavenly host;
Praise Father, Son, and Holy Ghost!

Bishop Ken's "Morning Hymn" begins

"Awake, my soul, and with the sun
Thy daily stage of duty run;
Shake off dull sloth, and joyful rise
To pay thy morning sacrifice."

Some things are to be noted with regard to this
first great Christian singer in the English tongue—
most particularly this, that the burden of his song is
gratitude. His two hymns have gone echoing down
the ages because they are so charged with this important element of the true hymn. No one has since
succeeded in compressing into four short lines so full
a measure as we find in his doxology. We will also

observe the reflex of the age, of his own trials and his own heroism, in such lines as

> "Teach me to live that I may dread
> The grave as little as my bed."

And these from his "Morning Hymn,"

> "Direct, control, suggest, this day,
> All I design, or do, or say;
> That all my powers, with all their might,
> In thy sole glory may unite.

JOSEPH ADDISON.—1672–1719

The reputation of Addison rests with the general student upon his literary work. He is known, in connection with his coadjutor, Sir Richard Steele, as the publisher of the "Spectator;" and his essays are still ranked as models of English prose. But Addison was more than a mere *litterateur*. He was a devout Christian as well. His dying remark to the Earl of Warwick is often quoted, "See in what peace a Christian can die." Addison was born in Wiltshire. His father, then rector at Milston, was soon after made Dean of Lichfield. His mother was sister of the Bishop of Bristol. So Addison grew up in the atmosphere of the English establishment, with an inherited attachment to Episcopacy and aristocracy. He married a countess, Charlotte of Warwick, and so passed his life among dignitaries of church and state, filling one government office after another until he became assistant secretary of state—a high-bred, accomplished, Christian gentleman, adorning every position he held and leaving behind him a legacy of refined thought seldom surpassed.

Five of his hymns are in common use to-day, chief of which is his "Creation," so called because sung to a selection from Haydn's great oratorio of that name:

"The spacious firmament on high,
With all the blue ethereal sky,
And spangled heavens, a shining frame,
Their great Original proclaim;
The unwearied sun, from day to day,
Does his Creator's power display,
And publishes to every land
The work of an almighty hand.

"Soon as the evening shades prevail
The moon takes up the wondrous tale;
And nightly, to the listening earth,
Repeats the story of her birth;
While all the stars that round her burn,
And all the planets in their turn,
Confirm the tidings as they roll,
And spread the truth from pole to pole.

"What though in solemn silence, all
Move round the dark terrestrial ball—
What though no real voice nor sound
Amid their radiant orbs be found—
In reason's ear they all rejoice,
And utter forth a glorious voice,
Forever singing as they shine—
'The hand that made us is divine.' "

His other hymns are almost equally popular.   That beginning

"When all thy mercies, O my God,
My rising soul surveys,"

is a great favorite in many congregations.   One is known as the "Traveler's Hymn." It was published in the "Spectator," after a stormy voyage upon the Mediterranean, in connection with an essay upon "The Sea." It begins

> "How are thy servants blest, O Lord!
> How sure is their defense."

The remaining hymns are those whose first lines read

> "The Lord my pasture shall prepare!"

and

> "When rising from the bed of death."

It is very unusual to find one in whose life blessings abounded so peculiarly sensitive to the goodness and care of God as Addison. In the essay in which he introduces his hymn on the mercies of God he says, "If gratitude is due from man to man, how much more from man to his Maker. The Supreme Being does not only confer upon us those bounties which proceed more immediately from his hand, but even those benefits which are conveyed to us by others. Any blessing which we enjoy, by what means soever derived, is the gift of him who is the great Author of good and the Father of Mercies."

Isaac Watts.—1674–1748

Watts and Wesley divide the first honors in English hymnody. Their names are always coupled together and placed at the head of all the writers of sacred song. A comparison of their respective productions is reserved for its proper place, but thus much is necessary in our introduction to the celebrated character whom we now consider.

Watts is called the "Father of English Hymnody," not because he was the first to write hymns, for as

we have seen he had his predecessors, but because
he gave a distinct impetus to the work and established its place in the worship of the Protestant
Church. He also so far surpassed those who had
gone before him, both in the extent and quality of his
productions, that he well deserves the title which has
been accorded him.

Isaac Watts was the son of a deacon in the Independent Church of Southampton. His mother was
the child of a Huguenot refugee. When this is taken
in connection with the history related in the preceding
chapter we may divine the story of his infancy and
youth. There were fourteen years of suffering for
his parents and their children following his birth until
1688, when William and Mary came to the throne
and better times began.

His father's pastor and the officers of his church
were persecuted for their non-conformity. His father
passed six months in jail, his pastor with him for a
part of the time at least, and the mother often sitting
disconsolate on the stone steps of the prison gate with
the infant Isaac in her arms.

He was an invalid all his life; a puny infant, and
only a trifle more than five feet tall as an adult. His
studies were frequently interrupted by sickness and
never completed as desired. He was never married.
For many years he had no home of his own, depend-
ing largely on the generosity of others.

When he was twenty-three years old he undertook
the charge of a congregation in London, where he
continued for fourteen years. But his services were

interrupted by repeated attacks of severe illness, so that he was obliged to abandon the pastorate in 1712. He was invited to the house of Sir Thomas Abney, at Theobalds to recuperate, with the result that he remained there a welcome guest for thirty-four years, "waiting God's leave to die." But he was not idle. He preached in various places, as his health permitted, and did a great deal of literary work, to the permanent enrichment of the church of Christ.

The story of Dr. Watts' introduction to hymn-writing is an interesting one. He was a poet from childhood. He wrote rhymes for his parents' amusement when he was only seven years old, and was writing Latin verses when he was not much older. When he was about eighteen he undertook to criticise the versification of the psalms sung in his father's church, when one of the officers said to him rather peremptorily, "Give us something which will be better, young man."

Watts accepted the task, wrote his first hymn, and heard it sung at the next evening service. This hymn is not generally found in our collections to-day, though we are bound to say we find many poorer ones. Its first verse is

"Behold the glories of the Lamb
Amidst his Father's throne;
Prepare new honors for his name
And songs before unknown."

The cordial reception of this hymn led its author to prepare others. He furnished one for each Sunday until over two hundred had been written. These were gathered together and published, and the first Watts' Hymn-Book appeared.

Watts' monumental work was his versification of the Psalms. It occupied his attention for several years, the several portions being published as prepared, until the entire task was completed. The peculiar feature of his version is the New Testament flavor which he gives to the Old Testament poetry. While the translation is rendered with great fidelity, it is fidelity to the spirit rather than to the form, and the terms employed are those of the Gospel age. He himself said, "I have expressed as I may suppose David would have done had he lived in the days of Christianity." Thus his seventy-second psalm begins:

> "Jesus shall reign where'er the sun
> Does his successive journeys run";

and his nineteenth psalm closes:

> "Nor shall thy spreading Gospel rest
> Till through the world thy truth has run,
> Till Christ has all the nations blessed
> That see the light or feel the sun."

For this reason many treat these poems simply as hymns, forgetting their Davidic origin; many reject them because they are not sufficiently literal to suit their theories, but it still remains that Watts' version of the Psalms is considered incomparably the best in existence.

By common consent Watts' greatest hymn is "The Wondrous Cross."

"When I survey the wondrous cross,
    On which the Prince of glory died,
My richest gain I count but loss,
    And pour contempt on all my pride.

"Forbid it, Lord! that I should boast,
    Save in the death of Christ, my God;
All the vain things that charm me most,
    I sacrifice them to his blood.

"See, from his head, his hands, his feet,
    Sorrow and love flow mingled down;
Did e'er such love and sorrow meet,
    Or thorns compose so rich a crown?

"His dying crimson, like a robe,
    Spreads o'er his body on the tree;
Then I am dead to all the globe,
    And all the globe is dead to me.

"Were the whole realm of nature mine,
    That were a present far too small;
Love so amazing, so divine,
    Demands my soul, my life, my all."

This is also, in the writer's judgment, the finest hymn in the English language. Its place is disputed only by Toplady's "Rock of Ages." Though it is not ranked with the Great Four of "Anglican Hymnology," its position is not dependent upon a single authority. The best literary critics and the usage of worshiping congregations determine its place. If any one would know its claim, let him simply observe how often it is announced in public worship. There is no temptation to analyze it, to dissect its lines, and point out its particular beauties. Let the devout reader simply dwell upon its subject, its description, its imaginative quality, its absolute self-surrender. Then let him sing it from his own responsive heart.

We will not undertake to catalogue all the hymns of Watts—it is too great a task.   Let the reader find them in any hymn-book.   A few among the finest are:

"Before Jehovah's awful throne."

"Great God, how infinite art thou."

"The heavens declare thy glory Lord."

"My God, how endless is thy love."

"Come let us join our cheerful songs."

"There is a land of pure delight."

"Our God! our help in ages past."

Watts was a pronounced Calvinist.   For this reason some of his hymns are omitted from present-day collections.   But it is well to give an example as indicative of the age in which he lived, when doctrine was particularly emphasized:

"Keep silence all created things,
    And wait your Maker's nod;
My soul stands trembling while she sings
    The honors of her God.

"Life, death, and hell, and world's unknown
    Hang on his firm decree;
He sits on no precarious throne,
    Nor borrows leave to be.

"Chained to his throne a volume lies
    With all the fates of men,
With every angel's form and size
    Drawn by the eternal pen.

"His providence unfolds the book
    And makes his counsels shine,
Each opening leaf and every stroke
    Fulfils some deep design.

"Here he exalts neglected worms
  To scepters and a crown;
Anon the following page he turns
  And treads the monarch down.

"Not Gabriel asks the reason why,
  Nor God the reason gives,
Nor dares the favorite angel pry
  Between the folded leaves.

"My God, I would not long to see
  My fate with curious eyes,
What gloomy lines are writ for me
  Or what bright scenes shall rise;

"In thy fair book of life and grace
  O may I find my name
Recorded in some humble place
  Beneath my Lord, the Lamb."

Whatever may be thought of the theology of this poem, or of its claims to suitable hymnic qualities, it must be admitted that many of its features are incomparably fine. What can surpass the reference to the throne of Jehovah in the second stanza or the lines concerning the "favorite angel" in the sixth? And how the exaltation of the providence of God must have stirred the souls of Watts' contemporaries, who had seen monarchs "trodden down" and "neglected worms exalted" to sovereignty!

Another hymn of Watts', now generally omitted from our collections, is also one of his finest. For use in a Christian burial there is nothing that equals it in connection with the committal service, and it serves to enforce a doctrine frequently ignored, if not even rejected.

"Unveil thy bosom, faithful tomb;
    Take this new treasure to thy trust,
And give these sacred relics room
    Awhile to slumber in the dust.

"Nor pain, nor grief, nor anxious fear
    Invade thy bounds; no mortal woes
Can reach the peaceful sleeper here,
    While angels watch the soft repose.

"So Jesus slept; God's dying Son
    Passed through the grave and blest the bed;
Rest here, blest saint, till from his throne
    The morning break, and pierce the shade.

"Break from his throne, illustrious morn!
    Attend, O earth, his sovereign word!
Restore thy trust; a glorious form
    Shall then ascend to meet the Lord."

We ought not to omit a reference to Watts' hymns for children. These were written during his life at Abney House, and published in a volume entitled "Divine and Moral Songs." It seems strange that a man with no children of his own should have undertaken such a task, but so it was, and many a mother has blessed him for it. For many years his children's hymns were in common use. Many of them linger to-day only in memory or popular quotation, as

"Let dogs delight to bark and bite,"

and

"How doth the little busy bee."

But one at least remains, as sweet and acceptable as ever, surpassed by no cradle-song in any language:

"Hush, my dear, lie still and slumber,
    Holy angels guard thy bed,
Heavenly blessings without number,
    Gently falling on thy head.

"Soft and easy is thy cradle,
    Coarse and hard thy Saviour lay
When his birthplace was a stable
    And his softest bed was hay.

"May'st thou live to know and fear him,
    Trust and love him all thy days,
Then go dwell forever near him
    See his face and sing his praise."

While many qualities unite to make the hymns of Watts what they are, their most conspicuous feature is their profound reverence.   His sense of the majesty, power, and holiness of God were overwhelming.   To him Jehovah's throne is "awful," the Saviour's cross "wondrous," his love "amazing."   The poet's thought runs into the "ages past," and forth into the "years to come," while he seeks to set forth the infinity and eternity of God's holy being.   He engages himself with high themes, with whose transcendent character he is deeply impressed, and his language is as well adapted to their expression as anything in which the thought of man has been contained.   And so his songs are still sung and every worthy collection contains twice as many by him as by any other author.

CHAPTER VIII

HYMNS OF THE FIRST PERIOD. II

The chronological list of the great hymn-writers of the First English Period is continued in this chapter.

PHILLIP DODDRIDGE.—1702–1751

Reverend Phillip Doddridge, D.D., was born in London, June 26, 1702. His grandfather had suffered persecution under the Commonwealth. His father was a pious layman of the Independent Church. His mother gave him a very careful training in Bible history and doctrine, and very interesting tales are told of her use, for this purpose, of the old Dutch tiles with which a portion of the wall of the family sitting-room was covered. Doddridge displayed in early youth so much talent that the Duchess of Bedford offered to educate him either at Oxford or Cambridge on condition of his becoming a clergyman in the English Church. This offer he declined. He was prepared for the ministry at a private Nonconformist seminary, at Kibworth, where he became pastor of the church. He soon removed to Harborough and opened an academy for the purpose of preparing young dissenting candidates for the ministry for their work. Here he resided for four years. In 1729 he was invited to become pastor of the church at Northampton, where he continued for twenty years, preaching and teaching in the theological seminary, and where he trained nearly two hundred students. His health now failed; consumption set in and he sailed for Portugal. He arrived at Lisbon in an exhausted condition, and soon died there, October 26, 1751.

Doddridge was a voluminous author, in both prose and poetry. The best known of his prose writings are his commentary on the New Testament, called "The Family Expositor," and his "Rise and Progress of Religion in the Soul."

He is entitled to rank as one of the great English hymn-writers, not because he has written any single hymn of the highest rank, but because he has written so many that have endured the test of time and are still eminently acceptable to the worshiping church. While he never rises to the heights which Watts and Wesley attain, he never falls below a certain level. He is remarkably even, in all the qualities of a good hymn. For this reason we cannot select one or two hymns of Doddridge and say "These are his best." There are at least fifteen between which we find it impossible to choose. The following will perhaps furnish as good an illustration as any of his spirit and style:

> "Jesus! I love thy charming name,
>   'Tis music to mine ear;
> Fain would I sound it out so loud
>   That earth and heaven should hear.
>
> "Yes! thou art precious to my soul,
>   My transport and my trust;
> Jewels, to thee, are gaudy toys,
>   And gold is sordid dust.

"All my capacious powers can wish,
  In thee doth richly meet;
Not to mine eyes is light so dear,
  Nor friendship half so sweet.

"Thy grace still dwells upon my heart,
  And sheds its fragrance there;
The noblest balm of all its wounds,
  The cordial of its care."

The student, however, will be surprised to find how many very familiar and oft-sung hymns must be assigned to Doddridge, the following among them:

"Now let our cheerful eyes survey."

"Why will ye waste on trifling cares."

"Awake, my soul, stretch every nerve."

"Do not I love thee, O my Lord?"

"Grace,'tis a charming sound."

"Dear Saviour, we are thine."

"Triumphant Zion, lift thy head."

"O happy day that fixed my choice."

"Eternal source of every joy."

"Hark the glad sound the Saviour comes."

The striking characteristic of Doddridge's hymns is their scripturalness. Most of them are substantial paraphrases of some Bible passage. Many were written to be sung following his sermons and applying their lessons. It is easy to trace this connection in the hymns to which we have referred, and the student may often recognize and identify them by observing this feature.

CHARLES WESLEY.—1708–1788

Rev. Charles Wesley, brother and associate of Rev. John Wesley, the distinguished founder of Methodism, divides with Isaac Watts, as we have already noticed, the first honors in English hymnody. His fame, indeed, rests almost exclusively upon his hymns, though he was an able prose-writer also. The fame of his brother John, on the other hand, rests almost exclusively upon his prose works, though John also wrote hymns.   But the hymns with which John's name is generally associated are translations from the German, such as

"Give to the winds thy fears,"

from Paul Gerhardt; and

"Jesus thy blood and righteousness,"

from Count Zinzendorf.

But the hymns of Charles Wesley are originals; evangelical, spiritual, immortal.

Wesley was born at Epworth, Lincolnshire, December 18, 1708.   He was the eighteenth child and youngest son in a family of nineteen.   His father was Rev. Samuel Wesley, a clergyman of the English Church.   His mother was Susannah Annesly, daughter of Rev. Samuel Annesly, LL. D., a learned Nonconformist minister in London.   She was by far the more gifted of his parents, and to her character and training the remarkable career of her children is chiefly to be attributed.

In 1726 Wesley was elected to Christ Church College, Oxford, where the serious manners and severe methods of himself and a few friends won for them the title by which a great religious departure was soon to be known—"Methodists." This was before his older brother, John, had joined the society.

After taking his degree Wesley remained at the college, as tutor, until 1735, when he was persuaded to accompany his brother John on a mission to Georgia.

Before sailing he was ordained to the English priesthood by Bishop Gibson of London. His voyage to America was attended by many privations, so that his health suffered, and he was compelled to return to England within a year.

It was then that a providential circumstance occurred which was destined to change the whole course and aspect of his own life as well as that of his brother's. They fell in with a devout Moravian, Peter Böhler by name, whom Charles undertook to instruct in English. But the great outcome to his own heart was the revelation of his real spiritual condition, for he discovered that, priest though he was, he was without saving grace or hope. Again he was taken ill, but in his sickness he received the blessed sense of pardon through Jesus Christ.

The week following, his brother John enjoyed a similar experience. This was in May, 1738. Thenceforth the character of their labors entirely altered, and Methodism, instead of being as its name implied a thing of mere methods, became a system of vital, evangelical faith.   The preaching of Charles at once became such as to incur the disapprobation of his bishop; the curacy of St. Mary's, Islington, London —the only place which he had ever occupied in the Church of England—was taken from him, and he was denied access to any other.   So, though he was ardently attached to the church and deeply devoted to her spiritual interests, he was compelled to seek a field of labor elsewhere.

From 1739 to 1756 he was actively engaged with his brother John, itinerating through Great Britain. But his constitution was too feeble, his spirit too gentle, to continue in this work, and he could not heartily adopt some of the measures which John so earnestly advocated.   He therefore withdrew from active service and spent the balance of his life in retirement.   In 1771 he removed to London, where he died, March 29, 1788.

Wesley wrote over six thousand hymns.   Many of these have been received by all evangelical denominations, and are sung the world over.   There can be no question with regard to the most acceptable of all Wesley's hymns.   There is one which the entire church, with absolute unanimity, assigns to the first place.

"Jesus! lover of my soul,
　　Let me to thy bosom fly
While the billows near me roll,
　　While the tempest still is high;
Hide me, O my Saviour, hide,
　　Till the storm of life is past;
Safe into the haven guide;
　　Oh, receive my soul at last!

"Other refuge have I none;
    Hangs my helpless soul on thee;
Leave, ah! leave me not alone,
    Still support and comfort me.
All my trust on thee is stayed;
    All my help from thee I bring;
Cover my defenseless head
    With the shadow of thy wing.

"Thou, O Christ, art all I want;
    More than all in thee I find;
Raise the fallen, cheer the faint,
    Heal the sick, and lead the blind.
Just and holy is thy name,
    I am all unrighteousness;
Vile and full of sin I am,
    Thou art full of truth and grace.

"Plenteous grace with thee is found,
    Grace to pardon all my sin;
Let the healing streams abound,
    Make and keep me pure within;
Thou of life the fountain art,
    Freely let me take of thee;
Spring thou up within my heart,
    Rise to all eternity."

The title originally given to this hymn was "In Temptation"—the author probably using the word in the sense of trial. It is said that Wesley wrote it after he and his brother had been driven from the place in which they were holding service by a furious mob. Another and very pretty story is told of the poet sitting by an open window when a little bird pursued by a hawk flew in and took refuge in the folds of his coat. These stories, however, cannot be verified; nor does the lyric have need of them to enhance its beauty.

The tributes which it has received are many and emphatic. Dr. George Duffield, himself a hymn-writer, and author of "Stand up, stand up for Jesus," says, "If there is anything in Christian experience of joy and sorrow, of affliction and prosperity, of life and death, that hymn is *the* hymn of the ages!" President Finney sang it through the night before his death. The *Methodist Hymn-book* pronounces it "the queen of all the lays of holy love." Dr. Louis F. Benson, in his little book, *The Best Hymns*, gives it third place among all English hymns, ranking above it only Toplady's "Rock of Ages" and Watts' "Wondrous Cross."

And yet the place of this hymn is disputed by another, according to some authorities.

> "Hark! the herald angels sing
> 'Glory to the new-born King;
> Peace on earth and mercy mild,
> God and sinners reconciled!'
> Joyful, all ye nations, rise,
> Join the triumph of the skies;
> With the angelic host proclaim,
> Christ is born in Bethlehem!

> "Christ, by highest heaven adored;
> Christ, the everlasting Lord;
> Late in time behold him come,
> Offspring of the Virgin's womb;
> Veiled in flesh the Godhead see;
> Hail the incarnate Deity,
> Pleased as man with men to dwell;
> Jesus, our Immanuel!

> "Hail! the heaven-born Prince of Peace!
> Hail the Sun of Righteousness!
> Light and life to all he brings,
> Risen with healing in his wings;

> Mild he lays his glory by,
> Born that man no more may die;
> Born to raise the sons of earth,
> Born to give them second birth."

This, according to the *Anglican Hymnology*, is Wesley's greatest hymn, and is named, as we have already noted, among the "Great Four."

Another hymn is invested with very peculiar interest from its associations, as well as from the intensity of its expressions.

> "Oh, for a thousand tongues to sing
> My dear Redeemer's praise!
> The glories of my God and King,
> The triumphs of his grace!
>
> "My gracious Master and my God!
> Assist me to proclaim,
> To spread, through all the earth abroad,
> The honors of thy name.
>
> "Jesus—the name that calms my fears,
> That bids my sorrows cease;
> 'Tis music to my ravished ears;
> 'Tis life, and health, and peace.
>
> "He breaks the power of canceled sin,
> He sets the prisoner free;
> His blood can make the foulest clean;
> His blood availed for me.
>
> "Let us obey, we then shall know,
> Shall feel our sins forgiven;
> Anticipate our heaven below,
> And own that love is heaven."

Wesley entitled this hymn, "For the Anniversary Day of One's Conversion." No doubt it is the record of his own heart experiences, for it was written on the day indicated in its title.

One other hymn of this author should be quoted as illustrating the communion of saints.

"I know that my Redeemer lives,
   And ever prays for me;
A token of his love he gives,
   A pledge of liberty.

"I find him lifting up my head;
   He brings salvation near;
His presence makes me free indeed,
   And he will soon appear.

"He wills that I should holy be;
   What can withstand his will?
The counsel of his grace in me
   He surely shall fulfill.

"Jesus, I hang upon thy word;
   I steadfastly believe
Thou wilt return, and claim me, Lord,
   And to thyself receive."

The Wesleys were, as we have seen, pronounced Arminians. Their opposition to Calvinistic doctrine was emphatic, almost violent, and the earnest doctrinal controversies of their day estranged and separated them from friends and divided the Methodists themselves into two camps. But what Calvinist could ever have asked a hymn more to his mind than this of the great Arminian. Neither Watts nor Toplady could have surpassed it. Surely here is evidence of the substantial agreement of the people of God even upon those subjects upon which they apparently disagree when dogmatically discussed.

Other great hymns of Wesley begin:

"Ye servants of God, your Master proclaim."

"Hail the day that sees him rise."

"Our Lord is risen from the dead."

"Come thou long expected Jesus."

"A charge to keep I have."

"Arise, my soul, arise."

"Sinners turn, why will ye die?"

"Love divine all love excelling."

"Depth of mercy can there be."

"Soldiers of Christ arise."

The hymn beginning

"Come thou Almighty King,"

long associated with the name of Wesley, was certainly not written by him. It must, apparently, go down the ages anonymously.

It is not hard to discover the distinguishing characteristic of Wesley's hymns. Beyond question it is loyalty to Jesus Christ as King. Perhaps for this very reason the "Come thou Almighty King" has been attributed to him; it is so like him. Were it a work of plastic art rather than of poetic, we would be warranted in labeling it, "Wesley, or one of Wesley's pupils."

The student has but to run back over the hymns to which we have referred to note this prevailing feature. And it is this feature which marks the great contrast with the hymns of Watts and explains why to some minds Wesley is greater than Watts, while to others Watts is greater than Wesley. Watts is so profoundly impressed with the majesty of God that he appears to shrink from familiarity in his expressions of divine fellowship. We cannot imagine the man who wrote "Great God, how infinite art thou," also writing "Jesus, lover of my soul."

Wesley, on the other hand, seems so intimate with his Redeemer as to be incapable of expressing a sense of his awful majesty. Watts is more reverential; Wesley more loving. Watts is stronger; Wesley sweeter. Watts appeals profoundly to the intellect; Wesley takes hold of the heart. Watts will continue to sing for the Pauls and Peters of the church; Wesley for the Thomases and the Johns. Where both are so great it would be idle to attempt to settle their priority. Let us only be grateful that God in his gracious providence has given both to the church to voice the praises of various classes.

ANNA STEELE.—1716–1778

Miss Anna Steele is noted not only as one of the great hymn-writers of the first English period, but also as the earliest of women in this field. She was born at Broughton in Hampshire. Her father was a merchant, and also a minister. He served the Baptist Church in Broughton for sixty years and for the most part without pay. She united with her father's church when she was fourteen years old, and lived all her life in the same town, quietly and without special experience.

Like Watts, who lived only fifteen miles from her, she never married; though Watts was cruelly jilted and Miss Steele lost her lover, to whom she was deeply attached, by drowning.   Like Watts also, her health was very poor, and for many years she was a great sufferer, so her soul found relief, as his, in sacred song.   She has frequently been compared to Miss Havergal, as we shall observe under the latter's name.

Miss Steele's most familiar and best beloved hymn is the following:

> "Father! whate'er of earthly bliss
>   Thy sovereign will denies,
> Accepted at thy throne of grace
>   Let this petition rise:
>
> " 'Give me a calm, a thankful heart,
>   From every murmur free;
> The blessings of thy grace impart,
>   And make me live to thee.
>
> " 'Let the sweet hope that thou art mine
>   My life and death attend;
> Thy presence through my journey shine,
>   And crown my journey's end.' "

We cannot determine the date of this hymn.   It seems to have been among her first, if not the very first.   Doubtless it contains a reference to her great bereavement.   This hymn, however, is outranked in the judgment of some authors by the following:

> "Dear Refuge of my weary soul,
>   On thee, when sorrows rise,
> On thee, when waves of trouble roll,
>   My fainting hope relies.
>
> "To thee I tell each rising grief,
>   For thou alone canst heal;
> Thy word can bring a sweet relief
>   For every pain I feel.

"But oh, when gloomy doubts prevail,
　I fear to call thee mine;
The springs of comfort seem to fail
　And all my hopes decline.

"Yet, gracious God, where shall I flee?
　Thou art my only trust;
And still my soul would cleave to thee,
　Though prostrate in the dust.

"Thy mercy-seat is open still,
　Here let my soul retreat,
With humble hope attend thy will,
　And wait beneath thy feet."

Another fine hymn by this author, beginning "Father of Mercies in Thy Word," receives extended notice in Dr. Benson's *Studies of Familiar Hymns.*

It is a fine example of the "movement Godward" in connection with the theme, "The Excellency of the Holy Scriptures."

Other hymns of Miss Steele are:

"O thou whose tender mercy hears."

"Great God, to thee my evening song."

"My God, my Father, blissful name."

"Thou lovely source of true delight."

"The Saviour, O what endless charms."

"He lives, the great Redeemer lives."

"Thou only Sovereign of my heart."

"Alas! what hourly dangers rise."

The longing for the presence and power of the Saviour which Miss Steele expresses is truly wonderful. He is the "Refuge of her soul," the "Sovereign of her heart," the "Source of her delight," her "joy," and "assurance." Her songs are not great poetry, but they are great lyrics, nevertheless. There are very few metaphors in her verses—they are almost prose creations in the form of rhyme. But there is such sweet simplicity in them, such artless faith, such serene resignation, that the church has continued to cherish and sing them. Her chief petition, as given in the first hymn quoted, may be particularly commended to the worshipers of this busy and troubled age, and many a soul, wearied with the multiplied cares and anxieties of the week-day world, will sing itself to rest in her lines and thank God for Anna Steele.

WILLIAM WILLIAMS.—1717–1791
JOHN CENNICK.—1718–1755

These two names may well be associated in the student's memory. They were kindred spirits— though the one was a Welshman and the other an Englishman. They were of the same age, adopted the same form of faith, and each wrote one great hymn. Both were identified with the Wesley's for a time, though with Williams the connection was not so intimate as with Cennick, who for a time assisted Wesley as a lay preacher, but finally parted from him on account of their doctrinal differences. Both were instrumental in organizing the Calvinistic Methodist body, which Cennick subsequently abandoned for the Moravian Church.

William Williams is called the "Sweet singer of Wales," and the "Watts of Wales." He was ordained a deacon in the Established Church, but served in this capacity only for a short time. For thirty-five years his life was spent in travel as a revivalist. His great hymn is

> "Guide me, O thou great Jehovah,
>   Pilgrim through this barren land;
> I am weak, but thou art mighty;
>   Hold me with thy powerful hand;
>   Bread of heaven,
>   Feed me till I want no more.
>
> "Open thou the crystal fountain
>   Whence the healing streams do flow;
> Let the fiery, cloudy pillar
>   Lead me all my journey through;
>   Strong Deliverer,
>   Be thou still my Strength and Shield.
>
> "When I tread the verge of Jordan,
>   Bid my anxious fears subside;
> Death of death! and hell's Destruction!
>   Land me safe on Canaan's side;
>   Songs of praises
>   I will ever give to thee.

This hymn was originally published in Welsh. It was translated into English by Rev. Peter Williams, 1771. The author then accepted the English translation, revised it, and sent it down the years as his own.

Williams is generally known by but one other hymn, by no means the equal of this, though often effectively used in missionary meetings. Let us observe in this connection that we are approaching the missionary period in hymnology.

The first line of this hymn is

> "O'er the gloomy hills of darkness."

John Cennick was a more prolific hymn-writer than Williams. He is particularly distinguished as the author of one of the "Great Four" of the Anglican Hymnology. The hymn which has made him famous is the following:

"Lo, he comes, with clouds descending,
    Once for favored sinners slain;
Thousand thousand saints attending
    Swell the triumph of his train;
        Hallelujah!
    God appears on earth to reign.

"Every eye shall now behold him,
    Robed in dreadful majesty;
Those who set at naught and sold him,
    Pierced, and nailed him to the tree,
        Deeply wailing,
    Shall the true Messiah see.

"Yea, Amen; let all adore thee,
    High on thine eternal throne;
Saviour, take the power and glory;
    Claim the kingdom for thine own.
        Oh, come quickly,
    Hallelujah!   Come, Lord, come."

This is truly a majestic poem.   It reminds us of the *Dies Iræ* in theme and treatment.   The rhyme is double, the description graphic, the language chaste, the adoration of the Saviour profound.   The wonder is that it should have been writtten by a comparatively illiterate layman—a Quaker by birth, a reckless youth, then, after his conversion, a school teacher, a Methodist exhorter, and finally a Moravian deacon!

The hymn above is in the form given to it by Charles Wesley.   There are other versions of it, however; at least twenty; which indicates its deep hold upon the heart of the church.

Another well-known hymn of Cennick's is that beginning

"Children of the heavenly King."

This is preferred by some to his more famous poem.

The only other one in general use begins,

"Jesus my all to heaven is gone."

If now we place the two great hymns of Williams and Cennick, respectively, side by side, we will discern at once their great similarity, and observe why these men whom we have associated because of the incidents of their lives, may also be associated in their hymns.

They are written in the same meter; there is similar elevation in sentiment, and the imagery is closely related. Williams' hymn recalls the experiences of the Israelites in the wilderness—the manna, the smitten rock, the pillar of cloud and fire, the passage of the Jordan, and the entrance upon the Promised Land. Cennick's hymn brings before us the scenes of the last great day; the Saviour returning with the clouds, his appearance to all mankind including those that pierced him, the last judgment, and the cry of the waiting church—"Come, Lord Jesus." The subjects are very different, indeed, but the style is the same. These two hymns have laid the church under deep obligation to these two Calvinistic Methodists.

CHAPTER IX

HYMNS OF THE FIRST PERIOD. III

The chronological notice of the great English hymn-writers of the first period is concluded in this chapter.

JOHN NEWTON.—1725–1807
WILLIAM COWPER.—1731–1800

These names will be forever associated in hymnology, as those that bore them were in life. They were intimate friends for many years, dwelling under the same roof, engaged in the same occupations, contributing to the same great poetical composition. While the external features of their early experiences were very unlike, their intrinsic characters corresponded very closely—especially in spiritual results; and while the physical natures and mental states of the two men were totally dissimilar, their temperaments and tastes were almost identical. For these reasons their hymns are such that some have pronounced them "indistinguishable," and yet in certain respects they are separable as oil and water, and as unlike as sunshine and shadow. Both were rendered motherless at a very early age, Newton when he was seven years old, Cowper when he was six. Both in consequence passed a miserable, wretched youth, but with opposite effects: self-reliance and strength of character to Newton, timidity and melancholia to Cowper.   Newton became a wild, disbelieving, blasphemer;   Cowper an irresolute, despairing, would-be suicide.   One was driven to Christ by the violence of his sins, the other by the violence of his sufferings.   Both, therefore, needed the grace of God; sought it, found it, and sang of it to the ages following.

John Newton was born in London.   His mother was a pious woman who improved the few years in which she was spared to him in storing his mind with the truths of Scripture.   His father was a sea-captain, and when Newton was only eleven years old he went to sea with him, and thence continued to follow the life for eighteen years.   These were years full of stirring adventure, narrow escapes, vacillating purposes, and ungodly recklessness.   At times he seemed under conviction of sin and about to enter upon the religious life, and again he seemed wholly skeptical and unconcerned.   He is said to have changed his religious professions four times before he was sixteen years old.   He was impressed into the navy; flogged for deserting; engaged in the slave trade; and passed through many similar experiences which cannot be recounted.   Finally the chance discovery of a volume of Thomas à Kempis added to the influence of a godly sea-captain, led to the reconstruction of his life. In 1754 he left the sea forever.   He was now twenty-nine years old; but his true life was only begun.   He resided for the next nine years at Liverpool, fitting himself for such a work as the remaining portion of his life would permit; but in the good providence of God there yet remained fifty-three years of signal usefulness before him.   His time was spent in hard study, in exercises of devotion, and occasional preaching. He had frequent intercourse with Whitefield, the Wesleys, and other prominent leaders of the evangelical movement, and caught their spirit.   In 1764, at the age of thirty-nine, he was ordained to the curacy of Olney, and here the most fruitful period of his life was passed.   His physical powers were vigorous and his labors were abundant.   Sixteen years later he removed to London, as rector of Saint Mary Woolnoth.   He continued to preach almost up to the time of his death, declaring "Shall the old African blasphemer stop while he can speak?"   And so he passed to his reward; another Saul of Tarsus, we might almost say, or another Jacob, with characteristics and a career reminding us of both.

William Cowper's father was rector of the church at Berkhampstead.   He was a sensitive, feeble child upon whom were early laid burdens too heavy for him to bear.   Not long after his mother's death he was sent to Westminster school, where he was goaded almost to madness by the persecutions of older and stronger lads, "lying down," as he himself writes, "in horror and rising up in despair."   It was prophetic, alas, of his whole life!

After leaving school he spent three years in a lawyer's office, after which he was himself admitted to the bar.   During this time he fell in love with his cousin; but the marriage was forbidden by her father—another circumstance adding to all he had experienced conspiring to affect his mind.

He became subject to fits of melancholia, sinking at times into positive madness, until, after nine years of attempts to practice his profession, he became a sedentary invalid, dependent on his friends. Three times he attempted suicide, but was graciously prevented from succeeding. Certain friends of his, named Unwin, residing at Huntingdon, now took him into their home and tenderly cared for him for two years, after which he removed to Olney and was for six years the guest of his devoted friend John Newton. He left Olney in 1786 and removed to Weston. He died in East Dereham, April 25, 1800.

Newton and Cowper were authors of other works besides their hymns. Little else that Newton wrote, however, is esteemed to-day. Cowper is best remembered by "John Gilpin"—a strange composition for such a mind as his.

The great work in hymnody with which the names of the two men are associated is the "Olney Hymns." It was originally prepared for use in Newton's services; but it has been suggested, and not without reason, that its real origin lay in Newton's loving attempt to occupy the mind of his afflicted friend with pleasant, soothing subjects. It was in process of construction from 1767 to 1779, and from it are derived most of the pieces by which its authors are known.

In the light of the foregoing history it will not be a difficult task to interpret the hymns of these two

companions, both in their similarity and dissimilarity.
Take the following, for example, and compare them.
Newton wrote:

> "Amazing grace! how sweet the sound
>   That saved a wretch like me!
> I once was lost, but now am found—
>   Was blind, but now I see.
>
> " 'Twas grace that taught my heart to fear,
>   And grace my fears relieved;
> How precious did that grace appear
>   The hour I first believed!
>
> "Through many dangers, toils, and snares
>   I have already come;
> 'Tis grace hath brought me safe thus far,
>   And grace will lead me home."

Cowper wrote:

> "God moves in a mysterious way
>   His wonders to perform;
> He plants his footsteps in the sea,
>   And rides upon the storm.
>
> "Ye fearful saints, fresh courage take!
>   The clouds ye so much dread
> Are big with mercy, and will break
>   In blessings on your head.
>
> "Judge not the Lord by feeble sense,
>   But trust him for his grace;
> Behind a frowning providence
>   He hides a smiling face.
>
> "His purposes will ripen fast,
>   Unfolding every hour;
> The bud may have a bitter taste,
>   But sweet will be the flower.
>
> "Blind unbelief is sure to err,
>   And scan his work in vain;
> God is his own interpreter,
>   And he will make it plain."

Might we not readily assign each to its own author, even though we were not informed of their respective origin?   It is evident that Newton's hymn is a reference to his own peculiar experience of sin, and Cowper's to his own peculiar experience of sorrow.   We know, indeed, what Newton had in mind, for he entitled this hymn ''Faith's Review and Expectation,'' and it is said that Cowper's was written soon after one of his suicidal attempts, when his mind had regained its balance.

But let us compare two other hymns.   Newton wrote:

> "Approach, my soul, the mercy-seat
>   Where Jesus answers prayer;
> There humbly fall before his feet,
>   For none can perish there.
>
> "Thy promise is my only plea,
>   With this I venture nigh:
> Thou callest burdened souls to thee,
>   And such, O Lord, am I.
>
> "Bowed down beneath a load of sin,
>   By Satan sorely pressed;
> By war without and fears within,
>   I come to thee for rest.
>
> "Be thou my shield and hiding-place,
>   That, sheltered near thy side,
> I may my fierce accuser face,
>   And tell him—thou hast died.
>
> "Oh wondrous Love—to bleed and die,
>   To bear the cross and shame,
> That guilty sinners, such as I,
>   Might plea thy gracious name!"

Cowper wrote:

> "Jesus, where'er thy people meet,
> There they behold thy mercy-seat;
> Where'er they seek thee thou art found,
> And every place is hallowed ground.
>
> "For thou, within no walls confined,
> Inhabitest the humble mind;
> Such ever bring thee where they come,
> And going, take thee to their home.
>
> "Great Shepherd of thy chosen few,
> Thy former mercies here renew;
> Here to our waiting hearts proclaim
> The sweetness of thy saving name.
>
> "Here may we prove the power of prayer
> To strengthen faith and sweeten care
> To teach our faint desires to rise
> And bring all heaven before our eyes."

It is from the comparison of such hymns that some have been led to say that their songs are "indistinguishable," and certainly in their superficial aspects these before us are very much alike. Both introduce the "mercy-seat" in the first stanza; both make use of similar expressions. Newton says, "where Jesus answers prayer;" Cowper says, "Here we may prove the power of prayer." Newton says, "None can perish there," and Cowper, "Where'er they seek thee thou art found."

Yet a closer examination reveals the same characteristic differences as before. Where Newton has "burdened souls," Cowper has "waiting hearts;" where Newton has "guilty sinners," Cowper has the "chosen few." To the first the mercy-seat is a "hiding-place;" to the second "hallowed ground."

The one comes that he "may his fierce accuser face;" the other "to strengthen faith and sweeten care." Similar comparisons may be made between other hymns noted hereafter, and the student will be much interested and instructed in doing so.

While most of the hymns of these authors are on nearly the same level, each has one that rises considerably above that level to the dignity of a great hymn.

Newton's great hymn, written in all the buoyancy of his strong nature, is the following:

"Glorious things of thee are spoken,
  Zion, city of our God!
He, whose word cannot be broken,
  Formed thee for his own abode:
On the Rock of Ages founded,
  What can shake thy sure repose?
With salvation's walls surrounded,
  Thou may'st smile at all thy foes

"See! the streams of living waters,
  Springing from eternal love,
Well supply thy sons and daughters,
  And all fear of want remove:
Who can faint, while such a river
  Ever flows their thirst to assuage?—
Grace, which like the Lord, the Giver,
  Never fails from age to age.

"Round each habitation hovering,
  See the cloud and fire appear
For a glory and a covering,
  Showing that the Lord is near!
Thus deriving from their banner
  Light by night and shade by day,
Safe they feed upon the manna
  Which he gives them when they pray."

Cowper's great hymn, expressive of his one only solace is:

"There is a fountain filled with blood,
    Drawn from Immanuel's veins;
And sinners plunged beneath that flood,
    Lose all their guilty stains.

"The dying thief rejoiced to see
    That fountain in his day;
And there may I, though vile as he,
    Wash all my sins away.

"Dear dying Lamb, thy precious blood
    Shall never lose its power
Till all the ransomed church of God
    Be saved to sin no more.

"E'er since, by faith, I saw the stream
    Thy flowing wounds supply,
Redeeming love has been my theme,
    And shall be, till I die.

"Then in a nobler, sweeter song
    I'll sing thy power to save,
When this poor lisping, stammering tongue
    Lies silent in the grave."

Some literary critics have condemned the figure of speech contained in the first verse of this hymn; but it has never proved objectionable to those who looked beyond the figure to its deeper spiritual meaning. It has become precious to thousands of souls who have taken refuge and found the cure of their sin in that fountain of which the poet writes—"a fountain opened to the house of David and to the inhabitants of Jerusalem for sin and for uncleanness." Zech. xiii. 1.

But may we not say that these are the greatest hymns of their authors because that in each the author positively departs from his characteristic style of utterance? In fact, the authors seem to have changed places. Newton comes over to Cowper's standpoint and Cowper comes over to Newton's. Newton does not now write of the "guilty sinner," but of the dependent, trustful child of God, following the pillar of cloud and fire, drinking of the smitten rock, eating the heavenly manna. Cowper, on the other hand, forgets for the time his depression and suffering, and is consumed with the sense of his guilt and of the precious cleansing blood. He is now the "vile" sinner, and magnifies above all else the Redeemer's power to save.

It is evident, then, that either theme is sufficient to inspire the noblest song, and it is not because Newton usually wrote upon saving grace and Cowper on consoling grace that neither reached thereby the superior height; but it is because of that additional impulse in which their vision was extended beyond the themes ordinarily discussed, and in which they were drawn out of their own comparatively narrow selves to the broader experiences of a common nature.

Cowper is usually too introspective. His subjectiveness is intense. For this reason his hymns, useful as they are, should be used with some degree of caution, and with very special regard to the occasions and persons to which they apply. But although Newton's hymns are the more wholesome it might be justly inquired whether even they are not somewhat morbid. No doubt such expressions as "a wretch like me," "by Satan sorely pressed," and similar ones found in his other hymns, are absolutely descriptive of every sinner and would be accepted by all whose evil hearts have been fully revealed to themselves. And yet very few have had such experiences of continued sin and conscious rebellion against God as Newton suffered, and consequently such expressions on the lips of many who sing them are, to say the least, extravagant.

When, then, we come to the two hymns in which each author is at his best, we recognize that they have become such in the obliteration of self. The obtrusive personality has disappeared; the authors speak for all their fellow-Christians and we have two great typical lyrics in which God's gracious providence and God's gracious redemption are set forth in lofty strains.

Other well-known hymns by Newton begin

"How sweet the name of Jesus sounds,"

which is perhaps more generally sung than the one which we esteem his greatest.

"I saw One hanging on a tree."

"Come, my soul, thy suit prepare."

"Jesus who on his glorious throne."

"While with ceaseless course the sun."

"Saviour visit thy plantation."

Other familiar hymns by Cowper are

"Far from the world, O Lord, I flee."

"The Spirit breathes upon the Word."

"O for a closer walk with God."

"Sometimes a light surprises."

"Hear what God the Lord hath spoken."

"Hark my soul, it is the Lord."

EDWARD PERRONET.—1726–1792

Edward Perronet was a Christian genius; a man of distinguished pedigree, of great and varied native gifts, learned, witty, consecrated, and influential; and yet, like some others of like character and for some inscrutable reason, his name would have passed into oblivion and his deeds have been recalled only by the casual discovery of his works in some musty alcove, but for the single splendid hymn of which he was the author.

As his name indicates, he was of French extraction. His great grandfather was Pasteur Perronet, a refugee who fled into Switzerland and ministered there to a Protestant Congregation. His grandfather, David Perronet, came from Switzerland to England. His father, Vincent Perronet, entered the English Church, and in 1728, two years after Edward's birth, became vicar of Shoreham, in Kent. Vincent cordially embraced the methods of the Wesleys, and entered heartily into the evangelical revival, in which work he continued to the venerable age of ninety-two. His son Edward followed in his footsteps, and entered the English Church. But he was not indifferent to its defects, and his earliest work, published about 1757, known as *The Mitre*, is a satire on prevailing ecclesiastical sentiment.

Perronet early associated himself with the Wesleys and became one of their most industrious itinerants; but after some eight years of this work he broke with John Wesley at the same time as Charles Wesley.

The contention was chiefly over John's law that none of his ministers were to administer the sacraments, but were to direct their parishioners to attend for these purposes the regular parish churches. Perronet claimed that being an ordained clergyman it was his right and duty to do what Wesley forbade, so they separated.

He still continued, however, to evangelize until his death. His closing years were passed at Canterbury. He lived in a part of the archbishop's old palace, served as pastor of an Independent Church, and when he died was buried in the cloisters of the great cathedral.

The disagreement between Perronet and Wesley was not a quarrel. They still continued in mutual affection and admiration. Yet the feeling on questions of doctrine and order ran high, and Wesley would not even admit Perronet's hymns to his collection.

On one occasion Wesley discovered Perronet in his audience, and without consulting with him, announced that he would preach the next morning. Perronet was very loth to do this, and yet still more disinclined to make such a public remonstrance as might reflect upon his former leader. So he let the matter rest until the morning. He then entered the pulpit at the hour of service, and after explaining the situation to the worshipers, declared he was inadequate to the task assigned him; he would therefore offer nothing of his own, but would nevertheless furnish them with the best sermon they had ever heard.

Whereupon he proceeded to read the Sermon on the Mount from beginning to end, without comment, and when he had completed it, he dismissed the people. The incident is thoroughly typical of the character of the two great men of whom it is related.

Perronet published three volumes of hymns. The first consisted of Scripture paraphrases, the second of hymns proper, the third of "Occasional verses, moral and sacred." Copies are very rare. Selections from these will excite a wonder that more of Perronet's hymns are not in use. Here are three characteristic verses from as many poems:

> "Hail holy, holy, holy Lord!
>   Let powers immortal sing;
>   Adore the coeternal Word
>   And shout The Lord is King."

The next is from "The Master's Yoke":

> "O grant me, Lord, that sweet content
>   That sweetens every state;
>   Which no internal fears can rent,
>   Nor outward foes abate."

The last from a paraphrase of Hebrews xii. 1, 2:

> "Awake, my soul, arise!
>   And run the heavenly race;
>   Look up to Him who holds the prize
>   And offers thee his grace."

Perronet's great hymn, known from the tune to which it is generally sung, is "Coronation."

> "All hail the power of Jesus' name!
>   Let angels prostrate fall;
>   Bring forth the royal diadem,
>   And crown him Lord of all.

"Crown him, ye morning stars of light,
    Who fixed this floating ball;
Now hail the strength of Israel's might,
    And crown him Lord of all.

"Crown him, ye martyrs of our God,
    Who from his altar call;
Extol the stem of Jesse's rod,
    And crown him Lord of all.

"Ye chosen seed of Israel's race,
    Ye ransomed from the fall;
Hail him who saves you by his grace,
    And crown him Lord of all.

"Sinners, whose love can ne'er forget
    The wormwood and the gall,
Go, spread your trophies at his feet,
    And crown him Lord of all,

"Let every kindred, every tribe,
    On this terrestrial ball,
To him all majesty ascribe,
    And crown him Lord of all.

"Oh, that with yonder sacred throng
    We at his feet may fall;
We'll join the everlasting song,
    And crown him Lord of all."

In Dr. Benson's list this is ranked "21." We prefer to say that it ranks just as high as one desires to place it. It is superfine every way. It is particularly fine in its unusual scriptural allusions. These begin with the reference to the "*royal diadem*," of Revelation xix. 12, and a correction of the common idea, borne out by the King James version, that the King of kings wears only "many crowns," which others might wear besides kings, rather than the imperial "diadem." These references are beautifully continued in the "stem of Jesse's rod," "the wormwood and the gall," and other expressions.

There is splendid sweep in the psalm, as it contemplates the lordship of Jesus from the time when "the morning stars sang together" to the "everlasting song" of the New Jerusalem; though the last verse was added by Rev. John Rippon, in 1787. There is vast comprehensiveness in angels, martyrs, Israelites, Gentiles, every tribe and kindred and the heavenly throng. The rhythm is faultless, the double rhyme effective, and the recurring "Crown him Lord of all," most impressive. Surely the author has amply vindicated the claim of the Redeemer to his universal lordship; time and eternity, matter and mind, men and angels—these comprise the "all" over which he is enthroned.

AUGUSTUS MONTAGUE TOPLADY.—1740–1778

Rev. Augustus M. Toplady is the last of the great hymn-writers of the first English period. His father was an army officer, Major Richard Toplady. He died at the siege of Carthagena, while his son was yet an infant. His mother was a woman of fine and forceful character. She early removed to Ireland, and Toplady was in consequence graduated from Trinity College, Dublin. He was ordained to the English ministry in 1762, and served therein for about fourteen years. He then became minister of the Chapel of French Calvinists in London. But his constitution was feeble, and his energies were soon expended. He died at the early age of thirty-eight.

Concerning no great hymn-writer and his works have there been such varying opinions as concerning Toplady and his hymns.

The controversy seems chiefly to have grown out of Toplady's very pronounced Calvinisim. He was certainly more emphatic in defense of this system than any of his associates. Though never an active participant in the Methodist movement, he belongs to the same class as Whitefield and Cennick—intent upon evangelism, but differing from Wesley on doctrinal matters. By some it is claimed that he was harsh and bigoted, and his attacks upon Wesley are characterized as scurrilous. The Rev. Dr. Grosart, author of *Three Centuries of Hymns*, characterizes him as impulsive and reckless, yet concedes his genuine devoutness. Others assign to him a tender heart and rather gentle manners. Concerning his hymns Dr. Grosart admits that "Rock of Ages" has "given him a deeper and more inward place in millions of human hearts from generation to generation than almost any other hymnologist of our country, not excepting Charles Wesley;" yet, he says, "He is no poet or inspired singer. He climbs no heights; he sounds no depths; he has mere vanishing gleams of imaginative light; his greatness is the greatness of goodness; he is a fervent preacher not a bard." Yet in Benson's list his great hymn is ranked "1." Julian says of it, "No other English hymn can be named which has laid so broad and firm a grasp upon the English-speaking world." Dr. Robinson declares it to be "the first hymn of the first rank." It is as we have already observed, one of the great quartet of the *Anglican Hymnology*. We have already given reasons for outranking it only by Watts' "Wondrous Cross."

The following is the hymn almost exactly as Toplady wrote it:

"Rock of Ages, cleft for me!
  Let me hide myself in thee;
  Let the water and the blood,
  From thy wounded side that flowed,
  Be of sin the double cure:
  Cleanse me, from its guilt and power.

"Not the labor of my hands
  Can fulfil the law's demands;
  Could my zeal no respite know,
  Could my tears forever flow,
  All for sin could not atone;
  Thou must save, and thou alone.

"Nothing in my hand I bring,
  Simply to thy cross I cling;
  Naked, come to thee for dress;
  Helpless, look to thee for grace;
  Vile, I to the fountain fly;
  Wash me, Saviour, or I die!

"While I draw this fleeting breath,
  When my eyelids close in death,
  When I soar to worlds unknown,
  See thee on thy judgment throne,
  Rock of Ages, cleft for me!
  Let me hide myself in thee."

It would be a work of supererogation to analyze this splendid lyric. Comment is unnecessary. One of the finest compliments ever paid to it was its translation into Latin by W. E. Gladstone. The translation itself is a splendid piece of literary work.

"Iesus, pro me perforatus,
 Condar intra tuum latus,
 Tu per lympham profluentem,
 Tu per sanguinen tepentem,
 In peccata mi redunda,
 Tolle culpam, sordes munda.

"Coram te nec iustus forem,
 Quamvis tota vi laborem,
 Nec si fide nunquam cesso,
 Fletu stillans indefesso;
 Tibi soli tantum munus;
 Salva me, Salvator unus!

"Nil in manu mecum fero,
 Sed me versus crucem gero;
 Vestementa nudus oro,
 Opem debilis imploro;
 Fontem Christi quæro immundus,
 Nisi laves, moribundus.

"Dum hos artus vita regit;
 Quando nox sepulchro tegit;
 Mortuos cum stare iubes,
 Sedens iudex inter nubes;
 Iesus, pro me perforatus,
 Condar intra tuum latus."

The Calvinism of Toplady distinctly manifests itself in this hymn, yet not in such a way as to be at all offensive to any evangelical Christian. Wesley himself, as we have seen, could be even more Calvinistic—when he forgot himself. Yet this notice would be very incomplete without some reference to other hymns in which Toplady's very emphatic faith appears, the more so since for this very reason they are eliminated from many collections.

Here is one on

FULL ASSURANCE

"A debtor to mercy alone;
    Of covenant mercy I sing;
Nor fear, with Thy righteousness on,
    My person and offering to bring.

"The terrors of law and of God
    With me can have nothing to do;
My Saviour's obedience and blood
    Hide all my transgressions from view.

"The work which His goodness began,
    The arm of His strength will complete;
His promise is yea and amen,
    And never was forfeited yet.

"Things future, nor things that are now,
    Nor all things below nor above,
Can make Him His purpose forego,
    Or sever my soul from His love.

"My name from the palms of His hands
    Eternity cannot erase;
Impressed on His heart it remains
    In marks of indelible grace.

"Yes, I to the end shall endure,
    As sure as the earnest is given;
More happy, but not more secure,
    The glorified spirits in heaven."

Another very fine hymn is being fast forgotten, though it still holds an honored place, and is often sung as one of our most acceptable anthems.

"Inspirer and Hearer of prayer,
    Thou Shepherd and Guardian of thine,
My all to thy covenant care
    I sleeping and waking resign;

If thou art my shield and my sun,
    The night is no darkness to me;
And fast as my moments roll on ·
    They bring me but nearer to thee.

"Thy ministering spirits descend
    And watch while thy saints are asleep,
By day and by night they attend,
    The heirs of salvation to keep;
Bright seraphs, despatched from thy throne,
    Fly swift to their stations assigned,
And angels elect are sent down
    To guard the elect of mankind.

"Their worship no interval knows,
    Their fervor is still on the wing,
And while they protect my repose
    They chant to the praise of my king.
I, too, at the season ordained,
    Their chorus forever shall join,
And love and adore without end,
    Their gracious Creator and mine."

The second stanza has been sometimes marred by the substitution of the word "redeemed" for "elect" in the last line, perhaps in the hope of softening the doctrine. But thereby the beautiful thought of the author is absolutely obliterated—the relation between the elect of both orders of creation, angels and men.

Yet this is he of whom it has been written "he is not a bard!" Let his own lines answer.

The other hymns of Toplady in use to-day, begin

"Surely Christ thy griefs hath borne."

"Your harps ye trembling saints."

"If through unruffled seas."

It is a beautiful and most suggestive commentary on this whole period of doctrinal dispute, to the close of which we have now come, that when Toplady came to die he specially requested that his body should be buried beneath the gallery, opposite the pulpit, of the Totenham Court Chapel. And there he was laid to rest, in the historic building associated with early Methodism, erected by Whitefield, and where Wesley preached Whitefield's funeral sermon. And there all the bitterness of doctrinal controversy was buried with him. This era passes away, and—irrespective of literary merits, and without entering into any further questions of intrinsic merit—the two great songs of the heart, "Jesus, lover of my soul" and "Rock of Ages, cleft for me," go sounding down the ages together; one the work of a great Arminian, the other the work of a great Calvinist; but both, thank God! above and beyond all, great Christians. Their echoes will never cease until they that sing them are all gathered into the New Jerusalem and sing the "Song of Moses and the Lamb."

CHAPTER X

HYMNS OF THE SECOND PERIOD. I

We pass now to the hymn-writers of the second English period, the period of evangelism and missions. The contrast between this period and that which preceded it has already been indicated at length in Chapter V. The church has received a new vision and a new mission; which, whether or not they were greater or more important than those which were given her just before the opening of the first period, were certainly incomparably broader and brighter. At the former time her eyes were opened to her long-forgotten and true faith, and she was bidden to purify her doctrine and her life. Now she is quickened with the revelation of a fallen humanity and called to bestir herself for its redemption. Doctrine, though no less important than before, retires into the background and Christian zeal is to the front. New notes are struck and new songs are sung. It is the difference between a great army in its barracks, studying its tactics and perfecting its discipline, and the same army mobilizing for a great campaign, betaking itself to its tents, responding to the bugle-call, following the flag, and hastening into action. All this will be illustrated in the hymns which we proceed to review. So far, there have been no hymns written with a distinctively missionary purpose, and scarcely half a dozen which, like Watts' "Jesus shall reign where'er the sun," can be used in connection with missionary subjects; but they will now begin to appear. Among all the hymns we have considered there is but one in which the conversion of sinners is directly sought— Wesley's *Sinners turn; why will ye die?* But this class will be again and again addressed in the period which we now enter. The change from the doctrinal period to the evangelistic is as distinctly marked as the change from Catholic hymnody to Protestant.

The first great author of this period is

BENJAMIN BEDDOME.—1717–1795

It will be observed that Beddome was a contemporary of the later hymn-writers of the first period, and that both Cowper and Newton outlived him; and it may be asked, Why, then, is he placed in the second period rather than the first?

The answer is, that his hymns belong to it, and that for a special reason. He was a member of the Baptist Communion—the first to move in modern Protestant missions, and naturally the first to sing its songs. We have assumed that he was a member of the society organized in 1792. He must have contributed to the influences that created it. It will be remembered that Carey had been agitating his missionary projects for a number of years, and Beddome's heart seems to have been with him; for his fine missionary hymn, which was the first in English written for this express purpose, was published in 1787, five years before the Baptist Society was formed.

Beddome was the son of a Baptist minister at Henley, Warwickshire. In his youth he was apprenticed to a surgeon, but the cure of souls was more to his mind, and in 1740 he entered the ministry and settled at Bourton, Gloucestershire. He remained in the same parish until his death. This was not for lack of opportunity to remove elsewhere, but solely because of his own modesty. He was called to London, but replied, "I would rather honor God in a station much inferior to that in which he has placed me than intrude myself into a higher without his direction."

Beddome wrote eight hundred and thirty hymns. Most of them were prepared, as were Doddridge's, for use in his own services, in connection with his sermons. He published none himself. They were collected and edited by friends and admirers.

His missionary hymn is the following:

> "Ascend thy throne, Almighty King,
>   And spread thy glories all abroad;
> Let thine own arm salvation bring,
>   And be thou known the gracious God.
>
> "Let millions bow before thy seat,
>   Let humble mourners seek thy face,
> Bring daring rebels to thy feet,
>   Subdued by thy victorious grace.
>
> "Oh, let the kingdoms of the world
>   Become the kingdoms of the Lord!
> Let saints and angels praise thy name,
>   Be thou through heaven and earth adored."

This hymn places Beddome among hymn-writers where Carey, his co-Baptist fellow, is placed among ministers of the Gospel, and should bring him similar distinction.

Another hymn of Beddome's should be placed beside it:

> "Let party names no more
>   The Christian world o'erspread,
> Gentile and Jew, and bond and free,
>   Are one in Christ their head.
>
> "Among the saints on earth
>   Let mutual love be found;
> Heirs of the same inheritance,
>   With mutual blessings crowned.
>
> "Thus will the church below
>   Resemble that above,
> Where streams of pleasure ever flow,
>   And every heart is love."

Nothing could be more indicative of the dawn of the new era than these two hymns, especially when taken together.   The spirit of the one is the spirit of the other—brotherhood and the world for Christ.

The evangelistic tendency also appears in Beddome's hymns.   He wrote at least two hymns of the kind scarcely found before in English hymnody, as we have observed above—hymns directed to the unconverted.   These begin

> "Can sinners hope for heaven?"

and

> "Did Christ o'er sinners weep?"

Beddome is also remarkably prolific in his hymns to the Holy Spirit, and this should be construed in connection with his evangelism.

"Come, Holy Spirit, come
With energy divine."

"Come Spirit source of light."

"Come blessed Spirit source of light."

" 'Tis God the Spirit leads."

He has also a fine hymn on prayer:

"Prayer is the breath of God in man."

Finally, his most useful, if not indeed his best, hymn is emphatically evangelistic, though not directly addressed to the unconverted. In it the Gospel is beautifully and forcibly commended to those who need it.

"God, in the gospel of his Son,
  Makes his eternal counsels known:
  Where love in all its glory shines,
  And truth is drawn in fairest lines.

"Here sinners, of an humble frame,
  May taste his grace, and learn his name;
  May read, in characters of blood,
  The wisdom, power, and grace of God.

"The prisoner here may break his chains;
  The weary rest from all his pains;
  The captive feel his bondage cease;
  The mourner find the way of peace.

"Here faith reveals to mortal eyes
  A brighter world beyond the skies;
  Here shines the light which guides our way
  From earth to realms of endless day.

"Oh, grant us grace, Almighty Lord,
  To read and mark thy holy word,
  Its truth with meekness to receive,
  And by its holy precepts live."

It will be seen from this review why we place Beddome among the great English hymn-writers. He is not usually so classed, nor can he be indeed, if we judge him by the superior merits of any single hymn.

But what we call greatness is not all of one kind; neither is a hymn-writer great only because he has written a great hymn; nor does he fail of being great because he has not done so. Beddome is great in that prophetic foresight, by reason of which he was the first to catch the spirit of the dawning era and give it voice in so large a variety of ways.

JAMES MONTGOMERY.—1771–1854

Montgomery is specially distinguished as the only layman, besides Cowper, among the hymn-writers of the first rank in English.

He was born in Ayrshire, the section made famous as the native place of Robert Burns, November 4, 1771. His father was a Moravian minister. When he was sixteen years old he was apprenticed to a grocer at Mirfield, near Wakefield, from whom he ran away two years later. He was already writing poetry, and in 1790 went to London to secure its publication. The publisher, Mr. Harrison, refused the manuscript, but engaged Montgomery's services as shopman, and from this time forth he was engaged in newspaper work. In 1792 he removed to Sheffield as assistant to Mr. Gales, publisher of the *Sheffield Register*, a paper of revolutionary tendencies. Gales was threatened with prosecution for his political utterances and fled to America, and Montgomery secured the newspaper for himself.   He changed its name to the *Sheffield Iris* and continued to edit and publish it from July, 1794, to July, 1825.   His reform principles, however, did not meet with the favor of the authorities.   Soon after becoming an editor he was fined twenty pounds and imprisoned for three months. Two years later, in 1796, he was found guilty of sedition, fined thirty pounds, and imprisoned for six months.   These experiences, however, only added to his reputation, and together with the publication of his poems gave him wide celebrity.   He lectured in various places on poetry, notably at the Royal Institution, London, and was in demand for many religious gatherings, particularly those of missionary organizations and the Bible Society.   In 1833 his literary successes and his Christian character had won universal regard, and the government—perhaps to atone for its former severity—gave him an annual pension of two hundred pounds.   So he passed on into a beautiful and serene old age.

Theodore Cuyler, in his autobiography, gives an interesting account of his call upon the venerable poet in 1832.   He describes him as "a short, brisk, cheery old man.   His complexion was fresh and snowy hair crowned a noble forehead."

Montgomery died in his sleep, April 30, 1854. His fellow-townsmen of Sheffield revered his memory, gave him a public funeral, and erected a bronze statue in his honor.

Montgomery's fame rests exclusively upon his

hymns. His other works are scarcely known to-day, and never read. His hymns number about four hundred. They cover a wide variety of subjects, and many of them are in every good hymn-book. His best known and best beloved hymn is *The New Jerusalem.*

> "Jerusalem! my happy home!
>   Name ever dear to me!
> When shall my labors have an end,
>   In joy, and peace, in thee?
>
> "Oh, when, thou city of my God,
>   Shall I thy courts ascend,
> Where congregations ne'er break up,
>   And Sabbaths have no end?
>
> "There happier bowers than Eden's bloom,
>   Nor sin nor sorrow know;
> Blest seats! through rude and stormy scenes
>   I onward press to you.
>
> "Why should I shrink at pain and woe,
>   Or feel at death dismay?
> I've Canaan's goodly land in view,
>   And realms of endless day
>
> "Apostles, martyrs, prophets there,
>   Around my Saviour stand;
> And soon my friends in Christ below
>   Will join the glorious band.
>
> "Jerusalem! my happy home!
>   My soul still pants for thee;
> Then shall my labors have an end,
>   When I thy joys shall see."

It is perhaps apparent why this hymn has the popular favor beyond any other that Montgomery wrote. In Dr. Benson's catalogue it is number 10.

Yet it is truly surprising that it has attained such a rank either among its author's compositions or among hymns in general. Montgomery's finest hymn is probably his version of Psalm lxxii. It is worthy of being quoted entire.

"Hail to the Lord's anointed,
    Great David's greater Son!
Hail, in the time appointed,
    His reign on earth begun!
He comes to break oppression,
    To set the captive free,
To take away transgression,
    And rule in equity.

"He comes with succor speedy,
    To those who suffer wrong;
To help the poor and needy,
    And bid the weak be strong;
To give them songs for sighing,
    Their darkness turn to light,
Whose souls, condemned and dying,
    Were precious in his sight.

"He shall come down like showers
    Upon the fruitful earth,
And love, and joy, like flowers,
    Spring in his path to birth:
Before him, on the mountains,
    Shall peace the herald go,
And righteousness in fountains
    From hill to valley flow.

"Arabia's desert-ranger
    To him shall bow the knee;
The Ethiopian stranger
    His glory come to see:
With offerings of devotion,
    Ships from the isles shall meet,
To pour the wealth of ocean
    In tribute at his feet.

"Kings shall fall down before him,
    And gold and incense bring;
All nations shall adore him;
    His praise all people sing;
For he shall have dominion
    O'er river, sea, and shore,
Far as the eagle's pinion
    Or dove's light wing can soar.

"For him shall prayer unceasing
    And daily vows ascend;
His kingdom still increasing,
    A kingdom without end.
The heavenly dew shall nourish
    A seed in weakness sown,
Whose fruit shall spread and flourish,
    And shake like Lebanon.

"O'er every foe victorious,
    He on his throne shall rest;
From age to age more glorious,
    All-blessing and all-blessed.
The tide of time shall never
    His covenant remove;
His name shall stand forever,
    His great, best name of Love."

This hymn was written originally as a Christmas ode and was sung at one of the British Moravian settlements December 25, 1821. The next April he attended a Wesleyan missionary meeting in Liverpool and at the climax of his address repeated this poem. It was received with great enthusiasm. Dr. Adam Clark, who presided, subsequently printed it in his *Commentary*, and it has since gone round the globe. The student will do well to compare it with other versions of the same Psalm, particularly Watts' *Jesus shall reign where'er the sun*.

Montgomery is known by two other fine missionary hymns.   His "Song of Jubilee" is particularly fine.

"Hark! the song of jubilee,
　　Loud as mighty thunders roar,
Or the fullness of the sea,
　　When it breaks upon the shore;
Hallelujah! for the Lord
　　God omnipotent shall reign!
Hallelujah! let the word
　　Echo round the earth and main.

"Hallelujah! hark, the sound,
　　From the depths unto the skies,
Wakes above, beneath, around,
　　All creation's harmonies!
See Jehovah's banners furled!
　　Sheathed his sword! he speaks—'tis done!
And the kingdoms of this world
　　Are the kingdoms of his Son!

"He shall reign from pole to pole,
　　With illimitable sway;
He shall reign, when like a scroll
　　Yonder heavens have passed away;
Then the end: beneath his rod
　　Man's last enemy shall fall:
Hallelujah! Christ in God,
　　God in Christ, is all in all!"

This comes very near to being a hymn of the first rank.   In its literary quality it surpasses all his other hymns.   The rhythm, however, is defective and the changes too abrupt.

His third missionary hymn is:

"Lift up your heads, ye gates of brass."

Montgomery's poem on prayer is a classic.

> "Prayer is the soul's sincere desire,
>   Uttered or unexpressed;
> The motion of a hidden fire
>   That trembles in the breast.
>
> "Prayer is the burden of a sigh,
>   The falling of a tear,
> The upward glancing of an eye,
>   When none but God is near.
>
> "Prayer is the simplest form of speech
>   That infant lips can try;
> Prayer the sublimest strains that reach
>   The Majesty on high.
>
> "Prayer is the Christian's vital breath,
>   The Christian's native air;
> His watchword at the gates of death—
>   He enters heaven with prayer.
>
> "Prayer is the contrite sinner's voice,
>   Returning from his ways;
> While angels in their songs rejoice,
>   And cry—'Behold he prays!'
>
> "O thou, by whom we come to God—
>   The Life, the Truth, the Way—
> The path of prayer thyself hast trod;
>   Lord, teach us how to pray."

We call this a "poem"—it can scarcely be called a "hymn," and is only saved to hymnody by its last stanza. The author himself realized this, and is said to have added the stanza for this purpose.

But hymn or poem it is an exceedingly valuable aid to devotion and has helped multitudes to pray.

It is an interesting fact in this connection that the poet's last words on earth were used in family worship just before retiring. He closed the exercises with prayer, in which he seemed particularly fervent, and immediately went to his room.   He died before morning, and so "entered heaven with prayer."

Montgomery was urged to attempt a versification of the entire Psalter, but did not consider himself equal to the task.   But such of the Psalms as he rendered into meter have taken high rank.   They may well be compared with those of others.   For example, his Psalm xxiii.:

> "The Lord is my Shepherd no want shall I know";

his Psalm xlii.:

> "As the hart with eager looks";

and his Psalm lci.:

> "Call Jehovah thy salvation."

His hymn beginning

> "Forever with the Lord"

has been greatly admired.   Julian says "it is full of lyric fire and deep feeling."   Four of its lines are pronounced by Dr. Cuyler as fine as anything in hymnody.   They are:

> "Here, in the body pent,
>   Absent from thee I roam,
> Yet nightly pitch my moving tent
> A day's march nearer home."

Other hymns by Montgomery begin:

> "Holy, holy, holy Lord."

> "Sing we the song of those who stand."

> "To thy temple we repair."

> "Go to dark Gethsemane."

> "Come let us sing the song of songs."

"Oh! where shall rest be found?"

"Come to Calvary's holy mountain."

"Work while it is to-day."

"Sow in the morn thy seed."

"According to thy gracious word."

"When on Sinai's top I see."

"People of the living God."

Montgomery is a hymn-writer of the first rank; though he cannot be graded with Watts and Wesley. But surely few surpass him in positive usefulness. And after all, what better standard can we raise than this? What if Montgomery has written no hymn of the supreme quality, he has written many which admirably serve the purpose of devout worshipers on various occasions. His hymns are characterized by great simplicity. He has a scholar's erudition and a saint's faith united to the childlike spirit. The church will therefore continue to sing his songs through generations yet to be, and many of them will be as gratefully cherished in memory as those of any other author.

MISS HARRIET AUBER.—1773–1825

Miss Auber was born in London; became a communicant in the Church of England; lived a quiet life, and died in Hertfordshire. She published one book of poems, entitled "The Spirit of the Psalms" (another of the same title is by a different author), which was at first issued anonymously. From this book her hymns in present use are derived. She is entitled to a place among the great hymn-writers chiefly because of two very fine compositions. The first is a missionary hymn, founded like others which we have noted on Psalm lxxii.:

"Hasten, Lord! the glorious time
　When, beneath Messiah's sway,
Every nation, every clime,
　Shall the Gospel's call obey.
Mightiest kings his power shall own,
　Heathen tribes his name adore;
Satan and his host, o'erthrown,
　Bound in chains, shall hurt no more.

"Then shall wars and tumults cease,
　Then be banished grief and pain:
Righteousness and joy and peace
　Undisturbed shall ever reign.
Bless we, then, our gracious Lord;
　Ever praise his glorious name;
All his mighty acts record;
　All his wondrous love proclaim."

The other is an exquisite lyric in praise of the Holy Spirit, numbered "53" in the Anglican Hymnology:

"Our blest Redeemer, ere he breathed
　His tender, last farewell,
A Guide, a Comforter bequeathed,
　With us to dwell.

"He came in tongues of living flame,
　To teach, convince, subdue;
All-powerful as the wind he came,
　And viewless, too.

"He came, sweet influence to impart,
　A gracious, willing Guest,
While he can find one humble heart
　Wherein to rest.

"And every virtue we possess,
      And ever victory won,
    And every thought of holiness,
      Is his alone.

"Spirit of purity and grace!
      Our weakness pitying see;
    Oh, make our hearts thy dwelling-place,
      And worthier thee!"

Other hymns of Miss Auber are in use, but none equal to these.

MRS. VOKES.—1780–(?)

We come next to the greatest enigma in all hymnody.   Here is a name distinguished by its association with a number of the finest missionary hymns in the language, and more particularly in present-day collections, with hymns of no other class; and yet it is only a name—nothing more.   No one knows anything about the writer, nor has it been solved whether the name was a true name or only a *nom de plume*.   She has been traced back to the *Selection of Missionary and Devotional Hymns*, published by John Griffin, Portsea, 1797, in which all her hymns now known appear.   Dr. Robinson, however, states that two of her hymns should be credited to a Baptist clergyman, Rev. B. H. Draper, of Southampton, who was born 1775.   If this assumption be true the author was only twenty-two years of age when his hymns were published by Griffin as those of Mrs. Vokes!   Perhaps he *was* "Mrs. Vokes."   At all events, we shall assign the hymns according to the accepted tradition.

There are about thirty hymns in all to which Mrs.

Vokes' name is attached; but only four in common use. It is not easy to discriminate, but probably the most popular of these hymns is the following:

"Ye Christian heralds, go proclaim
  Salvation through Emmanuel's name;
  To distant chimes the tidings bear,
  And plant the Rose of Sharon there.

"God shield you with a wall of fire,
  With flaming zeal your breasts inspire,
  Bid raging winds their fury cease
  And hush the tempests into peace.

"And when our labors all are o'er,
  Then we shall meet to part no more;
  Meet with the blood-bought throng to fall,
  And crown our Jesus Lord of all."

But finer than this is another:

"Soon may the last glad song arise
  Through all the millions of the skies—
  That song of triumph which records
  That all the earth is now the Lord's!

"Let thrones and powers and kingdoms be
  Obedient, mighty God, to thee!
  And over land and stream and main,
  Wave thou the scepter of thy reign!

"Oh, let that glorious anthem swell,
  Let host to host the triumph tell,
  That not one rebel heart remains,
  But over all the Saviour reigns!"

Her remaining hymns are:

"Sovereign of worlds, display thy power";

and

"Ye messengers of Christ."

JOHN MARRIOTT.—1780–1825

The Rev. John Marriott was a clergyman of the English Church, a graduate of Rugby, and of Christ Church, Oxford. He took high honors in college, and was then engaged as private tutor by the Duke of Buccleuch, who after two years presented him with the living of Church Lawford, Warwickshire. This he kept to the end of his life. He wrote but three hymns, of which only one is in use. But this one belongs in the first rank, and entitles him to a place among the great hymn-writers:

> "Thou! whose almighty word
> Chaos and darkness heard,
>   And took their flight,
> Hear us, we humbly pray,
> And, where the Gospel's day
> Sheds not its glorious ray,
>   'Let there be light!'

> "Thou! who didst come to bring,
> On thy redeeming wing,
>   Healing and sight,
> Health to the sick in mind,
> Sight to the inly blind—
> Oh, now to all mankind,
>   'Let there be light!'

> "Spirit of truth and love,
> Life-giving, holy Dove!
>   Speed forth thy flight:
> Move o'er the waters' face,
> Bearing the lamp of grace,
> And in earth's darkest place,
>   'Let there be light!'

"Blessèd and holy Three,
  All-glorious Trinity—
      Wisdom, Love, Might!
  Boundless as ocean's tide,
  Rolling in fullest pride,
  Through the world, far and wide—
      'Let there be light!' "

This hymn will richly repay careful study. It is founded on Genesis i. 3, but with a very fine and suggestive reference to the three persons of the Trinity. The Father uttered the original mandate "Let there be light"; the Son declared himself to be the "Light of the World"; the Spirit enlightens the soul. The poem is usually classed with the missionary hymns of the church, and very properly so. It is profoundly pervaded with the missionary spirit, not only in its separate expressions, but also in its majestic undertone. Its metaphors are striking—the "chaos" and "darkness" of creation and of heathenism; the "sick in mind"; the "lamp of grace"; the "ocean's tide" of Wisdom, Love, and Might, and the like. The action is vigorous—"redeeming wing"; "speed forth thy flight"; "rolling in fullest pride." The survey and sweep are most comprehensive. Above all, the hymn is a broad, beautiful, and blessed evangel.

CHAPTER XI

HYMNS OF THE SECOND PERIOD. II

REGINALD HEBER.—1783–1826

With Bishop Heber we come again to a writer of the first rank, and to missionary hymns of the highest quality. In this particular class of sacred literature we rise with Heber to the very crest of the wave; his work is the climax.

Reginald Heber, the son of Rev. Reginald Heber, Sr., was born at Malpas, Cheshire, April 21, 1783. His father was a man of wealth and learning, and the boy enjoyed everything that ample means and generous culture could bestow upon him. He improved his opportunities. He added to rich native endowments and a genial, gentle spirit the most earnest devotion to the Saviour and laborious, systematic study. He entered Brazenose College, Oxford, at the age of seventeen. His first year he took the Chancellor's prize for the best Latin poem. Two years later he took the Newdigate prize for the best English poem, with his *Palestine*. He took other honors in addition to these. His student days were a series of brilliant successes.

After ordination to the ministry he settled at Hodnet, where he remained for sixteen years, during which period most of his hymns were composed. In

1822 he removed to London as the preacher of Lincoln's Inn. The next year he was made bishop of Calcutta, and entered upon his missionary career. He continued in this life only three years, but they were years of the holiest enthusiasm, filled with travel, administration, and various labors. It is worthy of note that he ordained the first native Hindu to the ministry—Christian David. April 3, 1826, he officiated at an unusually exhausting confirmation service, in which he admitted forty-two persons to the church. He became overheated, retired to his apartments, and went at once into a cold bath. He delayed so long that his servant was moved to enter the room only to find him dead.

Bishop Heber is not the greatest of hymn-writers, yet he is distinguished before them all in certain important particulars. Let us bear this in mind as we proceed to an examination of his hymns and recur to it when we have finished. He has given us, to begin with, that which is by common consent of Christendom the most inspiring of all missionary lyrics:

> "From Greenland's icy mountains,
>   From India's coral strand,
> Where Afric's sunny fountains
>   Roll down their golden sand—
> From many an ancient river,
>   From many a palmy plain,
> They call us to deliver
>   Their land from error's chain.
>
> "What though the spicy breezes
>   Blow soft o'er Ceylon's isle;
> Though every prospect pleases,
>   And only man is vile;

In vain, with lavish kindness,
  The gifts of God are strown,
The heathen, in his blindness,
  Bows down to wood and stone!

"Shall we, whose souls are lighted
  With wisdom from on high—
Shall we, to men benighted,
  The lamp of life deny?
Salvation, oh, salvation!
  The joyful sound proclaim,
Till earth's remotest nation
  Has learned Messiah's name.

"Waft, waft, ye winds, his story,
  And you, ye waters, roll,
Till, like a sea of glory,
  It spreads from pole to pole;
Till o'er our ransomed nature
  The Lamb for sinners slain,
Redeemer, King, Creator,
  In bliss returns to reign!"

The story of this hymn is as wonderful as the hymn itself. A fac-simile of the original manuscript was made at Wrexham, England, and is still preserved. On its fly-leaf its story is written by Thomas Edgworth, a solicitor of the place, as follows:

"On Whitsunday, 1819, the late Dr. Shipley, Dean of St. Asaph and Vicar of Wrexham, preached a sermon in Wrexham Church in aid of the Society for the Propagation of the Gospel in Foreign Parts. That day was also fixed upon for the commencement of the Sunday evening lectures intended to be established in the church, and the late Bishop of Calcutta (Heber), then rector of Hodnet, the Dean's son-in-law, undertook to deliver the first lecture. In the course of the Saturday previous, the dean and his son-in-law being together in the vicarage, the former requested Heber to write 'something for them to sing in the morning'; and he retired for that purpose from the table, where the dean and a few friends were sitting, to a distant part of the room. In a short time the dean inquired, 'What have you written?' Heber, having then composed the first three verses, read them over. 'There, there, that will do very well,' said the dean. 'No, no, the sense is not complete,' replied Heber. Accordingly he added the fourth verse, and the dean being inexorable to his repeated request of 'Let me add another, oh, let me add another,' thus completed the hymn, of which the annexed is a fac-simile, and which has since become so celebrated. It was sung the next morning, in Wrexham Church, the first time."

The tune to which the hymn is always sung was written by Dr. Lowell Mason. The story of the tune is almost equal to the story of the hymn. It is given in Robinson's *Annotations*, as follows:

"The tune, 'Missionary Hymn,' to which this piece is universally sung in America, was composed by Dr. Lowell Mason. The history of its composition is in like measure romantic; the family of the now deceased musician have very kindly supplied the facts.

"It seems that a lady residing in Savannah, Georgia, had in some way become possessed of a copy of the words, sent to this country from England. This was in 1823. She was arrested by the beauty of the poetry and its possibilities as a hymn. But the meter of 7s, 6s, D. was almost new in this period; there was no tune which would fit the measure. She had been told of a young clerk in a bank, Lowell Mason by name, just a few doors away down the street. It was said that he had the gift for making beautiful songs. She sent her son to this genius in music, and in a half-hour's time he returned with this composition. Like the hymn it voices, it was done at a stroke, but it will last through the ages."

This hymn was, in several particulars, a new departure in hymnody. It was written in a new meter; it was expressed in the choicest poetic terms; and beyond all else, it was such a trumpet-call as the church had never yet heard in sacred song. If we recall the missionary hymns which precede it we shall observe that they do not press the duty or the opportunity of missions upon the singing worshiper. There is only an approach to this in Mrs. Vokes' "Ye Christian Heralds." Heber's hymn, on the contrary, speaks to the deepest conscience—yet speaks most tenderly and persuasively.

The diction is incomparably beautiful. The alliterations are perfectly natural; there is no strife after mere effect in them, and they contribute immensely to the flowing style—"palmy plain," "prospect pleases," "gifts of God," "lamp of life," "pole to pole," and for "sinners slain" are examples. Every line indeed is as polished and refined as it can be. It is the art of the jeweler in the precious gems of language.

Another fine example of Heber's style is his "Star of the East."

"Brightest and best of the sons of the morning!
    Dawn on our darkness and lend us thine aid;
Star of the East, the horizon adorning,
    Guide where our infant Redeemer is laid.

"Cold on his cradle the dewdrops are shining;
    Low lies his head with the beasts of the stall;
Angels adore him, in slumber reclining,
    Maker, and Monarch, and Saviour of all!

"Say shall we yield him, in costly devotion,
    Odors of Edom and offerings divine?
Gems of the mountains, and pearls of the ocean,
    Myrrh from the forest, or gold from the mine?

"Vainly we offer each ample oblation,
    Vainly with gold would his favor secure:
Richer, by far, is the heart's adoration;
    Dearer to God are the prayers of the poor.

"Brightest and best of the sons of the morning!
    Dawn on our darkness and lend us thine aid;
Star of the East, the horizon adorning,
    Guide where our infant Redeemer is laid."

This also was unusual meter at the time it was written. In its other literary qualities it is much like the preceding.

We are also indebted to Bishop Heber for the finest of martial hymns:

"The Son of God goes forth to war,
    A kingly crown to gain;
His blood-red banner streams afar;
    Who follows in his train?

"Who best can drink his cup of woe,
    And triumph over pain,
Who patient bears his cross below—
    He follows in his train.

"A glorious band, the chosen few,
    On whom the Spirit came;
Twelve valiant saints, their hope they knew,
    And mocked the cross and flame.

"They climbed the dizzy steep to heaven
    Through peril, toil, and pain;
O God! to us may grace be given
    To follow in their train!

But great as are the foregoing, they are all surpassed by Heber's hymn of adoration:

"Holy, holy, holy, Lord God Almighty!
    Early in the morning our song shall rise to thee;
Holy, holy, holy, merciful and mighty,
    God in three persons, blessed Trinity.

"Holy, holy, holy! all the saints adore thee,
    Casting down their golden crowns around the glassy sea;
Cherubim and seraphim falling down before thee,
    Which wert and art and evermore shalt be.

"Holy, holy, holy! though the darkness hide thee,
  Though the eye of sinful man thy glory may not see;
Only thou art holy; there is none beside thee,
  Perfect in power, in love, and purity.

"Holy, holy, holy! Lord God Almighty!
  All thy works shall praise thy name, in earth and sky and sea;
Holy, holy, holy, merciful and mighty;
  God in three persons, blessed Trinity!

This hymn is invariably sung to Dr. Dykes's *Nicæa*, which was written expressly for it. The tune takes its name from the town in Asia Minor in which sat the Ecumenical Council of 325 A.D., in the course of whose deliberations the doctrine of the Trinity was finally elaborated. The tune is well adapted to the hymn, and taken together they comprise a sacred song which has never been surpassed.

In addition to the above, special attention should also be directed to Heber's beautiful children's hymn beginning

"By cool Siloam's shady rill."

Other well-known hymns begin

"Lord of mercy and of might."

"Hosanna to the living Lord."

"Bread of the world in mercy broken."

"Beneath our feet and o'er our head."

After this survey it will be plain why Bishop Heber is not the greatest of English hymn-writers, though surpassing all in certain particulars. He is the greatest poet among the hymn-writers; he is the most versatile; he is equally effective in all varieties; but he has not the Scriptural strength of some who thereby outrank him. His hymn in adoration of Trinity approaches very near to the supreme rank for this reason, that it has more of the majesty of inspired truth in its expressions than any other.

Nevertheless the whole story of his beautiful, brave, and gifted personality, including his hymns, promotes in those who have studied it a feeling of admiration akin to the warmest personal affection, though we have never seen his face in the flesh and he is to us only a historical record and an influence.

THOMAS HASTINGS.—1784–1872

With Thomas Hastings we note the introduction of several new features into hymnology. The chief of these are the beginning of American hymnody and the appearance of the Hymn and Tune Book.

Thomas Hastings, Mus. Doc., was born in Washington, Connecticut, October 15, 1784. His parents removed when he was yet a child to Clinton, New York, the seat of Hamilton College. The country was then an almost unbroken wilderness, and consequently educational advantages were meager. The boy, however, made the most of them, journeying six miles on foot every day to attend school. His musical talents were early manifested and cultivated. He was soon engaged in choir-conducting, and later, in 1816, issued his first publication, the "Musica Sacra." In 1832 he removed to New York, where the balance of his life was spent. His entire time was given to the elevation of sacred song. He composed music and wrote hymns; trained many choirs, and published a number of books. He will be best known and most celebrated as the author of "Top-lady," the tune for "Rock of Ages," written in 1830. His "Church Melodies," published in 1865, was the forerunner of a class of books, now greatly multiplied, in which tunes with the hymns adapted to them are printed together on the same page. An interesting study is derived from the comparison of this book with more modern ones.

Hastings' hymns are in the spirit of the age. Some are missionary; some evangelistic. His best hymn is the one entitled "Missionary Success," 1830:

"Hail to the brightness of Zion's glad morning!
    Joy to the lands that in darkness have lain!
Hushed be the accents of sorrow and mourning;
    Zion in triumph begins her mild reign.

"Hail to the brightness of Zion's glad morning,
    Long by the prophets of Israel foretold:
Hail to the millions from bondage returning;
    Gentile and Jew the blest vision behold.

"Lo! in the desert rich flowers are springing,
    Streams ever copious are gliding along;
Loud from the mountain-tops echoes are ringing,
    Wastes rise in verdure and mingle in song.

"See, from all lands—from the isles of the ocean—
    Praise to Jehovah ascending on high;
Fallen are the engines of war and commotion,
    Shouts of salvation are rending the sky."

It will be observed that this hymn is written in the meter which was first introduced into hymnody by Bishop Heber's "Brightest and Best." Both hymns are sung to "Wesley," the composition of Dr. Lowell Mason, the friend and fellow-worker of Hastings.

Another of his fine missionary hymns is "The Gospel Banner," beginning

> "Now be the Gospel banner
> In every land unfurled."

This does not, however, enjoy the popularity of the preceding.

The following is a very sweet and persuasive evangelistic hymn:

> "Delay not, delay not; O sinner, draw near,
>   The waters of life are now flowing for thee;
> No price is demanded; the Saviour is here;
>   Redemption is purchased, salvation is free.
>
> "Delay not, delay not; the Spirit of grace,
>   Long grieved and resisted, may take his sad flight,
> And leave thee in darkness to finish thy race,
>   To sink in the gloom of eternity's night.
>
> "Delay not, delay not; the hour is at hand;
>   The earth shall dissolve, and the heavens shall fade,
> The dead, small and great, in the judgment shall stand;
>   What helper, then, sinner, shall lend thee his aid?

Another of much the same character begins

> "Return, O wanderer, to thy home."

Other oft-sung hymns are

> "Now, from labor and from care."
>
> "Gently, Lord, O gently lead us."
>
> "Go tune thy voice to sacred song."
>
> "The Saviour bids thee watch and pray."

Hastings is not of the first rank.   Nevertheless there is a certain element in all his productions that will ever commend them to like spirits. It is particularly voiced in his "Gently, Lord, O gently."

PHŒBE BROWN.—1783–1861

This plain, unassuming woman deserves a place in this enumeration for the sake of her one hymn that is unspeakably precious to multitudes of the saints of God. Her life was full of unusual bitterness. She was born at Canaan, New York. Left an orphan at two years of age, she fell into the hands of a relative who kept the county jail. Here, according to the testimony of her son, she endured "such privations and cruel treatment and toil as it breaks my heart to read." She never recovered from the treatment, but through her life was timid and retiring. She married a house-painter, and her subsequent history was uneventful. But she reared a son, Rev. S. R. Brown, D.D., who became the first American missionary to Japan, and two grandchildren followed in the same mission.

About a dozen of her hymns are found in the collections, but the one to which we have referred is the following:

> "I love to steal awhile away
>   From every cumbering care,
> And spend the hours of setting day
>   In humble, grateful prayer.
>
> "I love in solitude to shed
>   The penitential tear,
> And all his promises to plead,
>   Where none but God can hear.

"I love to think on mercies past,
    And future good implore,
And all my cares and sorrows cast
    On him whom I adore.

"I love by faith to take a view
    Of brighter scenes in heaven;
The prospect doth my strength renew,
    While here by tempest driven.

"Thus, when life's toilsome day is o'er,
    May its departing ray
Be calm as this impressive hour,
    And lead to endless day."

The story of this hymn is as pathetic as it is interesting.   She was living at Ellington in a small, unfinished house, caring for four little children and a sick sister.   In order to gain a little quiet for her own private devotions, she would steal out at sunset to the boundaries of a beautiful garden in the neighborhood in which stood one of the finest residences of the place. There, in the fragrance of the fruits and flowers, she rested a while and poured out her soul to God. The lady of the mansion observing her actions, misinterpreted them, and rudely rebuked her as an intruder. The timid worshiper withdrew in tears, went to her room, and wrote "An Apology for my Twilight Rambles," and sent it to her critic.   This "apology," slightly amended, we have in the hymn above.

Mrs. Brown deserves special mention as the first of the leading American female hymnists.

SIR ROBERT GRANT.—1785-1838

Here is a writer of the first rank. Here also is a man born in the atmosphere of high political life and spending all his mature years in exalted official position, yet preserving always the fervor and simplicity of his faith, and known to those who come after chiefly through his volume of "Sacred Poems." His father was a member of Parliament for Inverness, and a director of the East India Company. The son graduated from Cambridge in 1806; practiced law for nineteen years; was member of Parliament for Inverness for five years; became privy counselor in 1831; governor of Bombay in 1834; died at Dapoorie, Western India, 1838.

Sir Robert wrote a number of fine hymns, among them three between which we find it hard to choose. The one which is most sung is

"Oh, worship the King, all-glorious above
And gratefully sing his wonderful love;
Our Shield and Defender, the Ancient of days,
Pavilioned in splendor and girded with praise.

"Oh, tell of his might, and sing of his grace,
Whose robe is the light, whose canopy space;
His chariots of wrath the deep thunder-clouds form,
And dark is his path on the wings of the storm.

"Thy bountiful care what tongue can recite?
It breathes in the air, it shines in the light,
It streams from the hills, it descends to the plain,
And sweetly distills in the dew and the rain.

"Frail children of dust, and feeble as frail,
In thee do we trust, nor find thee to fail;
Thy mercies how tender! how firm to the end!
Our Maker, Defender, Redeemer, and Friend."

This hymn is great in every element. Its spiritual features are particularly praiseworthy. Its adoration of the "King," his "might," his "grace," his "care," and his faithfulness to those who trust him, is elevated in the extreme. Its literary features are in keeping with the spiritual ones. The imagery is simply magnificent. The language is flowing, the measure unusually graceful, and the double rhyme—in the middle as well as the end of the lines—adds a wonderful beauty to the style. And what could be more suggestive and inspiring than the high use which is made of the majesty and might of the all-glorious King; namely, his tender mercies towards those "frail children of dust" who are introduced in the hymn in such striking antithesis. This hymn is twenty-three in Dr. Benson's list and thirty-two in Mr. King's. It deserves a higher place. It has very few superiors, and the more it is studied the more will its great merit be disclosed.

The second of Sir Robert's great hymns is

> "Saviour, when in dust to thee
> Low we bend the adoring knee;
> When, repentant, to the skies
> Scarce we lift our weeping eyes;
> Oh, by all thy pains and woe
> Suffered once for man below,
> Bending from thy throne on high,
> Hear our solemn Litany!
>
> "By thy helpless infant years,
> By thy life of want and tears,
> By thy days of sore distress
> In the savage wilderness;

By thy dread mysterious hour
Of the insulting tempter's power—
Turn, oh, turn a favoring eye;
Hear our solemn Litany!

"By thine hour of dire despair;
By thine agony of prayer;
By the cross, the nail, the thorn,
Piercing spear, and torturing scorn;
By the gloom that vailed the skies
O'er the dreadful sacrifice—
Listen to our humble cry,
Hear our solemn Litany!

"By thy deep expiring groan;
By thy sad sepulchral stone;
By the vault whose dark abode
Held in vain the rising God;
Oh, from earth to heaven restored,
Mighty reascended Lord!
Listen, listen to the cry
Of our solemn Litany!"

It will be observed that this is a paraphrase of the ancient litany, and is to be so construed. There is nothing just like this in the language as an example of that form of prayer in hymnody which is known as "pleading." The lyric is unique.

The third hymn follows:

"When gathering clouds around I view,
And days are dark, and friends are few,
On him I lean, who, not in vain,
Experienced every human pain;
He sees my wants, allays my fears,
And counts and treasures up my tears.

"If aught should tempt my soul to stray
From heavenly virtue's narrow way—
To fly the good I would pursue,

Or do the sin I would not do—
Still he, who felt temptation's power,
Shall guard me in that dangerous hour.

"When sorrowing o'er some stone, I bend,
Which covers all that was a friend,
And from his voice, his hand, his smile,
Divides me, for a little while,
My Saviour sees the tears I shed,
For Jesus wept o'er Lazarus dead.

"And, oh, when I have safely passed
Through every conflict but the last—
Still, still unchanging, watch beside
My painful bed—for thou hast died;
Then point to realms of cloudless day,
And wipe my latest tear away."

These hymns ought to be read in the light of Sir Robert Grant's history. They should be carefully compared, also, each with the others. What a range they cover! What majesty and what simplicity! There is the same graceful expression, the same deep spirituality in all; but how varied the subjects of which they treat and the sentiments which they inspire. What a treasure we have in them, yet how little known and how imperfectly understood.

HENRY KIRKE WHITE.—1785–1806

We come now to a very remarkable character, whose poems find a place in every collection and are much admired, though it is scarcely permissible to call them "hymns."

Henry Kirke White was the son of a butcher in Nottingham, and some have been seriously disturbed in their theories of heredity on that account, as though a butcher might not be possessed of superior mental qualities. White's mother, however, was a gifted woman, and for a number of years successfully conducted a ladies' boarding school. One of the teachers in this school started the boy on his illustrious career, teaching him Latin and other branches, in all which he made rapid progress.

At fourteen he was apprenticed to a stocking-weaver, but the work was so irksome and uncongenial that he was soon removed to an attorney's office. At fifteen he was awarded a silver medal for a translation of Horace, and other honors soon poured upon him. Following his conversion he determined to become a Christian minister and entered St. John's College, Cambridge. Here he greatly distinguished himself and his life seemed full of highest promise. But he was taken with an illness which ran into quick consumption, and he died before completing his course and before he had reached his twenty-second birthday.

He had already acquired such reputation that his untimely death was lamented on both sides of the ocean. Lord Byron wrote memorial verses. A monumental tablet was erected to his memory at Cambridge, a citizen of Boston, Massachusetts, bearing the expense. Southey published a sketch of his life.

The reason for all this will appear on an examination of his hymns. The best known is his "Star of Bethlehem":

"When, marshaled on the nightly plain,
    The glittering host bestud the sky,
One star alone, of all the train,
    Can fix the sinner's wandering eye.
Hark! hark! to God the chorus breaks
    From every host, from every gem;
But one alone the Saviour speaks—
    It is the Star of Bethlehem.

"Once on the raging seas I rode,
    The storm was loud, the night was dark,
The ocean yawned, and rudely blowed
    The wind that tossed my foundering bark.
Deep horror then my vitals froze;
    Death-struck, I ceased the tide to stem;
When suddenly a star arose,
    It was the Star of Bethlehem!

"It was my guide, my light, my all;
    It bade my dark forebodings cease,
And through the storm and danger's thrall
    It led me to the port of peace.
Now safely moored, my perils o'er,
    I'll sing, first in night's diadem,
For ever and for evermore,
    The Star, the Star of Bethlehem!"

This hymn is said to be a transcript of his own spiritual experience. He was very much disposed to skepticism, but the conversion of a former comrade who thereupon avoided him, so wrought upon his mind as to lead to his own conviction, in which he likens himself to a "foundering bark."

Another hymn of White's which deserves notice is the following:

"The Lord, our God, is full of might,
    The winds obey his will;
He speaks, and in his heavenly height,
    The rolling sun stands still.

"Rebel, ye waves, and o'er the land
  With threatening aspect roar;
The Lord uplifts his awful hand,
  And chains you to the shore.

"Howl, winds of night, your force combine;
  Without his high behest
Ye shall not, in the mountain pine,
  Disturb the sparrow's nest.

"His voice sublime is heard afar,
  In distant peals it dies;
He yokes the whirlwind to his car,
  And sweeps the howling skies.

"Ye nations, bend—in reverence bend;
  Ye monarchs, wait his nod,
And bid the choral song ascend
  To celebrate your God."

These are great poems, and as such worthy of all
the praise that has been given them; but they are not
often sung, though frequently printed, because they
do not meet the requirements of worship. Indeed,
they are scarcely lyrics; they have more power when
recited than when sung. But they are sacred compositions of a very high order. There is more sanctified imagination in them than in any of the works with
which they are classed. This quality demands the
student's special attention. The materials of this
imagination are most manifold—the sky, the ocean,
the winds, the waves, the mountain pine, and the
sparrow's nest. Its play vibrates between the most
terrible and the most tender of sentiments. The
language in which it is expressed is such as very few
writers would venture to employ even if it should

occur to them, yet in the hands of this poet it is every way attractive.

Such poems may well be treasured in the memory and quoted upon occasion, even though they be not employed in the distinctive praise of the Most High.

CHAPTER XII

HYMNS OF THE SECOND PERIOD. III

Miss Charlotte Elliott.—1789–1871

Miss Elliott is the greatest of English female hymn-writers. Though she wrote no single poem which has attained the celebrity of Mrs. Adams' "Nearer my God to Thee"—to be noted hereafter—the number and quality of her compositions advance her to the chief place.

Miss Elliott lived to be eighty-two years of age. For the greater part of her life she was an invalid. This fact appears in the title of her principal publication, "The Invalid's Hymn-Book."

She was born in Brighton, England, where most of her life was spent, though she resided for fourteen years on the Continent. There are no incidents of special importance to record in connection with her career. She lived very quietly with certain members of her family, passing her time in religious and literary employments.

Miss Elliott wrote the greatest evangelistic hymn in the language. Not only has it never been displaced by subsequent compositions, but it has never been fairly rivaled. Notwithstanding the multiplication of similar songs, particularly in connection with recent evangelism, this hymn continues to hold its high place;

and many a time, at the very climax of the revival, the revivalist has turned from modern "Gospel Songs," or other expressions of the penitent soul, to this wonderful hymn for his supreme argument and invitation.

Like other similar outbursts of emotion, this hymn has its history. We quote it from Robinson's "Annotations":

"The story has been told over and over, and yet it will never appear old, of the way in which this hymn of Miss Charlotte Elliott came to be written. In 1822 Dr. Cæsar Malan, of Geneva, was visiting at the house of this young woman's father. One evening, as they sat conversing, he asked her if she thought herself to be an experimental Christian. Her health was failing then rapidly, and she was harassed often with pain; the question made her petulant for the moment. She resented his searching, and told him that religion was a matter which she did not wish to discuss. Dr. Malan replied, with his usual sweetness of manner, that he would not pursue the subject then if it displeased her, but he would pray that she might "give her heart to Christ, and become a useful worker for him." Several days afterward the young lady apologized for her abrupt treatment of the minister, and confessed that his question and his parting remark had troubled her. 'But I do not know how to find Christ,' she said; 'I want you to help me.' 'Come to him *just as you are*,' said Dr. Malan. He little thought that one day that simple reply would be repeated in song by the whole Christian world. Further advice resulted in opening the young lady's mind to spiritual light, and her life of devout activity and faith began. She possessed literary gifts, and having assumed the charge of *The Yearly Remembrancer* on the death of its editor, she inserted several original poems (without her name) in making up her first number. One of the poems was "Just As I Am," 1836. The words of pastor Malan, realized in her own experience, were, of course, the writer's inspiration. Beginning thus its public history in the columns of an unpretending religious magazine, the little anonymous hymn, with its sweet counsel to troubled minds, found its way into devout persons' scrap-books, then into religious circles and chapel assemblies, and finally into the hymnals of the Church universal. Some time after its publication a philanthropic lady, struck by its beauty and spiritual value, had it printed on a leaflet and sent for circulation through the cities and towns of the kingdom, and in connection with this an incident at an English watering-place seems to have first revealed its authorship to the world. Miss Elliott, being in feeble health, was staying at Torquay, in Devonshire, under the care of an eminent physician. One day the doctor, who was an earnest Christian man, placed one of those floating leaflets in his patient's hands, saying he felt sure she would like it. The surprise and pleasure were mutual when she recognized her own hymn and he discovered that she was its author.''

The following is the hymn:

"Just as I am, without one plea
But that thy blood was shed for me,
And that thou bid'st me come to thee,
   O Lamb of God, I come!

"Just as I am, and waiting not
To rid my soul of one dark blot,
To thee, whose blood can cleanse each spot,
   O Lamb of God, I come!

"Just as I am, though tossed about
With many a conflict, many a doubt,
Fightings within, and fears without,
   O Lamb of God, I come!

"Just as I am—thou wilt receive,
Wilt welcome, pardon, cleanse, relieve;
Because thy promise I believe,
   O Lamb of God, I come!

"Just as I am—thy love unknown
Hath broken every barrier down;
Now, to be thine, yea, thine alone,
   O Lamb of God, I come!''

Could there be anything more completely evangelical than this? more faithfully, or more simply expressing the method of saving grace? It is the very epitome of the Gospel. The "sacrificial Lamb of God," his "shed blood," his "promise," and his "love" are all brought into sweetest and strongest association. The hindrances of the sinner, his guilt, doubt, conflicts, and procrastination are all met. The full work of the Saviour to welcome, forgive, sanctify, and comfort is exhibited. The boundless love on the one side and the full surrender on the other are set forth. In short, it is almost marvelous that so much can be contained in five short verses. In addition to all this, the rhythm is perfect, the poetical elements genuine, and the lyrical qualities unsurpassed.

We will not attempt to assign this hymn to any particular rank. As we have remarked in a previous instance, it is as high as we please to place it.

But if Miss Elliott wrote a great hymn for the penitent sinner, she also wrote an almost equally great one for the mature saint:

> "My God, my Father! while I stray
> Far from my home, in life's rough way,
> Oh! teach me from my heart to say,
> Thy will be done.

> "If thou shouldst call me to resign
> What most I prize—it ne'er was mine:
> I only yield thee what was thine
> Thy will be done.

> "If but my fainting heart be blest
> With thy sweet Spirit for its guest,
> My God, to thee I leave the rest—
> Thy will be done.

"Renew my will from day to day,
Blend it with thine, and take away
All now that makes it hard to say,
Thy will be done.

"Then when on earth I breathe no more
The prayer oft mixed with tears before,
I'll sing upon a happier shore,
Thy will be done."

In this hymn Miss Elliott shows her appreciation of the supreme elements in sanctification, just as she showed in the previous hymn her appreciation of the supreme elements in justification.

She wrote in all about one hundred and fifty hymns —all of fine quality, and generally in the same peculiar meter as those above. The best known begin

"My God, is any hour so sweet."

"There is a spot of consecrated ground."

"O Holy Saviour, Friend unseen."

"O Thou the contrite sinner's friend."

"When human hopes all wither."

"With tearful eyes I look around."

JOHN KEBLE.—1792–1866

At this stage in our study of Hymnology, the student should particularly inform himself concerning that significant and influential movement in the Church of England, which began in 1833 and practically ended in 1846, variously known as "Puseyism," "The Oxford Movement," or "The Tractarian Controversy." John Keble was one of the chief actors in this movement, and with him were associated several other hymn-writers, of whom we shall treat in their order.

Keble was the son of a clergyman in Fairford, Gloucestershire. His father, a man of many accomplishments, undertook the education of his two sons, John and Thomas, and they had no other teacher until they went to college. They entered Oxford together, and at once the very brilliant career of John Keble began. In 1806 he won a scholarship at Corpus Christi College, and in 1810 a Double First Class, a distinction never gained before except by Sir Robert Peel. Keble was at this time only nineteen years old.

The next year he was made fellow of Oriel and also took the university prizes in Latin and in English composition. Strange to say, however, the future poet was defeated in English verse by one who achieved little reputation subsequently, a student named Rolleston. In 1816 he was ordained to the English priesthood. From 1818 to 1823 he was a tutor at Oriel College, then, upon the death of his mother he left Oxford and returned to Fairford that he might care for his father and two sisters. Here he remained, serving in a very humble capacity, a beautiful example of filial and fraternal devotion, declining several very tempting offers because he would not neglect his own family. In 1836, released from these cares, he settled at Hursley for the balance of his life.

The year 1827 was made memorable by his publication of "The Christian Year," a very remarkable collection of poems, in which, as the title indicates, the author follows the church calendar, with an appropriate composition for each important day in order. This book passed through ninety-six editions in the author's lifetime, and before the copyright expired, in 1873, almost five hundred thousand copies had been sold. It is a book of permanent usefulness; from it most of Keble's hymns in common use have been derived, and it deserves a place in every Christian's library. It has been said that "what the Prayer-book is in prose the *Christian Year* is in poetry, and it would hardly be too much to prophesy that the *Christian Year* will live as long as the Prayer-book."

It was chiefly on the reputation of this book that Keble was elected to the professorship of poetry at Oxford. Here, in 1833, he preached his famous "Assize Sermon," which Cardinal Newman, himself one of parties to it, declared started the Oxford movement.

It is not for us to enter into details. It is enough to remember that this movement began in the earnest attempt to improve the spiritual state of the church. The Wesleyan revival had found little sympathy inside its bounds and so was compelled to work outside. Here was a movement which it was hoped would commend itself to those who desired better things for the church, but who would not accept Methodism. The other extreme was consequently adopted, and the result was a large and important perversion to the Church of Rome, in which Newman, Faber, and others were included. Many of their associates, however, shrank from the logical outcome and practical consequences of their course, and remained in the English church.   Among these was John Keble, himself a very leader in the discussion.

It is a noticeable fact that while the Oxford movement was ritualistic and sacramentarian to the last degree, its advocates were devoted Christians, and many emphatic evangelical features characterize their writings.   Some of these will appear in the hymns to be quoted.

In composing his "Christian Year" Keble followed the example of several predecessors, beginning with Bishop Ken, and introduced his poems with a Morning and Evening hymn.   From each of these respectively two of his favorite songs, in common use, are derived.   Both, however, are very seriously marred by the rupture of the selected verses from the context.   This is particularly noticeable in the Evening Hymn.   The Morning Hymn, as found in our books, is as follows:

> "New every morning is the love
>   Our wakening and uprising prove;
>   Through sleep and darkness safely brought,
>   Restored to life, and power, and thought.
>
> "New mercies, each returning day,
>   Hover around us while we pray;
>   New perils past, new sins forgiven,
>   New thoughts of God, new hopes of heaven.
>
> "If, on our daily course, our mind
>   Be set to hallow all we find,
>   New treasures still, of countless price,
>   God will provide for sacrifice.

"The trivial round, the common task,
  Will furnish all we need to ask,
  Room to deny ourselves, a road
  To bring us daily nearer God.

"Only, O Lord, in thy dear love
  Fit us for perfect rest above;
  And help us this, and every day,
  To live more nearly as we pray."

The original poem contains sixteen verses, and not one waste. The first verse above is immediately preceded by one which beautifully introduces it:

"O timely happy, timely wise,
  Hearts that with rising morn arise!
  Eyes that the beam celestial view
  Which ever more makes all things new."

Connect, now, the "new" of this last line with the first "new" above and how much more complete the sentiment, how much more uplifting!

In like manner between the third and fourth verses of the hymn as written above are a number of others in the original, among them this:

"We need not bid for cloistered cell,
  Our neighbor and our work farewell,
  Nor strive to wind ourselves too high
  For sinful man beneath the sky."

Then, with only a colon to break the continuity, the author continues:

"The trivial round, the common task," etc.

The verses, as known, are often quoted; in fact, they have become almost proverbial; but their beauty and suggestiveness are enhanced by reading them in connection with the other verses of the poem.

Keble's Evening Hymn, as commonly sung, is as follows:

"Sun of my soul, thou Saviour dear,
  It is not night if thou be near:
  O may no earthborn cloud arise
  To hide thee from thy servant's eyes.

"When the soft dews of kindly sleep
  My wearied eyelids gently steep,
  Be my last thought, how sweet to rest
  Forever on my Saviour's breast.

"Abide with me from morn till eve,
  For without thee I cannot live;
  Abide with me when night is nigh,
  For without thee I dare not die.

"If some poor wandering child of thine
  Have spurned, to-day, the voice divine,
  Now, Lord, the gracious work begin;
  Let him no more lie down in sin.

"Watch by the sick; enrich the poor
  With blessings from thy boundless store;
  Be every mourner's sleep to-night,
  Like infant's slumbers, pure and light.

"Come near and bless us when we wake,
  Ere through the world our way we take;
  Till in the ocean of thy love,
  We lose ourselves in heaven above."

This is indeed fine; and yet the force of the first verse is entirely broken by the omission of the verse preceding it in the author's edition. Let it be read first and then follow it with the first verse given above.

" 'Tis gone! that bright and orbéd blaze
  Fast fading from our wistful gaze;
  Yon mantling cloud has hid from sight
  The fast faint pulse of quivering light!"

But

"Sun of my soul!" etc.

Other familiar hymns of Keble are

"There is a book who runs may read."

"Blest are the pure in heart."

"When God of old came down from heaven."

Keble's reputation as a hymn-writer will rest almost exclusively on the two hymns which we have quoted, especially upon the Evening Hymn. Yet he is more of a poet than a hymnist, and it is his fine conception of the essential things in the religious life which gives his poems their high place in this class of literature. No better illustration of this can be given than to quote again his immortal expression, "SUN OF MY SOUL!"

HENRY FRANCIS LYTE.—1793–1847

This author is not only of the first rank, but by common consent he is the greatest hymn-writer of the second English period. He holds fifth place in Dr. Benson's list, with only Toplady, Watts, Wesley, and Ken above him; but those who are named before him belong to the first period.

Further, Lyte has two hymns in Dr. Benson's first ten, an honor accorded to no one else but Wesley. The Anglican Hymnology gives him two hymns of the first rank. Still further, his reputation is rapidly gaining, as we have seen in Chapter VI. He is full of the evangelistic and missionary spirit; but he is full of much besides. His work is worthy of all attention.

Lyte was born at Ednam, near Kelso, in Scotland,

June 1, 1793. He graduated at Trinity College, Dublin, in 1814. Here he took the prize in English poetry three separate times. He was ordained in 1815, and after serving in several places, he settled in Lower Brixham, Devonshire, England, in 1823, where he remained until his death, in 1847.

Brixham was a community of plain people, mostly sailors and fishermen, who, while they were kindly disposed, had little culture or sympathy with the higher education. This told heavily upon the author's spirits, and he bore in addition many severe crosses. His affections were betrayed, his ambitions disappointed, and his health failed at a comparatively early age. He sought rest and reinvigoration in travel, but died on his way to Rome in his fifty-fourth year, and was buried in Nice. His hymns are consequently the outgrowth of his own religious experiences. Yet so very delicately are they expressed, and with such careful veiling of the strictly personal element, that we might never imagine the secret of their origin. Lyte's best hymn is the following:

"Jesus, I my cross have taken,
　　All to leave, and follow thee;
Naked, poor, despised, forsaken,
　　Thou, from hence, my all shalt be!
Perish, every fond ambition,
　　All I've sought, or hoped, or known,
Yet how rich is my condition,
　　God and heaven are still my own!

"Let the world despise and leave me,
　　They have left my Saviour, too;
Human hearts and looks deceive me—
　　Thou art not, like them, untrue;

Oh, while thou dost smile upon me,
  God of wisdom, love, and might,
Foes may hate, and friends disown me,
  Show thy face, and all is bright.

"Man may trouble and distress me,
  'Twill but drive me to thy breast;
Life with trials hard may press me;
  Heaven will bring me sweeter rest!
Oh, 'tis not in grief to harm me
  While thy love is left to me;
Oh, 'twere not in joy to charm me,
  Were that joy unmixed with thee.

"Go, then, earthly fame and treasure!
  Come, disaster, scorn, and pain!
In thy service pain is pleasure,
  With thy favor, loss is gain.
I have called thee—Abba, Father!
  I have stayed my heart on thee!
Storms may howl, and clouds may gather,
  All must work for good to me."

This noble hymn, like Miss Elliott's "Just As I Am,"
was the product of a remarkable piece of history.
Lyte, like Wesley, was a minister before he was a
Christian—breaking for others that Bread of Life on
which he had not himself fed. But in 1818, when he
was living at Marazion, in Cornwall, and three years
after his ordination, a fellow-clergyman, who was very
ill, sent for him to visit and counsel him. Lyte discovered that he had nothing to offer him; that the
dying brother had a peace which he did not himself
possess, and to which he could not add. Concerning
the effect on his own mind, Lyte wrote: "I was
greatly affected by the whole matter, and brought to
look at life and its issue with a different eye than

before; and I began to study my Bible and preach in
another manner than I had previously done.'' In
this hymn he expresses his new-found hope. If
Saving Faith is the ''Confidence that surrenders,''
how could it be better expressed?

This hymn is scarcely inferior to ''Just As I Am,''
and is a worthy companion piece. Both are true to
the Gospel, though in different aspects. Both have
a wonderful record in their soul-saving influences.

When Lyte found that he could no longer continue
his work in the pastorate and prepared for his south-
ern journey, he girded himself for a final communion
service, although, as he afterwards wrote, he ''was
scarcely able to crawl.'' He closed the exercises with
a few tender words of admonition and retired to his
rooms. Then, as the shadows of the Sabbath evening
gathered about him, he wrote his farewell song:

> ''Abide with me: fast falls the eventide;
>   The darkness deepens; Lord, with me abide!
>   When other helpers fail, and comforts flee,
>   Help of the helpless, oh, abide with me!

> ''Not a brief glance I beg, a passing word,
>   But as thou dwellst with thy disciples, Lord,
>   Familiar, condescending, patient, free,
>   Come not to sojourn, but abide with me.

> ''I need thy presence every passing hour:
>   What but thy grace can foil the tempter's power?
>   Who like thyself my guide and stay can be?
>   Through cloud and sunshine, oh, abide with me.

> ''Swift to its close ebbs out life's little day;
>   Earth's joys grow dim, its glories pass away:
>   Change and decay in all around I see;
>   O thou, who changest not, abide with me!

"Come not in terrors, as the King of kings;
But kind and good, with healing in thy wings,
Tears for all woes, a heart for every plea;
Come, Friend of sinners, and abide with me.

"I fear no foe, with thee at hand to bless
Ills have no weight, and tears no bitterness:
Where is Death's sting? where, Grave, thy victory?
I triumph still, if thou abide with me."

"Hold thou thy cross before my closing eyes;
Shine through the gloom, and point me to the skies;
Heaven's morning breaks and earth's vain shadows flee:
In life, in death, O Lord, abide with me!

This hymn needs no comment; to read it is to interpret it; to sing it with any degree of seriousness is to realize its spiritual depth, purity, and beauty.

Lyte published a volume of versions of the Psalms, entitled "The Spirit of the Psalms," the same in title as Miss Auber's work, and as we have before noted, often confounded with it. Many of his hymns are derived from this book. His version of Psalm xlii., beginning

"As pants the hart for cooling streams,"

certainly surpasses all others. It reminds us of some beginning in similar terms, notably Montgomery's

"As the hart with eager looks."

Others from the same collection are

"Pleasant are thy courts above." Psalm lxxxiv.

"My spirit on thy care." Psalm xxxi.

"There is a safe a secret place." Psalm xci.

"Sing to the Lord our might." Psalm lxxxi.

The fine missionary spirit of this author is exhibited in the following hymn, founded in part on Psalm xiv. It is one of the very few hymns in which a petition is raised for the redemption of God's ancient people.

"Oh, that the Lord's salvation
　Were out of Zion come,
To heal his ancient nation,
　To lead his outcasts home!
How long the holy city
　Shall heathen feet profane?
Return, O Lord, in pity,
　Rebuild her walls again.

"Let fall thy rod of terror,
　Thy saving grace impart;
Roll back the vail of error,
　Release the fettered heart;
Let Israel, home returning,
　Their lost Messiah see;
Give oil of joy for mourning,
　And bind thy church to thee."

When we come to inquire the secret of Lyte's greatness in hymnody we find this comprehensive answer, his hymns fulfil all the conditions of true praise.　They are eminently Scriptural.　His mind was saturated with divine truth, his thoughts were clothed in the echoes of the words of Holy Writ. They are highly poetical, refined in their phraseology, beautiful in their imagery, deep with insight into spiritual realities.　They are readily wedded to music and they are particularly rich in Christian experience. In no other author is poetry and religion more exquisitely united.

WILLIAM CULLEN BRYANT.—1794–1878

This great American poet is too well known to require a special notice. His life is a part of our national history. His religious views are the subject of some question. In later life he connected himself with Dr. Bellow's church in New York City, and was reckoned as a Unitarian; but for more than thirty years he was identified with the Presbyterian Church of Roslyn, and habitually partook of the sacrament.

Bryant's name is connected with three very fine hymns. One of these was written for a church dedication. It begins

"O Thou, whose own vast temple stands."

Another, descriptive of human life, begins

"As shadows cast by cloud and sun."

But particular attention is asked for his unexcelled Home Missionary hymn:

"Look from thy sphere of endless day.
　O God of mercy and of might!
In pity look on those who stray,
　Benighted in this land of light.

"In peopled vale, in lonely glen,
　In crowded mart, by stream or sea,
How many of the sons of men
　Hear not the message sent from thee!

"Send forth thy heralds, Lord, to call
　The thoughtless young, the hardened old,
A scattered, homeless flock, till all
　Be gathered to thy peaceful fold.

"Send them thy mighty word to speak,
  Till faith shall dawn and doubt depart,
To awe the bold, to stay the weak,
  And bind and heal the broken heart.

"Then all these wastes, a dreary scene
  That makes us sadden as we gaze,
Shall grow with living waters green,
  And lift to heaven the voice of praise."

GEORGE WASHINGTON DOANE.—1799–1859

Bishop Doane has written several very acceptable hymns, some of which are rapidly growing in popularity.   He was born in Trenton, New Jersey, graduated from Union College, in 1818, was ordained in 1821.   He soon became rector of Trinity Church, Boston, and filled the pulpit made so conspicuous by its succession of great sacred orators —notably Phillips Brooks.   In 1832 he became Bishop of New Jersey.

His best hymn was scarcely appreciated until set to Calkin's spirited tune of "Waltham"; but with this music it has taken high rank and is sung perhaps as frequently as any other missionary hymn, Bishop Heber's alone excepted.

"Fling out the banner; let it float
  Skyward and seaward, high and wide;
The sun, that lights its shining folds,
  The cross, on which the Saviour died.

"Fling out the banner; angels bend
  In anxious silence o'er the sign,
And vainly seek to comprehend
  The wonder of the Love Divine.

"Fling out the banner; heathen lands
  Shall see from far the glorious sight;
And nations, crowding to be born,
  Baptize their spirits in its light.

"Fling out the banner; sin-sick souls
    That sink and perish in the strife,
Shall touch in faith its radiant hem,
    And spring immortal into life.

"Fling out the banner; let it float
    Skyward and seaward, high and wide;
Our glory only in the cross,
    Our only hope, the Crucified.

"Fling out the banner wide and high,
    Seaward and skyward let it shine;
Nor skill nor might nor merit ours;
    We conquer only in that sign."

What can be more stirring, more ringing, than these triumphant notes. Surely the missionary spirit—the spirit of the widest evangelization, is not subsiding while such trumpet-tones are sounded.

How original and striking is the reference in the fourth verse to the hem of the Saviour's garment and the use of the "In hoc signo" in the last verse. What a fine use is made of the Scriptural truth of the angel's interest in the work of redemption in the second verse. How unusual the conception of the spiritual birth of nations in "Crowding to be born." Take it for all in all, we can only say that if this hymn has not been assigned to the first rank among the missionary hymns it is because it has been strangely overlooked.

Bishop Doane's evening hymn may also be classed with Bishop Ken's and Keble's, and is little inferior to them:

"Softly now the light of day
　Fades upon my sight away,
　Free from care, from labor free,
　Lord, I would commune with thee.

"Thou, whose all-pervading eye
　Naught escapes without, within,
　Pardon each infirmity,
　Open fault, and secret sin.

"Soon, for me, the light of day
　Shall forever pass away;
　Then, from sin and sorrow free,
　Take me, Lord, to dwell with thee.

"Thou who, sinless, yet hast known,
　All of man's infirmity;
　Then from thine eternal throne,
　Jesus, look with pitying eye."

The only other hymn in common use by Bishop Doane is by no means the equal of the foregoing. "It rather stiffly and mechanically paraphrases" the passage on which it is founded.   It begins

"Thou art the Way; to thee alone."

JOHN HENRY NEWMAN.—1801–1890

Cardinal Newman's name has already been mentioned in connection with the Oxford Movement, in which he took a prominent part, and the most significant circumstances of his life have been noted under the name of John Keble.

He was born in London, graduated from Trinity College, Oxford, in 1820; ordained to the English ministry in 1824; received into the Roman Church October 8, 1845; became rector of the new Roman

Catholic University at Dublin in 1854; became a cardinal 1879; died in Birmingham, August 11, 1890. His celebrated *Apologia pro Vita Sua* is a defense of his own course and conduct. He wrote few hymns, and is generally known only in connection with the hymn below:

"Lead, kindly Light, amid the encircling gloom,
    Lead thou me on!
The night is dark, and I am far from home;
    Lead thou me on!
Keep thou my feet; I do not ask to see
The distant scene; one step enough for me.

"I was not ever thus, nor prayed that thou
    Shouldst lead me on;
I loved to choose and see my path; but now
    Lead thou me on!
I loved the garish day, and, spite of fears,
Pride ruled my will. Remember not past years!

"So long thy power hath blest me, sure it still
    Will lead me on
O'er moor and fen, o'er crag and torrent, till
    The night is gone,
And with the morn those angel faces smile
Which I have loved long since, and lost awhile!"

We notice this hymn only because of its great present popularity; but it can scarcely be called either a great poem or a great hymn, and it certainly is not a lyric. The rhythm is so very rough and confused that it is never sung successfully by a number of persons. Yet it has certain striking passages and appeals to those who for any reason are beset by darkness. Several stories are in circulation concerning its origin,

which, we fear, are apochryphal.   It can only be said
that both in sentiment and meter it well expresses the
state of mind of its author—a man who sincerely
desired to find the light, but whose curious mental
processes were his own confusion.

CHAPTER XIII

HYMNS OF THE SECOND PERIOD. IV

Sarah Flower Adams.—1805–1848

This author was the daughter of Benjamin Flower,
editor of *The Cambridge Intelligencer.*   She married
William Bridges Adams, a professional engineer, and
settled in London.   Here she came under the pastoral
care of Rev. William Johnston Fox, a Unitarian minister, and founder of the Westminster *Review.*   Her
pastor published a volume in 1841, entitled *Hymns
and Anthems,* to which Mrs. Adams contributed thirteen poems, among them the only one of hers to-day
in common use.   From the fact that she worshiped
with the Unitarians and contributed to their hymn-
books she has been persistently classed with them,
and zealous critics have read *into* her lines more Uni-
tarianism than can be found therein, and read *out* of
them the elements of evangelical faith which they
plainly contain.   If she was indeed a Unitarian, she
must have been a very high Arian, for her hymns
seem to be a close approach to orthodoxy.   She has
one to the Holy Spirit beginning

"Creator Spirit, Thou the first."

Another on Good Friday,

"Darkness shrouded Calvary";

and another, a rendering from Fénélon,

> "Living or dying, Lord, I would be thine."

Mrs. Adams is said to have joined the Baptist Church in later life.   We have not been able to verify this; but if it be so, it will solve the enigma of her personal faith.

Her great hymn is the following:

> "Nearer, my God, to thee!
>   Nearer to thee,
> E'en though it be a cross
>   That raiseth me;
> Still all my song shall be,
> Nearer, my God, to thee,
>   Nearer to thee!
>
> "Though like the wanderer,
>   The sun gone down,
> Darkness be over me,
>   My rest a stone,
> Yet in my dreams I'd be
> Nearer, my God, to thee,
>   Nearer to thee!
>
> "There let the way appear,
>   Steps unto heaven;
> All that thou sendest me,
>   In mercy given;
> Angels to beckon me
> Nearer, my God, to thee,
>   Nearer to thee!
>
> "Then, with my waking thoughts
>   Bright with thy praise,
> Out of my stony griefs
>   Bethel I'll raise;
> So by my woes to be
> Nearer, my God, to thee,
>   Nearer to thee!

> "Or if, on joyful wing
>   Cleaving the sky,
> Sun, moon, and stars forgot,
>   Upward I fly,
> Still all my song shall be,
> Nearer, my God, to thee,
>   Nearer to thee!"

This hymn will take rank among the best of the English language. It is the most widely popular of all written by female hymnists; yet no hymn has received such peculiar treatment at the hands of the critics. The English Baptists added a verse beginning "Christ alone beareth me," that the reference to the Saviour might be supplied. Others have quarreled with it because it sticks so closely to the figure supplied by the history of Jacob at Bethel. Bishop How of London wrote a paraphrase of the hymn in 1864, "expressing more definitely Christian faith and better adapted for Congregational worship." It omits every reference to Jacob and substitutes the history of Jesus during his passion. It is worth while to quote this hymn, that the student may compare the two.

> "Nearer, O God, to thee!
>   Hear thou our prayer;
> Ev'n though a heavy cross
>   Fainting we bear,
> Still all our prayer shall be
> Nearer, O God, to thee,
>   Nearer to thee!
>
> "If, where they led the Lord,
>   We too are borne,
> Planting our steps in his,
>   Weary and worn;

There even let us be
Nearer, O God, to thee,
    Nearer to thee!

"If thou the cup of pain
    Givest to drink,
Let not the trembling lip
    From the draught shrink;
So by our woes to be
Nearer, O God, to thee,
    Nearer to thee!

"Though the great battle rage
    Hotly around,
Still where our Captain fights
    Let us be found;
Through toils and strife to be
Nearer, O God, to thee,
    Nearer to thee!

"And when thou, Lord, once more
    Glorious shalt come,
Oh, for a dwelling-place
    In thy bright home!
Through all eternity
Nearer, O God, to thee,
    Nearer to thee!"

Other attempts to amend the hymn or displace it with a substitute of the same meter have been made, the most successful of which is a hymn by Mrs. Elizabeth Payson Prentiss, the author of *Stepping Heavenward*, in the following:

"More love to thee, O Christ,
    More love to thee!
Hear thou the prayer I make
    On bended knee;
This is my earnest plea—
More love, O Christ, to thee,
    More love to thee!

"Once earthly joy I craved,
Sought peace and rest;
Now thee alone I seek—
Give what is best;
This all my prayer shall be—
More love, O Christ, to thee,
More love to thee!

"Let sorrow do its work,
Send grief and pain;
Sweet are thy messengers,
Sweet their refrain,
When they can sing with me,
More love, O Christ, to thee,
More love to thee!

"Then shall my latest breath
Whisper thy praise,
This be the parting cry
My heart shall raise;
This still its prayer shall be—
More love, O Christ, to thee,
More love to thee!"

This may not have been written in deliberate imitation of *Nearer, My God, to Thee;* but the correspondence in meter, refrain, and progress of the thought is very close. As an imitation of the hymn of Mrs. Adams this is its only rival.

Without pursuing this matter further, it is enough to say that admitting the lack of distinct evangelical expression in the hymn under discussion, the devout worshiper will continue to sing it with his own interpretation. The "cross that raiseth" him will suggest the Crucified Redeemer, and the "steps unto heaven" will recall the Saviour's own application of Jacob's ladder to himself.

If it were not so great a hymn it would not have met with so many attempts to alter or displace it. But notwithstanding the seriousness and sincerity of these attempts the hymn still stands; none of its popularity has been surrendered, and its celebrity has received a decided increment in its pathetic association with the death of President McKinley.

There are a number of reasons apart from the beauty of the figure for the great popularity of this hymn, among them the following are conspicuous: It is an almost incomparable lyric; the striking refrain, "Nearer, my God to thee, Nearer to thee," is so graceful, so simple, and so completely a part of the whole that it ministers largely to lyrical effectiveness; the aspiration of the hymn is emphatic and its climax is in the refrain—the climax ascending with each verse to the last; but beyond all, the prevalence of this aspiration, even in our dreams, and the triumph of this aspiration over all trials, commends the hymn to every soul "stepping heavenward."

RAY PALMER.—1808–1887
SAMUEL FRANCIS SMITH—1808–1895

We associate these names together, not because the men that bore them were themselves associated during life, nor because they had anything in common beyond their common Christianity and their common poetical gifts, but their names should be recalled as those of the two greatest American hymn-writers; contemporaries; born in the same year; similarly distinguished by lives of great usefulness; equally beloved and admired; so that we need not enter into any dispute concerning their comparative rank. The early life of both was spent in Boston. Palmer was a Congregationalist; Smith a Baptist. Palmer was graduated from Yale, 1830; Smith from Harvard, 1829. Both were highly honored by their respective denominations and filled various positions of trust and responsibility. Smith had a peculiar advertising in early life in the lines of his class-mate, Oliver Wendell Holmes, in a class poem—

> "And there's a fine youngster of excellent pith,
> Fate tried to conceal him by naming him *Smith*."

Dr. Palmer's great hymn is the following:

> "My faith looks up to thee,
> Thou Lamb of Calvary,
>   Saviour divine!
> Now hear me while I pray,
> Take all my guilt away,
> Oh, let me from this day
>   Be wholly thine!
>
> "May thy rich grace impart
> Strength to my fainting heart;
>   My zeal inspire;
> As thou hast died for me,
> Oh, may my love to thee
> Pure, warm, and changeless be,
>   A living fire!
>
> "While life's dark maze I tread,
> And griefs around me spread,
>   Be thou my guide—
> Bid darkness turn to day,
> Wipe sorrow's tears away,
> Nor let me ever stray
>   From thee aside.

"When ends life's transient dream,
   When death's cold sullen stream
       Shall o'er me roll,
   Blest Saviour! then, in love,
   Fear and distrust remove;
   Oh, bear me safe above,
       A ransomed soul!"

This hymn was written in 1830, when the author was twenty-two years old. He wrote it for himself, to voice the deep feelings of his own soul, in special distress at the time through ill health. It was called forth from its hiding a year later on the special request of Dr. Lowell Mason for a contribution to the new *Spiritual Songs for Social Worship*, which he and Dr. Hastings were preparing. It is a hymn of the first rank, and may be safely pronounced the finest devotional lyric of the Second Period. Dr. Benson, in his "Familiar Hymns," says of it: "It is as well known and well loved as any American hymn. It seems to many people like a part of their own spiritual life."

Dr. Palmer wrote other hymns scarcely inferior to this. We have already referred in Chapter II. to his version of St. Bernard's "De Nomine Jesu." This perhaps ranks next to the one just quoted:

"Jesus, thou Joy of loving hearts,
   Thou Fount of life! thou Light of men!
From the best bliss that earth imparts
   We turn unfilled to thee again.

"Thy truth unchanged hath ever stood;
   Thou savest those that on thee call;
To them that seek thee thou art good,
   To them that find thee, All in All.

"We taste thee, O thou Living Bread,
    And long to feast upon thee still;
We drink of thee, the Fountain Head,
    And thirst our souls from thee to fill!

"Our restless spirits yearn for thee,
    Where'er our changeful lot is cast:
Glad, when thy gracious smile we see,
    Blest, when our faith can hold thee fast.

"O Jesus, ever with us stay;
    Make all our moments calm and bright;
Chase the dark night of sin away,
    Shed o'er the world thy holy light!"

Dr. Palmer's other hymns embrace the following:

"Come, Jesus, Redeemer abide thou with me."

"Wouldst thou eternal life obtain?"

"Take me, O my Father, take me."

"O Jesus, sweet the tears I shed."

"O Christ, the Lord of Heaven, to thee."

It should be noted that Dr. Palmer frequently expressed his own preference, above all his hymns, for the following:

"Jesus, these eyes have never seen
    That radiant form of thine!
The vail of sense hangs dark between
    Thy blessed face and mine!

"I see thee not, I hear thee not,
    Yet art thou oft with me;
And earth hath ne'er so dear a spot
    As where I meet with thee.

"Like some bright dream that comes unsought,
    When slumbers o'er me roll,
Thine image ever fills my thought,
    And charms my ravished soul.

"Yet, though I have not seen, and still
    Must rest in faith alone.
I love thee, dearest Lord!—and will,
    Unseen, but not unknown.

"When death these mortal eyes shall seal,
    And still this throbbing heart,
The rending vail shall thee reveal,
    All glorious as thou art!"

This was one of Dr. Palmer's latest hymns. It was written in 1858, and so falls without the boundary which we have assigned to the Second Period. For thirty years thereafter it was in the heart and on the lips of its author, and the day before his death, in his great feebleness, he was heard to repeat the last verse. They were the last intelligible words which he uttered. The hymn itself is beautiful; beautiful! very particularly so when the words of Christ on which it is founded are recalled: "Blessed are they that have not seen and yet have believed." (John xx. 29.)

Dr. Smith's best work is his missionary hymn:

"The morning light is breaking;
    The darkness disappears;
The sons of earth are waking
    To penitential tears;
Each breeze that sweeps the ocean
    Brings tidings from afar,
Of nations in commotion,
    Prepared for Zion's war.

"Rich dews of grace come o'er us,
    In many a gentle shower,
And brighter scenes before us,
    Are opening every hour:

Each cry to heaven going,
 Abundant answers brings,
And heavenly gales are blowing,
 With peace upon their wings.

"See heathen nations bending
 Before the God we love,
And thousand hearts ascending
 In gratitude above;
While sinners now confessing,
 The gospel call obey,
And seek the Saviour's blessing,
 A nation in a day.

"Blest river of salvation,
 Pursue thine onward way;
Flow thou to every nation,
 Nor in thy richness stay:
Stay not till all the lowly
 Triumphant reach their home:
Stay not till all the holy
 Proclaim, 'The Lord is come!' "

There is nothing "great" about this hymn, measured by the ordinary standards; but when Dr. Nutter, in his *Hymn Studies*, says of it that it is "pleasantly optimistic," he gives the very secret of its great popularity. It has probably gone further and been sung more frequently than any other missionary hymn, not even excepting Bishop Heber's. It is known to have been translated into Italian, Spanish, Portuguese, Swedish, Chinese, Siamese, and several of the Hindu dialects; and all because it voices the blessed optimism of the promises.

It is a very strange and noteworthy fact that while Dr. Smith wrote the most popular of missionary hymns he wrote also our National Anthem. All

lands were dear to him; but before all, his own.   He
is at once the most patriotic and the most cosmopoli-
tan of our hymn-writers:

> "My country! 'tis of thee,
>   Sweet land of liberty,
>   Of thee I sing;
>   Land where my fathers died!
>   Land of the Pilgrims' pride!
>   From every mountainside
>   Let freedom ring!
>
> "My native country, thee—
>   Land of the noble, free—
>   Thy name I love;
>   I love thy rocks and rills,
>   Thy woods and templed hills;
>   My heart with rapture thrills
>   Like that above.
>
> "Let music swell the breeze,
>   And ring from all the trees
>   Sweet freedom's song:
>   Let mortal tongues awake;
>   Let all that breathe partake;
>   Let rocks their silence break—
>   The sound prolong.
>
> "Our fathers' God! to thee,
>   Author of liberty,
>   To thee we sing:
>   Long may our land be bright
>   With freedom's holy light:
>   Protect us by thy might,
>   Great God, our King!"

The tune "America," to which this hymn is sung,
is of ancient origin; but its chief celebrity rests upon
its association with the National Anthem of Great
Britain—*God Save the King*.   It was a happy thought

in Dr. Smith to write in the same meter, and in Dr. Mason to set the words to the same tune, thus uniting our own land to the mother country in that form of expression which appeals most powerfully to the emotions—our country and our God!

Dr. Smith wrote a number of other hymns, but none which may be classed with the ones quoted.

The differences in the style of these two writers lie upon the surface. Palmer is engaged with the contemplative elements of the religious life; Smith with the active. Palmer's hymns abound with the invocation of Jesus and this name of the incarnate Son of God is again and again repeated. Smith's hymns deal almost exclusively with the work which the glorified Redeemer is carrying on in the world. Palmer is more evangelistic; Smith is more missionary. The poems of the one admirably supplement those of the other. Together they cover a wide range and illustrate all that is best in American hymnody. It will be observed that with Samuel F. Smith the era of great missionary hymns draws to its close. Some attempts have been made in later years, but none that reach the rank of those noted in this volume. This does not indicate any decline in missionary zeal or activity, but only, as before indicated, the removal of that initial impulse or passion out of which come all the great poems of a people. The evangelistic spirit is, however, continued in connection with two great names with which the Second Period closes.

HORATIUS BONAR.—1808–1889

Dr. Bonar is the most popular of all hymn-writers, except Watts and Wesley, if we are to judge by the number of hymns of each in the various collections. About one hundred of his hymns are in common use.

Horatius Bonar was born in Edinburgh, December 19, 1808. His father, James Bonar, was solicitor of the excise, a man of learning and piety. His father's ancestors for several generations were clergymen of the Church of Scotland, so that it was not strange that he gave himself to Christ in early youth and chose the ministry as his life-work. His education was pursued in the city of his birth, and there completed at the University of Edinburgh. His character was largely shaped by his familiar fellowship with Dr. Chalmers and the saintly McCheyne, and he gave himself to his calling with rare devotion.

His first settlement was at Kelso, on the banks of the Tweed, a district celebrated in song and story, and already associated in the mind of the reader with the name of Henry F. Lyte. A great revival soon developed at Dundee, under the preaching of McCheyne, into which Bonar threw himself with all his soul. He was very anxious for the extension of the blessed work, and to promote this he published the celebrated *Kelso Tracts*, which were largely circulated in Great Brittain and America, and which did much in promoting his reputation.

Then came the bitter controversy in the old Kirk

and the disruption. Bonar went with the Free Church, and inasmuch as he and his congregation were able to hold their property, his church became the center of power and influence.

In 1865 Dr. Bonar removed from Kelso to Edinburgh, where he continued to preach with unabated power for more than twenty years. He lived to be eighty-one years old. His age was serene and beautiful, and his death as sincerely mourned as any man's in his generation. Dr. Theodore Cuyler's account of his funeral service is particularly interesting. He says:

"In August, 1889, when I was on a visit to Chillingham Castle, Lady Tankerville said to me, 'Our dear Bonar is dead.' I left the next day for Edinburgh, and reached there in time to bear an humble part in the funeral services. There was a tremendous downpour, but in spite of the storm the Morningside Church was well filled by a representative assembly. The service was confined to the reading of the Scriptures, to two prayers, and the singing of Bonar's beautiful hymn, the last verse of which is

'Broken Death's dread hand that bound us,
Life and victory around us,
Christ the King himself hath crowned us,
Ah! 'tis heaven at last!'

I rode down to the Canongate Cemetery with grand old Principal John Cairns (who had offered the prayers at the service) and under weeping skies we laid down to his rest the mortal remains of the man who attuned more voices to praise than any Scotchman of the century."

There is such uniformity of merit in Dr. Bonar's hymns that we cannot select one, before all others, and say, "This is the best."

Probably the one which would be first mentioned by his admirers would be

"I lay my sins on Jesus,
The spotless Lamb of God;
He bears them all, and frees us
From the accursèd load;
I bring my guilt to Jesus,
To wash my crimson stains
White in his blood most precious
Till not a stain remains.

"I lay my wants on Jesus;
All fullness dwells in him;
He healeth my diseases,
He doth my soul redeem:
I lay my griefs on Jesus,
My burdens and my cares;
He from them all releases,
He all my sorrows shares.

"I long to be like Jesus,
Meek, loving, lowly, mild;
I long to be like Jesus,
The Father's holy child.
I long to be with Jesus,
Amid the heavenly throng;
To sing with saints his praises,
And learn the angels' song."

The beauty of this hymn is in its spiritual comprehensiveness. Beginning with the removal of the sinner's guilt it passes to the supply of his wants, the comfort of his sorrows, his imitation of the Saviour's example, his growth in his likeness and the everlasting enjoyment of his presence.

The next hymn to be mentioned would probably be the following:

"I heard the voice of Jesus say,
  'Come unto me and rest;
Lay down, thou weary one, lay down
  Thy head upon my breast!'
I came to Jesus as I was,
  Weary, and worn, and sad;
I found in him a resting-place,
  And he hath made me glad.

"I heard the voice of Jesus say,
  'Behold, I freely give
The living water; thirsty one,
  Stoop down, and drink, and live!'
I came to Jesus, and I drank
  Of that life-giving stream;
My thirst was quenched, my soul revived,
  And now I live in him.

"I heard the voice of Jesus say,
  'I am this dark world's light;
Look unto me, thy morn shall rise,
  And all thy day be bright!'
I looked to Jesus, and I found
  In him my Star, my Sun;
And in that light of life I'll walk
  Till all my journey's done."

This is, if we may use the expression, one of the most ingenious hymns in the language. The balancing of the call of Jesus and the soul's response is exceedingly graceful, forceful, and suggestive. This is perfectly represented in the tune *Vox Delicti*, written for the hymn by Rev. John B. Dykes, in which the plaintive minor of the first half of each verse is followed by the glowing major of the second half. The hymn, sung to this tune, is seldom surpassed in church music.

Other well-known hymns by Bonar begin

"When the weary seeking rest."

"Beyond the smiling and the weeping."

"Go labor on, spend and be spent."

"Jesus whom angel hosts adore."

"Yes, for me, for me he careth."

"This is not my place of resting."

"A few more years shall roll."

"The church has waited long."

"I was a wandering sheep."

Dr. Bonar would not admit to his own worship the hymns which he taught so many saints to sing. Many of them were first written for use in his Sunday school, to the work of which he was particularly devoted. He encouraged the children to sing them, but would not permit his adult congregation to do so. He enforced this rule until near the end of life, and when at last he introduced them in the church service two of his elders rose from their places and strode indignantly out of church.

Bonar's hymns cover a wide range of subjects, yet they are much alike in some particulars. Their use of the name "Jesus" is as noticeable as in the hymns of Ray Palmer—indicating in both cases the near approach of the Third Period. The emotional preponderates in them. Even when they urge activity, it is not so much as a call to duty, but as an encouragement to the worker. They are in other respects a psychological study; for Dr. Bonar had the reputa-

tion of a war-horse.   Dr. Cuyler says: "Behind that
benign countenance was a spirit as pugnacious in
ecclesiastical controversy as that of the Roman
Horatius"—a reference to Bonar's first name—yet
his hymns are as balmy as a May morning.   Let the
student solve the riddle for himself.

HENRY ALFORD.—1810–1871

Alford is the last hymn-writer of the Second Period.
He should need no introduction to the student, but
his name is not so familiar to those of the present day
as to those of the last half century.   For two generations it has been a household word among all students
of the Bible, because of his monumental work, his
Greek Testament with Notes, upon which he labored
for twenty years, and which the majority of divinity
students through two continents studied.

Alford was born in London, October 7, 1810,
where his father was an English Church clergyman.
He was graduated from Trinity College, Cambridge.
After serving with great success in several positions
he became in 1857 dean of Canterbury, and there
remained fourteen years, until his death.   His memory is almost exclusively associated with this office,
and he is known everywhere only as "Dean Alford"
—as though his Christian name were forgotten.   He
was a man of great learning, taste, piety, and eloquence; and is remembered by those who knew him
with much affection.   Dean Alford wrote many hymns,
but most of them added little to his reputation.   They
are generally "cold and conventional," so that few

have been cherished by the church and remain in common use. Those which are found in our collections, however, possess much merit.

"Ten thousand times ten thousand,
　　In sparkling raiment bright,
The armies of the ransomed saints,
　　Throng up the steeps of light;
'Tis finished, all is finished,
　　Their fight with death and sin;
Fling open wide the golden gates,
　　And let the victors in.

"What rush of hallelujahs
　　Fills all the earth and sky!
What ringing of a thousand harps
　　Bespeaks the triumph nigh!
Oh, day, for which creation
　　And all its tribes were made!
Oh, joy, for all its former woes,
　　A thousand-fold repaid!

"Oh, then, what raptured greetings
　　On Canaan's happy shore,
What knitting severed friendships up,
　　Where partings are no more!
Then eyes with joy shall sparkle,
　　That brimmed with tears of late,
Orphans no longer fatherless,
　　Nor widows desolate.

"Bring near thy great salvation,
　　Thou Lamb for sinner slain;
Fill up the roll of thine elect,
　　Then take thy power, and reign;
Appear, Desire of nations—
　　Thine exiles long for home—
Show in the heaven thy promised sign;
　　Thou Prince and Saviour, Come!"

This hymn was written only four years before his death. It represents the maturity of his hope and faith. It was sung at his funeral service in Canterbury Cathedral. Dykes' tune (Alford) gives it great dignity; but it is scarcely a lyric. It has more power when eloquently repeated than when sung. It can scarcely either be called a hymn, though the last verse saves it to hymnody. Nevertheless it is so full of the courage of the Church Militant, soon to become the Church Triumphant, that it cannot be spared from our hymn-books.

Two other hymns of Alford deserve mention. They begin

"Forward be our watchword,"

and his fine harvest song,

"Come, ye thankful people, come."

CHAPTER XIV

HYMNS OF THE THIRD PERIOD

We pass now from the second period in English hymnology to the third. The change in the character of the hymns is not so immediately marked, but it is fully as positive as that which was noted in passing from the first period to the second. The decadence of this period is marked in the large preponderance of translations and it would almost seem as though the ability of original utterance in sacred song of high character were departing from the church. The rise of the devotional and sentimental is also apparent in the multiplication of female hymn-writers.

MISS JANE BORTHWICK.—1813–
MRS. SARAH FINDLATER.—1823–
MISS CATHERINE WINKWORTH.—1829–1878

These three women are distinguished by their excellent work in the translation of the best German hymns. Their work has been already noted and a number of their translations quoted in Chapter III. Miss Borthwick and Mrs. Findlater were sisters and labored together in preparation of their work entitled *Hymns from the Land of Luther*. They were born in Edinburgh. Miss Sarah Borthwick married Rev. Eric John Findlater and resided for a time in Perthshire. Miss Winkworth was born in London and lived subsequently in Manchester and Clifton. Her *Lyra Germanica* is the work from which the more important of her translated hymns have been drawn.

The only hymn which need be quoted in addition to those already given in the previous chapter is the following by Miss Borthwick:

"My Jesus, as thou wilt!
  Oh, may thy will be mine;
Into thy hand of love
  I would my all resign;
Through sorrow, or through joy,
  Conduct me as thine own,
And help me still to say,
  My Lord, thy will be done!

"My Jesus, as thou wilt!
  Though seen through many a tear,
Let not my star of hope
  Grow dim or disappear;
Since thou on earth hast wept,
  And sorrowed oft alone,
If I must weep with thee,
  My Lord, thy will be done!

"My Jesus, as thou wilt!
  All shall be well for me;
Each changing future scene
  I gladly trust with thee:
Straight to my home above
  I travel calmly on,
And sing, in life or death,
  My Lord, thy will be done!"

This is a rendering of "Mein Jesu, wie du willst," by Benjamin Schmolck, a Lutheran pastor of Brauchitzchdorf, in Silesia, one of the most popular hymn-

writers of his day.   It was written about 1704.   The
hymn is one of the most acceptable to American congregations, and while the German original belongs to
an earlier date, the English translation is one of the
very best exponents of the period we are now con-
sidering.

FREDERICK WILLIAM FABER.—1814–1863

There is scarcely an English poet concerning whose
compositions such varying opinions have been expressed as Faber's.   Yet there is scarcely another of
the past century whose poems have been more frequently quoted by Christians of every name.   Many
single lines have become almost proverbial; though
many who make use of them are ignorant of their
origin.   His special admirers are intensely devoted
to him, with an admiration amounting almost to a
passion.   To say the least, his work is worthy of
careful examination.

Faber was the son of an English clergyman.   He
was born in Yorkshire, June 28, 1814.   He was
graduated from Baliol College, Oxford, in 1836,
ordained the year following, and became rector of
Elton, Huntingdonshire, 1843.   He came under the
influence of the Oxford movement and this, with his
great affection for Newman, carried him into the
Roman Church, which he joined in 1846.   He established in London, in 1849, one of the branches of the
Congregation of St. Philip Neri, of which Newman
was father superior.   In 1854 the Oratory was
removed to Brompton, where Faber continued to

reside. He died September 26, 1863, at the early age of forty-nine.

Dr. Faber was a very voluminous writer in both prose and poetry. Many editions of his hymns have been published, some of which for Protestant use omit those addressed to Mary and the saints, and modify the language of others. Yet a considerable number need no change, as they were written before the author's secession to Romanism.

In making our selections for quotation from Faber's hymns we find it difficult to select such as are fairly representative of his style and also generally known. The following seems to meet the conditions as well as any:

"There's a wideness in God's mercy
  Like the wideness of the sea;
There's a kindness in his justice
  Which is more than liberty.
There is welcome for the sinner,
  And more graces for the good;
There is mercy with the Saviour;
  There is healing in his blood.

"There is no place where earth's sorrows
  Are more felt than up in heaven;
There is no place where earth's failings
  Have such kindly judgment given.
There is plentiful redemption
  In the blood that has been shed;
There is joy for all the members
  In the sorrows of the Head.

"For the love of God is broader
  Than the measure of man's mind;
And the heart of the Eternal
  Is most wonderfully kind.

If our love were but more simple,
   We should take him at his word;
And our lives would be all sunshine
   In the sweetness of our Lord."

This hymn contains the very elements for which Faber has been both praised and blamed. He is very much given to just such expressions as this, "A kindness in his justice." He mixes qualities that are apparently incongruous, in his effort to exhibit spiritual truth. He is fond of such terms as this, "the sweetness of the Lord"; and indulges in a familiarity that is offensive to some minds. He uses words in unusual meanings and strange connections. His language is fulsome and extravagant. Some say that his meaning is obscure; that his words often lack sense; that his style is burdened with excrescences.

These criticisms may be just to the letter of his poems; but they are certainly very unjust to their spirit. Faber must be understood to be appreciated. To those who have read his works at some length his peculiar power is plainly revealed. His imagination was exceedingly vivid, and at the same time, most unusual in its play. It led him out and on into a realm of strange associations and combinations. He brought things together in the spiritual world that seemed far apart in the natural world, and in order to state his thought he invested his terms with unusual meanings. He got more out of language than any other poet of the English tongue, and used words— even simple words—so that they rendered him a service which no other poet ever secured from them.

This might be illustrated at length did the plan and space of this work permit.

In studying his hymns, therefore, we may seek the general impression which they are intended to convey and value it, when found, in spite of what may seem to be verbal infelicities.

Faber's peculiarities appear very strikingly in two of his hymns, which have become great favorites in many churches, as follows:

> "Hark, hark, my soul! angelic songs are swelling
>   O'er earth's green fields and ocean's wave-beat shore:
> How sweet the truth those blessed strains are telling
>   Of that new life when sin shall be no more.
>
> REF.—"Angels of Jesus, angels of light,
>   Singing to welcome the pilgrims of the night.
>
> "Onward we go, for still we hear them singing,
>   Come, weary souls, for Jesus bids you come;
> And through the dark, its echoes sweetly ringing,
>   The music of the gospel leads us home.—REF.
>
> "Far, far away, like bells at evening pealing,
>   The voice of Jesus sounds o'er land and sea;
> And laden souls, by thousands meekly stealing,
>   Kind Shepherd, turn their weary steps to thee.—REF.
>
> "Angels, sing on, your faithful watches keeping,
>   Sing us sweet fragments of the songs above;
> Till morning's joy shall end the night of weeping,
>   And life's long shadows break in cloudless love."—REF.
>
> "O Paradise! O Paradise!
>   Who doth not crave for rest?
> Who would not seek the happy land
>   Where they that loved are blest?
>
> REF.—"Where loyal hearts and true
>   Stand ever in the light,
> All rapture through and through,
>   In God's most holy sight.

"O Paradise! O Paradise!
  The world is growing old;
Who would not be at rest and free
  Where love is never cold?—REF.

"O Paradise! O Paradise!
  I greatly long to see
The special place my dearest Lord
  In love prepares for me.—REF.

"Lord Jesus, King of Paradise,
  Oh, keep me in thy love,
And guide me to that happy land
  Of perfect rest above!

REF.—"Where loyal hearts and true
  Stand ever in the light,
All rapture through and through,
  In God's most holy sight."

Other hymns of Faber begin

"Sweet Saviour bless us ere we go."

"O God! thy power is wonderful."

"O God! how wonderful thou art."

"O gift of gifts! O grace of Faith!"

"Thy home is with the humble Lord."

"God's glory is a wondrous thing."

EDWARD CASWALL.—1814–1878
JOHN MASON NEALE.—1818–1866

These names are associated as those of the most celebrated translators of the Greek and Latin hymns.

Their work has been noticed and some of their best translations quoted in Chapter II. Caswall's *Jesus, the very thought of thee* and Neale's *Jerusalem the Golden*—the originals by the two Bernards—are the only hymns of the third period which find a place in Dr. Benson's list. Both Caswall and Neale were affected by the Oxford movement, Caswall becoming a Roman Catholic and Neale remaining in the English Church, while adopting many of the Romish practices.

Caswall was born in Hampshire, July 15, 1814. His father was a clergyman. He was educated at Brazenose College, Oxford, graduating with honors. He was ordained in 1840, and after ten years of service, entered the Roman Church. He joined Newman's Oratory at Birmingham and thenceforth to the end of his life devoted himself to the duties of his order, manifesting an unusual tender interest in the needy, the sick and little children.

Neale was born in London, January 24, 1818. His father, also, was a clergyman. Neale entered Trinity College, Cambridge, where he soon took rank as the best scholar in his class. He was awarded many honors, chiefly classical, and became a devoted student of mediæval church literature. In 1846 he became warden of Sackville College, East Grimstead, an obscure almshouse, where he continued to labor, on the meager salary of twenty-seven pounds per year, until his death. Here he founded a number of institutions after Roman models, the most important of which was a sisterhood, the members of which were devoted to acts of charity. His work brought him into disfavor with the ecclesiastical authorities, but he was able to live down all opposition by his transparent sincerity, his gentle manners, and the abounding charity which he showed to Christians of every name. He was a high ritualist, and a pronounced mystic, and seemed more like a mediæval saint than a modern clergyman.   His voluminous writings, however, have greatly enriched the literature of Christendom, while he and Caswall have done more to familiarize the average student with ancient hymnody than all other authors combined.

Caswall's most celebrated hymn is taken from Bernard's *De Nomine Jesu*, the first line being *Jesus, the very thought of thee*.   It has been already quoted in Chapter II.   The following, scarcely inferior, is from the same original:

> "O Jesus! King most wonderful,
>   Thou Conqueror renowned,
> Thou sweetness most ineffable,
>   In whom all joys are found!
>
> "When once thou visitest the heart,
>   Then truth begins to shine,
> Then earthly vanities depart,
>   Then kindles love divine.
>
> "O Jesus, Light of all below!
>   Thou Fount of life and fire!
> Surpassing all the joys we know,
>   All that we can desire—
>
> "May every heart confess thy name,
>   And ever thee adore;
> And, seeking thee, itself inflame
>   To seek thee more and more.
>
> "Thee may our tongues forever bless,
>   Thee may we love alone;
> And ever in our life express
>   The image of thine own."

Caswall has very few original hymns in our collections.   The following deserves notice as one of them:

"O Jesus Christ, if sin there be,
  In all our former years,
That wrings the soul with agony,
  And chokes the heart with tears;
It is the deep ingratitude
  Which we to thee have shown,
Who didst for us in tears and blood
  Upon the cross atone.

"Alas, how with our actions all
  Has this defect entwined;
And poisoned with its bitter gall
  The spirit, heart, and mind!
Alas, through this, how many gems
  Have we not cast away
That might have formed our diadems
  In everlasting day!

"Yet though the time be past and gone;
  Though little more remains;
Though naught is all that can be done,
  Ev'n with our utmost pains:
Still, Jesus, in thy grace we try
  To do what in us lies;
For never did thy loving eye
  The contrite heart despise."

Dr. Robinson admits this hymn to his editions of *Laudes Domini* and yet criticises it rather severely in his *Annotatious*.   He raises the question "Whether any one can hope to be supremely poetical when he is unfortunate enough to select a special sin, or possibly a notable immorality, for his theme."   Perhaps not. But does the criticism apply in this instance?   Is ingratitude a "special sin"?   It surely cannot be properly called an "immorality." Rather it is generally the chief defect in renewed character and the source of many special sins. So the author himself declares in the second verse. There are those to whom this hymn has appealed with a power scarcely equaled by other compositions. It fills a place in hymnody otherwise almost neglected and the very peculiarity of its theme will maintain its high place among our sacred songs.

Neale's reputation rests chiefly on his beautiful translation of Bernard of Cluny, *Jerusalem the Golden*. Several verses of this hymn are given in the previous chapter. Another form by Dr. Neale is given here.

> "Jerusalem, the glorious!
>   The glory of the elect—
> O dear and future vision
>   That eager hearts expect!
> Ev'n now by faith I see thee,
>   Ev'n here thy walls discern;
> To thee my thoughts are kindled,
>   And strive, and pant, and yearn!

> "The Cross is all thy splendor,
>   The Crucified, thy praise:
> His laud and benediction
>   Thy ransomed people raise
> Jerusalem! exulting
>   On that securest shore,
> I hope thee, wish thee, sing thee,
>   And love thee evermore!

> "O sweet and blessed Country!
>   Shall I e'er see thy face?
> O sweet and blessed Country!
>   Shall I e'er win thy grace!

Exult, O dust and ashes!
   The Lord shall be thy part;
His only, his for ever,
   Thou shalt be, and thou art!"

Another translation from St. Stephen of Mars Saba, has also been noted in the same chapter. It is one of Dr. Neale's most beautiful poems:

"Art thou weary, art thou languid,
   Art thou sore distressed?
'Come to me,' saith One, 'and coming,
   Be at rest.'

"Hath he marks to lead me to him,
   If he be my Guide?—
'In his feet and hands are wound-prints,
   And his side.'

"Is there diadem, as Monarch,
   That his brow adorns?—
'Yea, a crown, in very surety;
   But of thorns.'

"If I find him, if I follow,
   What his guerdon here?—
'Many a sorrow, many a labor,
   Many a tear.'

"If I still hold closely to him,
   What hath he at last?—
'Sorrow vanquished, labor ended,
   Jordan passed.'

"If I ask him to receive me,
   Will he say me nay?—
'Not till earth, and not till heaven
   Pass away.'

"Finding, following, keeping, struggling,
   Is he sure to bless?—
'Saints, apostles, prophets, martyrs,
   Answer, Yes.'"

Dr. Neale is known by a few original hymns, the most familiar, probably, beginning

"Holy Father thou hast taught me."

Miss Anna Letitia Waring.—1820–

Little can be learned of this author beyond that she was born at Neath, South Wales, and that she is the author of several little books of hymns from which those in common use have been taken. She is the author of one of the finest hymns of this period, as follows:

"In heavenly love abiding,
    No change my heart shall fear,
And safe in such confiding,
    For nothing changes here:
The storm may roar without me,
    My heart may low be laid,
But God is round about me,
    And can I be dismayed?

"Wherever he may guide me,
    No want shall turn me back;
My Shepherd is beside me,
    And nothing can I lack:
His wisdom ever waketh,
    His sight is never dim:
He knows the way he taketh,
    And I will walk with him.

"Green pastures are before me,
    Which yet I have not seen;
Bright skies will soon be o'er me,
    Where darkest clouds have been:
My hope I cannot measure;
    My path to life is free;
My Saviour has my treasure,
    And he will walk with me."

In this hymn we have a new and very free rendering of the twenty-third Psalm. It is a superb lyric. The rhythm is faultless and has a peculiarly charming movement. The antithesis in "I will walk with him," and "He will walk with me" is striking, and, as Dr. Robinson well remarks, "the closing verse is fairly jubilant with confident hope and unfaltering trust."

Another hymn by the same author begins

"Father, I know that all my life."

CECIL FRANCES ALEXANDER.—1823–

This gifted woman is the wife of the Rev. Dr. William Alexander, Bishop of Derry, Ireland. She has published a number of volumes of poems, but particularly excels in her hymns for children, of which she has written many. Apart from these she is best known as the author of *The Burial of Moses*, a very fine descriptive poem. The hymn on which her reputation rests beyond all other of her compositions is the following:

"There is a green hill far away,
    Without a city wall,
Where the dear Lord was crucified
    Who died to save us all.
We may not know, we cannot tell,
    What pains he had to bear;
But we believe it was for us
    He hung and suffered there.

"He died that we might be forgiven,
    He died to make us good,
That we might go at last to heaven,
    Saved by his precious blood.

There was no other good enough
    To pay the price of sin;
He only could unlock the gate
    Of heaven, and let us in.

"Oh, dearly, dearly has he loved,
    And we must love him, too,
And trust in his redeeming blood,
    And try his works to do.
For there's a green hill far away,
    Without a city wall,
Where the dear Lord was crucified
    Who died to save us all."

This was first published in her "Hymns for Little Children," which accounts for the great simplicity of the language; but it furnishes a complete illustration of the fact that *child-like* simplicity—if it be not *childish*—is the most popular and profitable form of truth, even with adults.   Simple as this hymn is in its style, it voices the most profound doctrines.   The incomprehensible character and extent of our Lord's sufferings upon the cross is plainly indicated; as also the justifying and sanctifying influences of his grace, his sole merit, and the very foundation of all Christian living—love for him who first loved us.

Another of Mrs. Alexander's hymns of almost equal merit is

"When, wounded sore, the stricken soul
    Lies bleeding and unbound,
One only hand, a piercéd hand,
    Can heal the sinner's wound.

"When sorrow swells the laden breast,
    And tears of anguish flow,
One only heart, a broken heart,
    Can feel the sinner's woe.

"When penitence has wept in vain
Over some foul, dark spot,
One only stream, a stream of blood,
Can wash away the blot.

" 'Tis Jesus' blood that washes white,
His hand that brings relief;
His heart that's touched with all our joys,
And feeleth for our grief.

"Lift up thy bleeding hand, O Lord!
Unseal that cleansing tide;
We have no shelter from our sin
But in thy wounded side."

This hymn is most evangelical, intensely spiritual, and withal, full of poetic thought and refinement. The hand that was pierced heals our wounds; the heart that was broken feels our woe; the blood that flows washes away our stains!

Other fine hymns by Mrs. Alexander begin

"Once in David's royal city."

"He is coming! He is coming!"

"Jesus calls us o'er the tumult."

FRANCES RIDLEY HAVERGAL.—1836–1879

We come now to the last of the English hymn-writers whose work it is our privilege to study. In this distinctively woman's period, this is the name of a woman—the greatest of the period in those elements of hymnody for which the period is distinguished.

Miss Havergal's father was a minister of the Church of England, himself a poet and musician of no mean order, as a reference to any modern hymn-book will show. She was born at Astley in Wor-

cestershire, December 14, 1836.   In 1851 she says:
"I committed my soul to the Saviour and earth and
heaven seemed brighter from that moment." She
began to write poetry when she was only seven years
old, and this was only an index of her many intellectual gifts.   She was a great linguist, conversant not
only with several modern languages, but with Greek
and Hebrew as well.   She was a most accomplished
musician, and played familiarly from memory the finest strains of Handel, Beethoven, and Mendelssohn.
But she was greatest of all as a Christian, attaining a
degree of consecration which few have reached.

She was an invalid most of her life, yet the literary
and philanthropic work accomplished by her industry
surpassed that of most persons in good health.   Hers
was a life full of faith, courage, and intense devotion,
and her influence will abide through many generations.

Her hymns deserve a more complete study than
we are able to give them, but certain features may
well be indicated as a guide to the student who would
pursue the subject at some length.   It is most important to note the development of her character as indicated in her hymns, and in the same connection to
observe how fully she reflects the spirit of the age
and its relations to the preceding periods.   It is also
important to observe in her hymns the climax of that
devotional element by which this third period is distinguished.   She herself said indeed, "Writing is
praying with me."   Let us take one of her earliest
compositions:

"Holy and infinite! viewless! eternal!
    Vailed in the glory that none can sustain,
None comprehendeth thy being supernal,
    Nor can the heaven of heavens contain.

"Holy and infinite! limitless, boundless,
    All thy perfections, and powers, and praise!
Ocean of mystery! awful and soundless
    All thine unsearchable judgments and ways!

"King of eternity! what revelation
    Could the created and finite sustain,
But for thy marvelous manifestation,
    Godhead incarnate in weakness and pain!

"Therefore archangels and angels adore thee
    Cherubim wonder, and seraphs admire;
Therefore we praise thee, rejoicing before thee,
    Joining in rapture the heavenly choir.

"Glorious in holiness, fearful in praises,
    Who shall not fear thee, and who shall not laud?
Anthems of glory thy universe raises,
    Holy and infinite! Father and God!"

This is very fine poetry. The style is elevated, the rhythm smooth, the thought profound. But it is poor hymnody. It reminds us very forcibly of the hymns of the first period in its doctrinal features, but with the best elements of the first period eliminated. What is the explanation? Miss Havergal herself tells us, "I know I did not love God at this time. The very thought of him frightened me. My thoughts did not naturally flow heavenward, but I forced them into a definite channel by a half-whisper, 'How good it was of God to send Jesus to die!' "

But by and by a great change came over her life. She tells of a certain painting with a legend inscribed upon it, by which her whole heart was won to the Saviour. As she was an attendant upon a certain school in Dusseldorf, it is supposed to have been the celebrated *Ecce Homo* of that splendid gallery. This painting represents Christ crowned with thorns, with the words above it, "All this have I done for thee. What doest thou for me?" Count Zinzendorf was converted by the sight and probably Miss Havergal. At all events, according to her own showing, it was such a picture with such words attached. Then began the second stage of her life, and her hymnody with the verses below. As Miss Havergal herself wrote them, they began. "I gave my life for thee," and followed in the same person throughout the hymn. The lines have been changed so that the address is in the second person rather than the first:

> "Thy life was given for me,
>   Thy blood, O Lord, was shed,
> That I might ransomed be,
>   And quickened from the dead;
> Thy life was given for me;
> What have I given for thee?

> "Long years were spent for me
>   In weariness and woe,
> That through eternity
>   Thy glory I might know;
> Long years were spent for me;
> Have I spent one for thee?

> "Thy Father's home of light,
>   Thy rainbow-circled throne,
> Were left for earthly night,
>   For wanderings sad and lone;
> Yea, all was left for me;
> Have I left aught for thee?

"Thou, Lord, hast borne for me
  More than my tongue can tell
Of bitterest agony,
  To rescue me from hell;
Thou sufferedst all for me;
What have I borne for thee?

"And thou hast brought to me
  Down from thy home above
Salvation full and free
  Thy pardon and thy love;
Great gifts thou broughtest me;
What have I brought to thee?

"Oh, let my life be given,
  My years for thee be spent;
World-fetters all be riven,
  And joy with suffering blent;
Thou gavest thyself for me,
I give myself to thee.

This hymn was followed by many others in like strain, full of sweet resignation and complete self-surrender.

Then as years passed by there came the third stage in her experience, when she reached Beulah, heaven was very near, and the very serenity of the eternal state seemed to be anticipated in her soul. Then she wrote:

"Our yet unfinished story
  Is tending all to this:
To God the greatest glory
  To us the greatest bliss;
Our plans may be disjointed,
  But we may calmly rest;
What God has once appointed
  Is better than our best.

"We cannot see before us,
    But our all-seeing Friend
Is always watching o'er us,
    And knows the very end;
And when amid our blindness
    His disappointments fall,
We trust his loving kindness
    Whose wisdom sends them all.

"They are the purple fringes
    That hide his glorious feet;
They are the fire-wrought hinges
    Where truth and mercy meet;
By them the golden portal
    Of Providence shall ope,
And lift to praise immortal
    The songs of faith and hope."

We may not quote others of Miss Havergal's hymns, but who does not know some of them, at least by heart?

"Take my life and let it be."

"Jesus, Master, whose I am."

"I could not do without thee."

"I am trusting thee, Lord Jesus."

"Thou art coming, O my Saviour!"

"Lord, speak to me, that I may speak."

"O Saviour, precious Saviour."

Rev. James Davidson, in *Julian's Dictionary of Hymnology*, says of Miss Havergal: "She carved out a niche which she alone could fill. Simply and sweetly she sang the love of God and his way of salvation. To this end and for this object her whole life and all her powers were consecrated. She lives and speaks in every line of her poetry. Her poems are permeated with the fragrance of her passionate love of Jesus.''

As we have already intimated in advance, under the name of Anna Steele, we must go back to the first great female hymn-writer of the English language to find the counterpart of this, its last great hymn-writer. Miss Havergal is called the ''Theodosia'' of the nineteenth century, in so many respects does she resemble her. Yet Jesus is presented to them in different aspects. Both manifest the same deep devotion, but with Miss Steele the aspect is physical, with Miss Havergal moral. Miss Steele dwells on his work and sufferings; Miss Havergal on his sympathy and love. Miss Steele sees him as he was in the past; Miss Havergal as he will be in the future.

The student will be richly repaid if he take now the hymns of these two distinguished writers and read them in conjunction.

While this closes our review of those authors that may properly be classed as great hymn-writers, there are others to be named belonging to that peculiar form of hymnody which developed in connection with the lay evangelism of the past half-century. Their work will be considered in the later chapter, under the subject, ''Gospel Songs and Singers.''

PART II. TUNES

CHAPTER XV

THE HISTORY OF HYMN-TUNES
PERIOD I

The Homophonic Era

Our modern hymn-tunes come to us originally from the Greeks. Hebrew music was not long employed in the early Christian church. Greek thought and Greek art had obtained a hold upon all civilized life. The Gospels were written in Greek, the preachers of the Cross generally employed the same language. So when the apostles and their successors entered Gentile communities their entire method of worship was affected by the dominant form of culture. The most ancient hymns were written in Greek and were naturally set to Greek music, so that in the course of three centuries Hebrew models were entirely abandoned. We are now to trace so much of the development of this Christian song as is necessary to the purposes of this volume.

The history of Church Music may be divided into three periods, as follows: Period I., from the earliest times to Hucbald, 930 A. D.; Period II., from Hucbald to Palestrina, 1563 A.D.; Period III., from Palestrina to the present time. We shall note the special characteristics of each period in order.

PERIOD I. THE HOMOPHONIC ERA

The word "homophonic" means "sameness of sound." The music of the homophonic era had but one part, corresponding to that which we call the "air" or "melody." This extended over hundreds of years. There is no record of any other kind of music until we reach the tenth Christian century.

For many generations this one-part music was little else than a rude chant, subjected in time to certain rules or customs, and corresponding closely to the intonation of the Roman liturgy.

GREEK SCALES

The earliest Greek "scale," or arrangement of successive notes of different pitch in order, of which we have any knowledge was the "tetrachord of Olympus." From it all modern music has been developed. The notes of this scale, like those of its successors for many generations, tended downward, not upwards, as ours do to-day. Hence the word "cadence," indicating the falling of the voice. In this the vocal art followed the natural inflection used in speaking. The voice naturally falls to the end of every sentence, except in an interrogative.

The tetrachord of Olympus contained only three notes, which stood related to each other as do A, F, and E in our system.

It may then be expressed thus:

After a time the note G was added, and we have

This was at first known as the Doric or Dorian tetrachord. It is the nucleus of the entire Greek system. Still later similar groups of four notes each were added to this tetrachord, either above or below it, thus forming the scale and increasing the range to which the voice was extended. The later Dorian scale may then be written thus

In this scale the slur indicates a half step, or semitone, which fell between the 2d and 3d and the 5th and 6th notes of the Dorian scale.

This scale was subsequently modified by changing the position of the semitones and several other scales were the result. That beginning on E was the Phrygian, thus:

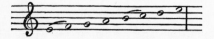

That beginning on F was the Lydian, thus:

That beginning on G was the Mixolydian, thus:

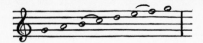

There were other forms which need not be here included. Those given above were the principal ones.

These scales are called "modes," to distinguish
them from modern forms. The word "mode" is
more strictly equivalent in modern musical nomen-
clature to our word "key," as when we speak of the
"key of G," and the music sung to these modes had
each its distinctive character, such as we recognize
to-day in our modern major or minor scales. The
Spartan boys were taught the Dorian mode exclusively,
because it was supposed to express courage and dignity. The Phrygian mode expressed pleasure and
excitement, the Lydian was considered effeminate and
voluptuous.

The early church doubtless availed itself of these
modes, but without any attempt at a definite ecclesiastical system, and so matters remained until near the
close of the fourth century.

AMBROSE

St. Ambrose, Bishop of Milan (384 A.D.), is
generally credited with the first orderly arrangement
of sacred song. There is considerable dispute with
regard both to the extent and the character of his
work, but it is certain that he regulated the ritual of
the church, introduced into Europe the Eastern prac-

tice of dividing the verses of the psalms between responsive choirs, and rearranged the hymns of the regular service. Whatever may have been his personal influence in the matter, there now appeared a new set of musical scales, based upon the four principal Greek modes given above, but so simplified as to meet the culture of his comparatively rude parishioners. Nothing like this music had ever been heard in the West, and it exercised a mighty influence. St. Augustine, in his "Confessions," tells of his weeping with deep emotion as he listened for the first time to these new melodies in the great congregation at Milan.

The Greek modes selected by St. Ambrose were chosen because of their apparently severe religious character. Others were used in the heathen temples and theaters, but were forbidden to the church. Hence the authorized scales were called *authentic*, and are still distinguished by this term.

GREGORY THE GREAT

There was no further development in the forms of church music for two hundred years. Then, with the accession of Pope Gregory the Great (590 A.D.) certain improvements were introduced destined to exercise salutary and permanent influence upon the worship of Christendom.

Gregory made a large number of reforms in connection with church music, among which was the revision of the Ambrosian hymns, the founding of a musical school at Rome, and the modification of the scales in use, with the addition of others. The music which resulted, and which has been maintained in the Roman Church ever since, is known as "Gregorian."

Gregory added to the "authentic" scales or "modes" of St. Ambrose four subordinate ones. These were formed by adding three successive notes below the lowest note of each scale respectively and on that account they were distinguished by the prefix "hypo," meaning "under" or "beneath." They are represented, and the relation of each to its corresponding Ambrosian scale shown as below.

Dorian

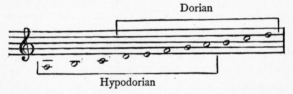

Hypodorian

The Hypophrygian, Hypolydian, and Hypomixolydian were constructed in the same way.   These scales were called "plagal."

But the authentic and plagal scales differed in another very important particular, affecting vitally all subsequent church music. The word "plagal" means "athwart," or "oblique."   It was applied to the new scales because such was their movement, in distinction to that of the authentic scales.   Observe the following:

Dorian; Authentic

Final   Final   Final

Mixolydian; Plagal

Final   Final   Final

It will readily be seen that in the authentic scale the *final*, that is, the tone which governs the scale, and on which it almost always closes, lies at the beginning of the series of consecutive notes, while in the plagal scale it lies in the middle of the series.

In the one case, the voice rises regularly from final to final and then descends regularly; in the other case, the voice first rises above the final, then descends below it, and again rises and finishes upon it.

The character of the music produced upon these two diverse systems is at once apparent. They promoted variety of the most pleasing and emphatic kind, and this variety is frequently illustrated in our modern hymn tunes.* *Old Hundred* is a fine illustration of a tune in the plagal form and *Antioch* of one in the authentic. It will be seen that the plagal melodies were more apt to be grave and dignified, the authentic more joyous and inspiring.

We must be careful, however, not to associate the harmony of four parts in which our modern tunes are written with the Gregorian melodies. They were not *tunes*, as we understand the term, but *chants*, and the style of music to which they belonged is called "plainsong." They were soon in use throughout Christen-

---

* The student should pursue this subject with some good hymn and tune book at hand and make use of the illustrations derived from tunes which they contain.

dom.   Trained singers were sent out from Rome to introduce the Gregorian music in all the principal centers of religious life, all variations from the system were rigorously restrained and this method established.

The following is a fair example of the usual Gregorian tones:

There were certain variations from this form, of a more or less florid character, but this gives a good idea of the method.   But the whole subject is one of vast dimensions.   The chant melodies were very numerous and varied greatly in length and character according to the particular ritual for which they were prepared. Many were highly elaborated, but all were dignified and impressive. The student who desires to inform himself concerning them will find them discussed in terms which may be readily understood by those who are not technical musicians, in Professor Dickinson's *Music in the History of the Western Church.*

Such is the form in which the liturgy of the Catholic Church has been clothed from the days of Gregory. It is regulated to a nicety in every particular, from the cadences of the officiating priest to the elaborate responses of the choir. Not a single note is extemporized, as might be imagined, but all adjusted to the one profound effect.

Another important advance dates from St. Gregory. Though he himself may have had nothing to do with it, yet the influence of his system was such that it begat an intense desire upon the part of those who made use of it, to invent some method of preserving the melodies which it evoked. A sentence from St. Isodore, the friend of St. Gregory, indicates both that this was impossible in his day and also that he longed to make it possible. He says: "Unless sounds are retained in the memory they perish because they cannot be written."

But how should they be written? The question was answered in the invention of a strange system of signs, known as *neumes*, from the Greek word meaning "wind," or "a breath." These neumes were written

above the syllables to which they were sung and re-
sembled somewhat the characters employed to-day in
phonography.   There was a vast variety of them, and
it is hard to understand how they could have been
mastered.

About the beginning of the tenth century a certain
improvement was introduced of immense significance,
inasmuch as it indicates the first element in the creation of the modern staff.   Up to this time the neumes
indicated only the rise and fall of the voice, but with
nothing whatever to indicate the pitch.   The melody
might be pitched high or low, at the pleasure of the
singer.   But now a red line was drawn across the
page and the neumes arranged with reference to this
line, which always represented the note F, corresponding to the F below our middle C.   Neumes thus written appeared thus; the corresponding syllables being
written below:

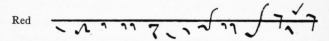

One note being thus fixed, the location of other notes
might be more readily determined.

But no sooner was one note located than it became
a speedy and easy matter to locate a second.   At first
this second line was yellow and stood for the note C,
the middle C of the modern keyboard.   But as it was
not convenient to employ colors on all occasions, both
lines were soon drawn in black with the letters C and
F placed opposite, thus:

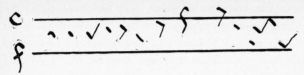

Here, then, was the origin of the modern bass and treble clefs—the G clef having been added subsequently.

HUCBALD

But as the one line suggested a second, so the two lines suggested the use of as many as the need of the musician required. Hucbald, a monk of Flanders, in the tenth century (930) discarded the use of neumes and added the needed lines. He used as many lines as there were notes to be sung, placing the syllables between the lines, thus employing the spaces only. The letters T and S were placed at the end of the lines to indicate tones and semitones, and his method of notation appeared thus:

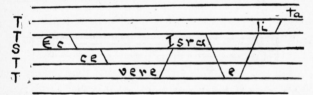

This, of course, is very unlike our modern staff, but it certainly foreshadows it. We might say its invention could not now be long delayed.

But Hucbald must be credited with still another and equally important invention, full of even greater promise and significance, in which the homophonic era is brought to its close, and harmony, in several parts, begins to appear.

He arranged a voice accompaniment to the chant, which beginning on the same note as the chant, continued a fourth or fifth below and ended on the same note as it began.   In another form it consisted simply in prolonging one note—the tonic, for example, while the chanting voice moved up and down.   It is represented thus:

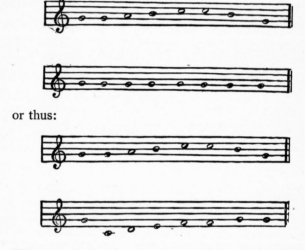

or thus:

This sounds harsh—almost unendurable to modern ears—but it was a marvelous thing to those upon whose ears had never fallen the sounds that attempted harmony.

Hucbald's system was approved by the church, and called the *sacred organum*.   Another method was soon introduced, employing other notes, but as it lacked ecclesiastical sanction it was known as the *profane organum.*

Hucbald was most industrious and enthusiastic in promoting his inventions. He might well have been. They contained the seeds of more splendid fruit than anything of which he had ever dreamed. A period of rapid and wonderful development was at hand, which we consider in the next chapter.

CHAPTER XVI

THE HISTORY OF HYMN-TUNES
PERIOD II

The Development of Polyphony

We know that the inventions of Hucbald promoted much experiment by the musicians of the tenth century, but little came of it until we reach the year 1024.

GUIDO ARENTINO

Another monk now appears, the inmate of a Benedictine convent near Ravenna, Guido Arentino by name, or Guido of Arezzo. He is credited by tradition with the invention of the musical scale or staff, though this is denied him by certain authorities. Perhaps he only represented the results of a hundred years of progress, but at all events a number of most important improvements are associated with his name, and with him the second period fairly begins.

To the first six tones of the scale, called a "hexachord," Guido applied the syllables *ut, re, mi, fa, sol, la*. These were taken from a hymn to John the Baptist, dating from the sixth century, which was very generally sung at the time. The syllables were the first of each line.

Ut queant laxis.
*Re*sonare fibris.
*Mi*ra gestorum
*Fa*muli tuorum.
*Sol*ve polluti.
*La*bii reatum.
 Sancte Johannes.

Each one of these syllables represented a definite note—the syllable was, so to speak, its name. This will more plainly appear by reference to the hymn as set to music.

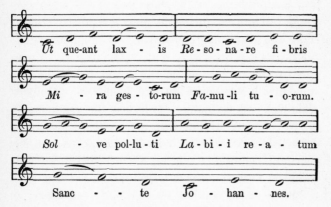

A glance at the above will show the relation of these notes to each other. In this instance the hexachord of six notes began on C. *Ut* was C, *re* was D, and so on. Other hexachords, however, began on F and on G. This involved certain difficulties, because the notes were also named by letters, as they had been from the days of Gregory, and therefore the letters and syllables did not always correspond, thus:

The art of changing the syllables with the change of the hexachords was called *solmization*. Another change, involving the position of the semitones, which it is not necessary to explain, was called *mutation*. These two arts comprised the great invention of Guido.

It was a startling innovation. It simplified musical instruction to a very remarkable degree. Compared with our present methods and judged by our standards it was awkward and inefficient. Guido's scale had only six notes. It lacked the one remaining to complete it; but that note, with its designating syllable, *Si*, was not added until the end of the sixteenth century, *Ut* being also discarded for *Do*, except in France where it is still retained.

But we must not judge Guido by the standards of to-day, but by those which preceded him. As he himself declared, the methods of his age were such that one might sing a hundred years and still need careful drill in order to render a simple response.

Guido accomplished what one has well called "hearing with the eyes" or "seeing with the ears." The choir-boys under his instruction were able to sing at sight melodies with which they were previously unfamiliar. Their hearers were confused and amazed.   It was a work beyond their comprehension.

His brother monks seemed to have connected some occult influence with his work and they procured his expulsion from the convent.   This came to the ears of the pope, who became sufficiently interested to summon Guido to Rome.   Here he demonstrated his system so practically that the pope himself succeeded in "hearing with his eyes" and was able to sing musical phrases from the manuscript without a leader.   This made Guido's reputation and established his permanent influence.   He was invited to remain in Rome to instruct the clergy in the principles of his system, and though he was unable to do so, as the climate was unendurable to him, he returned with honor to his own convent.   Thenceforth his reforms were accepted and the new era in musical development was inaugurated.

COUNTERPOINT

While all this was in progress another great reform in music was being developed.   It passed through several stages, which need not be described.   It was not therefore associated with any single name, but was probably the result of general effort.   Thereby the *organum* of Hucbald was to be greatly modified and a long stride taken towards modern harmony.   This was *discant*, meaning, as the word implies, *something apart from the song*.   It was a second voice-part sung at the same time as the principal part.   In order to its performance the chant in use was sung in long notes in regular measures, that the singer of the *discant* might be sure to accommodate himself to it. The leading part was therefore called *tenor*, from the Latin *teneo, to hold*. It was also known as the *cantus firmus—the fixed song*. Thenceforth the tenor was the leading part and carried the air until the days of Palestrina. Singers then might improvise any melody they chose for the discant. The most curious, and to our notion comical, results were thus obtained; but it must be borne in mind that there was as yet no notion of what we call "chords," and therefore no attempt at harmony. The solemn words of the chant might be sung at the same time and in connection with some trivial or even indecent secular song, the words of the chant being all-important and those of the discant being lightly regarded. Some of the bolder musicians even attempted to unite two secondary songs with the canto firmo; but as the number increased the task became the more difficult. It was therefore seldom attempted.

As the discant was never written down we have no positive means of judging of its success. But it would seem that it must have become, in skillful hands, more mellifluous than we may imagine.

Discant, however, though very useless in itself, filled a most important part in the transition from organum to counterpoint, and so was a signal advance toward the creation of our modern hymn-tunes.

And now that counterpoint is so nearly ready to appear, let us seek to understand its character and uses. In the olden times the notes were called "points," because they were pricked into the parchment. Written music was on this account called "prick-song." A "counter-point" was therefore a counter-note; that is, a note set over against another note. But the succession of counter-notes must have their own movement or melody. They must furnish something more than a mere voice accompaniment, such as a natural bass. In some modern hymn-tunes the parts other than the "air" may form perfect chords with it, but nothing else. The harmony may be good, but the counterpoint defective. In other tunes the parts are free and rich, even the bass moving independently and melodiously. In such counterpoint is developed.

Take, for example, the tunes known as *Ewing* or *Emmelar* (Merrial), and let each part be played or sung by itself alone, that its own movement may be clearly discerned. It will not only reveal the character of the counterpoint, but also the place which it holds in modern musical composition.

Johann Sebastian Bach (born 1685) is the greatest master of counterpoint. The character of his music and its application to the hymn-tune is indicated in the following selection from his *Passion Music*, the tune being known as *Passion Chorale:*

O sacred Head, now wounded, With grief and shame weighed down;

Now scorn-ful-ly surrounded With thorns, Thine only crown:

O sacred Head, what glo - ry, What bliss till now was Thine!

Yet, tho' despised and gory, I joy to call Thee mine. A-men.

Such, then, is counterpoint. It is the natural—almost the inevitable—outgrowth of discant. But before it can make its appearance other improvements must be made whereby the connecting link shall be supplied.

FRANCO

A third monk now appears upon the scene, a worthy successor of Hucbald and Guido, Franco of Cologne. Franco wrote the earliest book on measured or timed music, about 1175 A.D. Until he pro-

pounded his theories there had been no way of indicating the length of any given note. It must either be
borne in memory or governed by the taste of the
singer. But it will be readily understood that there
could be no adaptation of one part to another until
the length of every note was clearly and positively
indicated. Two parts could not be played together,
and much less could they be sung. Harmony was
impossible.

Franco had three signs by which to express the
length of his notes, thus:

The first sign indicated a note three times as long as
the second. The second sign indicated a note three
times the length of the third. This was because all
music of a sacred character was, at that period, sung
in triple time. As there were three persons in the
Trinity, this was held to be the only form permissible
for religious themes. The value of Franco's notes
may therefore be expressed thus:

The "long" note—equal to three of the "breve,"

or to nine of the "semi-breve";

This was soon found to be too awkward and inconvenient for practical purposes, and therefore another
note-sign was added, while the length of each was so
altered that each possessed the value of two of the
notes immediately below it, thus:

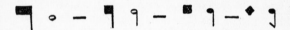

Triple rhythm kept the field for a time in connection with the quadruple.   It was known as "perfect
time" and quadruple as "common time."   When
triple time was used it was indicated by the signature
of a circle, thus:

When common time was used, the circle was broken,
thus:

which is still used when common time is indicated,
and the letter C is employed.   Originally, however,
it was not the letter C, but the broken circle.

Certain variations of Franco's forms were subsequently introduced, which need not be indicated,
resulting finally in such as we employ to-day.

And now, at last, the way was open to full harmony.   The location of the notes might be indicated,
their duration could be determined, the musician

"heard with his eyes" both their pitch and their
length and the organum followed by discant had suggested the adjustment of part to part.   Discant need
no longer be improvised, as it must be heretofore; it
could now be written.   So note was pricked opposite
note and incipient counterpoint began.

At first it was very formal and severe, to suit the
long notes of the chants to which the discant had been
sung.   This was called *plain* counterpoint—one note
set against another, thus:

Then two notes against one, thus:

Then it became syncopated and florid, thus:

Many other variations were introduced. It was a wonderful revelation to the musicians of that age. The capabilities of harmonic measures, thus set before them, fairly intoxicated them with pleasure, and they began to play with notes and chords as children with new toys in which all their inventive talent is evoked. They inverted the counterpoint, placing it first in the bass and then in the treble, thus:

Inverted.

They made still further variations. At first only two voices were employed, but with increasing dexterity others were added, until even eight or more parts were written on one score.

Then came the "canon," a musical composition in which the part of the first voice is exactly repeated by other voices, each beginning at a separate time. This was the invention of a member of the Belgian school, to which the development of counterpoint is to be chiefly credited, Guillaume Dufay, about the opening of the fifteenth century.

The canon led the way for a still greater variety and more extravagance of expression. It began in a simple manner, as follows:

This form, being brought to conclusion, was called a *finite* canon.

Then came the "infinite canon," which might continue forever, as follows:

But still more fantastic forms were invented by these merry musicians. They wrote canons that could be sung as well backwards as forwards, called "cancri-zans," or even upside down, or both, thus:

Canons were also written in curious forms, such as triangles and circles. Some were even composed in such a shape as to embody a monogram or suggest an enigma. Music was, however, attaining its major-ity. It was in the stage corresponding to that of the youth just approaching manhood—full of nonsense, experiment, and pretension, the subject of vicious temptation and frequent imposition, but still full of hope and promise and passing rapidly to the glorious era of self-mastery and service.

The more complex and intricate the arrangement, the greater the success of the composer. All kinds of technical problems were attempted, difficulty was added to difficulty, and musicians reveled in the mere mechanical effort involved in a multitude of parts and a variety of chords. But out of it all came the knowledge of the relation of tones and consequent harmonic combinations. All that is needed now is some master-hand to grasp all these wild and untamed elements and subject them to control. The materials were all furnished, the organizing mind alone was lacking.

PALESTRINA

In the good providence of God the hand and mind were forthcoming.

Giovanni Pierluigi, the son of a poor peasant, was born at Palestrina—the ancient Praeneste, a town in the Apennines, twenty miles from Rome,—A.D., 1514. We know nothing of his boyhood. When he was twenty-six years old he came to Rome to study music. Here he came under the influence of Orlando di Lasso, the last and greatest of that Belgian school which had done so much in the development of counterpoint. Returning to his own town, Giovanni, who is ever after to be himself known by its name, as Palestrina, became chapel master in the village church, and so continued for ten years. In 1551 he returned to Rome, where for a number of years he was busy as composer and director. Meanwhile the Council of Trent, in 1552, had resolved upon musical reform. It was sadly needed. Counterpoint was running mad, not only with all the extravagances of which we have spoken, but with many of the abuses inherited from the age of discant.   The solemn chant had become in many instances a trivial madrigal, and the sacred words of the *Gloria* or *Credo*, in the leading part, were accompanied by secular or even lewd strains from profane sources.

But no one was found to direct the reform until it was determined to appoint Palestrina, who by this time had become chapel master of the Vatican.   Pope Pius IV. thereupon directed him to compose a mass which should be the embodiment of the reform. Palestrina accepted the task.   Master as he was of all the contrivances known to his contemporaries, he was also a true scholar, a refined artist, and a devout churchman.   He particularly excelled the musicians of his day in his gift of melody, which invests his work with special artistic value.   As Louis C. Elson says, "In the use of choral-like simplicity Palestrina causes the commentator involuntarily to draw a comparison between him and John Sebastian Bach. Palestrina may stand as the typical Catholic, as Bach represents the earnest Protestant, in music."   He proceeded to subject all the current devices to the principles of divine praise, and produced a work which has since continued to be the model of sacred musical composition.   It is known as the "Missa Papæ Marcelli," the "Mass of Pope Marcellus"—so called from the name of the immediate predecessor of Pius IV.

The work was received with the greatest enthusiasm. Some even pronounced it a miracle. Palestrina himself claimed that he had produced "a new style," as indeed he had. With him the era of the development of harmony closes and the modern era begins. Palestrina is to the reformed music what Luther is to the reformed faith.

Little remained for his successors to accomplish except to carry on the work which he had inaugurated, with improvement, perhaps, in form, but with no change in fundamental principle.

The foundation principle in Palestrina's music was embodied in what he called the "plain" or "familiar style" (*stile famigliare*), of which the following is an example:

re - re   no - bis   Qui - a tu cre-

a - sti nos; tu   re - de -mi - sti nos.

præ - ti - o - sis—

San - gui -ne tu - o præ - ti - o - sis - si mo.

"This style," as Professor Dickinson remarks, "is peculiarly tender and gracious, and may be found reflected in the sweetest of modern Latin and English hymn-tunes. It is suggestive of the confidence and repose of spirit which is the most refined essence of the devotional mood. . . . . . The most obvious feature of the design is that each part appears quite independent of the others. The melody does not lie in one voice, while the others act as an accompaniment, but each part is as much a melody as any other, the voices apparently not subject to any common law of accent or rhythm, but each busy with its own individual progress. The whole effect is measured, subdued, solemn."

The modern hymn-tune is then upon its way and there is a remarkable conspiracy of providential agencies and circumstances in preparation of its coming. Palestrina himself will contribute the most effective material in his general influence, and his very music will also survive in some of its noblest illustrations. The following arrangement will enable the student to judge the dignified and enduring character of his work.

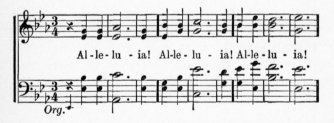

1. The strife is o'er, the bat - tle done; The vic - to-
ry of life is won; The song of tri - umph
has be - gun. Al - le - lu - ia! A - men.

The student will observe that in this chapter we
have joined together the names of Palestrina and
Bach. They are particularly worthy of his special
study. But since Protestants owe more to Bach than
to any other composer of all time, he should make a
special study of his life and work, even if others be
neglected.

CHAPTER XVII

THE APPEARING OF THE HYMN-TUNE. PERIOD III

The student will observe the historic period to which we have now been brought. It is the last quarter of the sixteenth century. The Protestant Reformation is in progress. The growth of the Huguenot faith is exciting the malice that shall soon break forth in the Massacre of St. Bartholomew. The Church of England has been established. Prussia is rising into power. Holland is about to revolt from Spain. The new world of thought and action has appeared and the people are to have a voice in both church and state. Such was the juncture in which the modern hymn-tune appeared. It was but one of the many exponents of the age, the product and the index of those fresh and mighty influences which culminated in the sixteenth century. This is well expressed by C. H. H. Parry, Mus. Doc., in his *Evolution of the Art of Music.* "The harmonic phase of music has been exactly coeval with the development of that particular kind of intellectual disposition which continued to manifest itself more and more as modern Europe slowly emerged from the chaos which followed the collapse of the Roman empire. It is as if harmony, the higher intellectual factor in music, began with the first glimmerings of modern mental development and grew more and more elaborate and comprehensive and more adapted to high degrees of expression and design, simultaneous with the growth of men's intellectual powers.   As long as the church reigned supreme, harmony remained more or less in the background, and made its appearance mainly as the result of the combination of the separate melodies which various voices sung at once.   But towards the end of the sixteenth century it began to assert itself as the basis of certain new principles of design, and in the succeeding century, as secular life grew more and more independent of ecclesiastical influences, it became more and more the center and basis upon which the whole system of artistic musical design was founded.''

The hymn-tune then must be regarded as one of the most expressive features of the age which produced it.   Its harmony, its intellectuality, its popular uses, and its sacred character all have the most profound meaning.   They speak of awakening mind, of larger brotherhood, of the sovereignty of the people, and of vital religion.   Its appearance must be also explained in connection with hymnody, for here is wedlock of the most positive kind.   The hymn and the hymn-tune are a substantial unity.   The one without the other has a barren existence, is but half a self, and perishes in its unproductiveness.

German Chorals

Most of the best tunes in common use to-day are from English composers, but we must go back to

Germany for their origin. The Lutheran Reformation was the fountain from which flowed the main stream of sacred song, though it has been greatly enriched by tributaries, which, taking their rise in the same sources, had flowed on for a time in separate channels.

The Catholic Church had consistently and persistently confined the office of song to a select body of priests and minor clergy; the people had no share in it. This was regarded as a liturgical necessity, intimately connected with the Romish theory of the priesthood.

This theory was rejected by Protestantism, and with it all its corollaries. Congregational song, therefore, became an expression of the very faith of the Reformers, not a mere form of their worship. Luther was the first to perceive its relations to his doctrines and the first to promote its use. Fortunately he was both poet and musician himself, and capable of directing the reform.

But with the Catholic theory he rejected also the Catholic forms. The hymns of the church were written in Latin; he would write his in the vernacular. They were elegant and scholarly and breathed the atmosphere of the cloister; his should be plain and simple, and breathe the air of practical life. They were sung in stately Gregorian tones, scarcely heard or used beyond the sacred walls of the church; his should be more like the strains which the people sung in the woods and fields. He himself said, "I am not of the opinion that through the Gospel all arts should

be banished and driven away, as some zealots want
to make us believe, but I wish to see all arts, principally music, in the service of Him who gave and
created them.'' So the new epoch was ushered in
and the German chorals began to be.

The Germans were singers from the earliest times.
Even before their conversion to Christianity they had a
vast number of religious songs which they sung in praise
of their heathen deities, and their songs for festivals
and similar occasions were equally numerous. In the
era before the Reformation many of these tunes had
been sung to religious songs, and although they were
discountenanced by the church they could not be
wholly repressed. (See Chapter III.) The people
therefore had their own hymns, even before Luther,
but they were separated from the hymns of the church
by an impassable chasm.

The wisdom and skill of Luther and his associates
appear in this, that they made use of the popular tunes
for religious purposes, not exactly by employing them,
but by employing their method. His work was substantially twofold: the reconstruction of the music of
the Catholic Church and the adaptation of popular
melodies, so that both might be harmoniously used in
worship. A number of Gregorian chants were employed without special alteration. Tunes were constructed upon Gregorian models; such, for example, as
the celebrated *Ein' Feste Burg*, and the secular folk-
song furnished others.

These tunes were called *chorals* because they were
written purely for the voice and were sung without

accompaniment. At first they were not harmonized
—all voices sang in unison. Later, when the development of counterpoint began, the congregation sang
the melody only and the choir supplied the parts.
Then, as the knowledge of music progressed, they
were much improved and elaborated.

Some of our most inspiring tunes in common use
are the product of these German chorals, and there is
little finer music for congregational purposes. We
have already referred (in Chapter III.) to one of the
best illustrations from Johann Crüger, who was the
author of a large number.

It was written in 1648, and is set to Martin Rinkart's hymn as translated by Miss Winkworth.

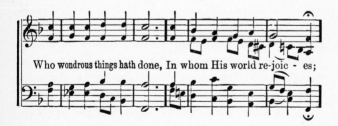

1. Now thank we all our God With heart and hands and voices,

Who wondrous things hath done, In whom His world re-joic - es;

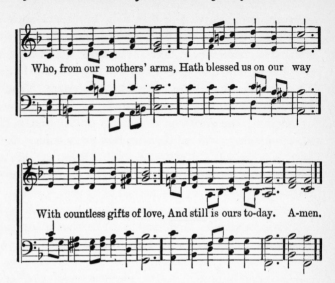

The illustration of Bach's music given in the preceding chapter is itself an arrangement of an old German choral by Hans Leo Hassler, composed in 1601. *Ein' Feste Burg* is too well known to the student to require our repeating it.   These must suffice as examples of that very large body of song which Germany contributed to Protestant worship.

FRENCH TUNES

But Germany, though it was the primal source and chief agent in this work, was not alone in it.   France and Geneva, so closely allied, as we have already seen, took an important part in it.   The psalms of the Marot-Beza collection were set to old French tunes as early as 1552.   They soon came into very general use, and were widely sung by French-speaking Protestants. An interesting account of their influence upon the people of Geneva is given by a visitor to that city in 1557, who writes of the large attendance upon Protestant worship, where "each one draws from his pocket a small book which contains the psalms with notes and out of full hearts, in the native speech, the congregation sings before and after the sermon. Every one testifies to me how great consolation and edification is derived from this custom."

It 1565 a collection of hymn-tunes was published in Paris by Claude Goudimel, a Netherlander, one of the last of the great school of Belgian contrapuntists and one of the first musicians of his age. He had given much attention to the purification of counterpoint and had written music substantially in the "plain style" even before Palestrina had named and developed it. In 1540 he was at the head of a music school at Rome, and Palestrina was one of his pupils. Coming to France, he attached himself to the Huguenots, and thereby incurred the hostility of their persecutors. He was a "shining mark" for their malice and perished in the massacre of St. Bartholomew.

Goudimel's faith and training fitted him to become a leader in fixing the forms of Protestant praise and his influence was incalculable. Many of his tunes were derived from secular sources. Others were arrangements of Gregorian chants. One of the latter was *Old Hundred*, which appears for the first time in his collection, but set to the 134th Psalm. It was afterward embraced, as we have seen, in the Anglo-Genevan psalter, united to the 100th Psalm, with which it has been associated ever since.

There can be no doubt that there was an interchange of these new tunes between Germany and France, while the indebtedness of the English, and more particularly the Scotch psalmody to these sources has been already noted.

The effect, however, upon English tune-music was not altogether salutary. The initial impulse was vigorous and hopeful; but the development was soon arrested. The Calvinistic Protestants of Geneva and Scotland, on conscientious grounds, repressed the artistic element in music as savoring of papacy, and consequently made little headway. Their hymn-tunes were not "hymn-tunes" at all, but *psalm-tunes*. The first sacred song-books in English were composed exclusively of the psalms in meter, and the tunes corresponded. English tune-music, therefore, like English hymnody was delayed for more than a hundred years, awaiting that burst of praise which was introduced in hymnody with Watts and Wesley, and which in turn promoted the development of music suited to itself. The psalms of Sternhold and Hopkins with the "apt notes to sing them withal" was the first complete psalm-book with tunes published in England. This was in 1562. The music was simple and severe, and was written in one part only, but the English Protestants were chiefly dependent upon it for one hundred and thirty years.

ANGLICAN MUSIC

In the mean time, however, a great work was in progress in English sacred music in general, which gives it historic interest exceeded only by Italy and Germany, and which is increased by the fact that this music was very largely indigenous. It had already developed the Anglican chant, a decided modification of the Gregorian, as any one may note who is familiar with what remains of it in the services of the Episcopal Church, and thus established for English music a character of its own.

Then came the Reformation. But the Reformation in England effected altogether different results in church music from those achieved on the Continent, from the fact that in England it developed along two diverse lines, which we may call the Anglican and the Puritan. The Anglican clung to many of the old forms of worship; the Puritan disowned them all. So that Anglican music followed Catholic precedents, while Puritan music struck out upon a new path.

The hymn-tune suffered and was long delayed in consequence; but when at last there came a better understanding and wiser musical co-operation, those, splendid tunes began to appear which are to-day the glory and the joy of all English-speaking worshipers.

In the opening of the Reformation the first decided development of the chant was the Anglican anthem; that is, the *anti-hymn*, or alternate hymn. At first the anthem was a comparatively simple composition, differing from the chant in that its parts were sung responsively and were somewhat more elaborate and florid. But its limitations were emphatic, as it was sung without any accompaniment. Soon, however, with the rapid improvement and multiplicaton of musical instruments, accompaniments were added, until in some cases they were of equal value with the voice parts, and thus gradually the English anthem with which we are familiar was evolved.

The English Church, however, could not long continue to practice a musical system which, like the Catholic, deprived the people of the privilege of concerted song. As they had their "Common Prayer," they must also be given their common praise. So in process of time the early form of cathedral service was modified, to adapt it to general parochial use.

In such cases the service was not intoned, but rendered in the natural voice, and even if the anthem was retained—as it might not be—metrical versions of the psalms were sung at proper intervals.

This, led to a development of hymn-tune melodies on a different basis from that of the Genevans, and thus began the contributions of the Anglican Church to this form of sacred song.

Thomas Tallis

The most notable name in this connection is that of Thomas Tallis, called the "Father of English Cathedral Music." He was a contemporary of Palestrina, and with this single exception, the most distinguished and capable musician of his day. He was chapel-master to Henry VIII. and retained the place under Edward VI., Mary, and Elizabeth, until his death, in 1585. His contributions to the development of the art of music and to the general store of musical compositions were prodigious, yet he is best known to-day by his labors in behalf of common praise. He was an indefatigable student of counterpoint and harmony, and arranged many of the old plain-song chants for part-singing. Indeed, he is the father of the English harmonized chant.

His best work for posterity, however, was done in his hymn-tunes. They were written by him in four parts—the melody being, however, in the tenor according to the custom not as yet displaced.

In 1560 John Daye published his "Morning and Evening Prayer and Communion." Tallis contributed to this book eight tunes, several of which may be found in our collections. One of these, slightly modified to suit the modern distribution of parts, is a favorite tune to-day with many congregations, and is found in most hymn and tune books. As it is set to Bishop Ken's evening hymn, "Glory to thee, my God, this night," it is known as *Tallis's Evening Hymn*.

It will be observed that the collection in which this hymn first appeared was published five years before Goudimel's and two years before Sternhold and Hopkins'. This should be particularly noted as indicative of the two lines—Puritan and Anglican—along which the hymn-tune was being developed. *Daye's psalter is the first collection of hymn-tunes in which the music is written in four parts*. Tallis' Evening

Hymn, therefore, possesses certain features of interest surpassing those of all other tunes now employed in Protestant worship, so that while we refer the student to the collections in use for illustrations of well-known tunes, we do well to introduce here this remarkable composition, in its present form.*

1. Glo-ry to Thee, my God, this night, For all the blessings of the light;

Keep me, O keep me, King of kings, Beneath Thy own almighty wings. A-men.

If due attention has been given to the preceding history a world of instruction is afforded us with regard to the most important features of hymn-tune music. Let this composition be compared with *Old Hundred* and we perceive at once the characteristic differences of the Puritan and Anglican methods.

Old Hundred and *Tallis' Hymn* are respectively the oldest representatives of two different styles, which were at first antagonistic. They still have their peculiar illustrations and ardent champions. The

* In modern hymnals "All praise" is substituted for the word "Glory" for the sake of the musical accent.

massive dignity of the one is set over against the flowing freedom of the other. The simple, radical chords of the first are in sharp contrast to the contrapuntal variety of the second. Which is the most suitable to public worship? The question has excited long and learned discussion. It is enough for the student, at this point, to observe the comparison, and to connect in his mind the various illustrations of the two forms, even in their extreme manifestations, from the most severe upon the one hand to the most gleeful upon the other.

Yet it ought to be said, that while Tallis' hymn is a fine exponent of the Anglican style it should not be inferred that Tallis departed from legitimate ecclesiastical forms. He was as truly devoted to sacred principles as Palestrina, and most of his compositions are written in what might be called the "familiar style." The student should confirm this by reference to some of his other tunes. He introduced no learned complications into his music merely to astonish his hearers. He endeavored by the use of pure, rich harmonies to promote true devotion, and never paraded his ingenuity at the expense of intrinsic truthfulness to his high themes. The Anglican style which he introduced was not therefore another genus, so to speak, but only another species within the same genus to which tunes like *Old Hundred* belong, and therefore the chief controversy is not between the Anglican and the Puritan, but between the sacred and the profane. Ere long this distinction began to be observed and the results appeared in the best tunes which we now possess. It ought to be thoroughly understood and observed to-day, that our services may be thoroughly purged of many tunes which are entirely inappropriate to the worship of God, while a liberal latitude is allowed for tunes of various styles and expressive of manifold sentiments, while yet devotion is never displaced nor reverence forgotten.

The history of English church music in general would be sadly incomplete without some reference to Orlando Gibbons (1583–1625), and Henry Purcell (1658–1695).   But as their names are not particularly associated with the development of the hymn-tune we must omit any reference to their influential labors. The student, however, is urged to inform himself concerning them.

With Thomas Tallis, then, the modern hymn-tune may be said to have appeared.   The work of perfecting and adapting it yet remains.   This will be discussed in the next chapter.

CHAPTER XVIII

THE PERFECTING OF THE HYMN–TUNE

The work of Thomas Tallis in hymn-tune music was bright with promise, and when we reach this period we feel confident that the development, now brought to such a high degree, will be rich and rapid. But our confidence is at once disappointed, and for several generations the promise is simply promise and nothing more. The reason will appear to any one who consults a good historical atlas. In France he reads of Richelieu and Louis XIV. and the Revocation of the Edict of Nantes and the War of the Spanish Succession; in Germany, of the Thirty Years' War and Frederick the Great; in Great Britain, of the Spanish Armada and the Gunpowder Plot and Cromwell and the Restoration. Nothing was done for the hymn-tune during this period. In fact, there was sad and positive retrogression.

THE OLD PSALM-TUNES

The Scotch Psalter of 1635 contained one hundred and forty-three tunes. Eight of these were "Rapports" (from the French "rapporter," to *carry back*, i. e., fugue-tunes). Forty-two were taken from the Genevan Psalter and the rest from various musicians on the Continent and in Great Britain. Fifteen years later (1650) the authorized version of Rous was published, but without tunes. Music was thereby turned adrift, to seek refuge with such individuals as might afford it a shelter, and consequently many tunes fell into disuse, were forgotten, and abandoned. The unsettled state of society, tossed to and fro in the struggles of commonwealth and monarchy, contributed to the deterioration of sacred song, and when the Restoration came, in 1660, the only tunes in use were the few old melodies to which the Psalms were sung, and these grew less and less in number until not more than half a dozen were generally known. A variety of circumstances conspired to continue this state of things. Chief among these was the general use of Rous' version of the Psalms, in which, with scarcely an exception, every number was rendered in common meter, compelling the use of a tune in similar measure.

The custom of "lining out" the hymns, which was rendered imperative by the scarcity of books, confined the worshiper to tunes of a certain class and almost destroyed any musical charm which they might possess, and the absence of instrumental accompaniment completed the barrenness of their performance. In addition to this, a certain veneration attached to the tunes that were distinctly associated with the Reformation and discredited the attempt to add to them. The Psalms in meter had come to the congregations united to certain tunes, which seemed to be a very part of them and to form an indivisible entity, thus inspiring such a spirit as was shown by the old family servant of Dr. Guthrie, who vowed she "wad sing

the Psaams o' Daavit to the tunes o' Daavit and nae-
thing else.''

So between the pharisaic routine of the Established Church and the stolid dullness of the Dissenters, music remained *in statu quo.*   Twelve ''orthodox
tunes'' were sanctioned by the Scotch Presbyterians.
Good tunes they were, however, well suited to their
age and purpose; but sadly similar in general structure and most monotonous.   Burns refers to them with
much feeling in his ''Cotter's Saturday Night,'' and
indicates the sentiments with which they were cherished and sung.

> ''Those strains that once did sweet in Zion glide
>   He wales a portion with judicious care,
> And 'Let us worship God,' he says, with solemn air.

> ''They chant their artless notes in simple guise,
>   They tune their hearts—by far the noblest aim;
> Perhaps *Dundee's* wild, warbling measures rise,
>   Or plaintive *Martyrs*, worthy of the name;
> Or noble *Elgin* beats the heavenward flame,
>   The sweetest far of Scotia's holy lays.
> Compared with these Italian trills are tame,
>   The tickled ear no heart-felt raptures raise,
> Nae unison hae they with our Creator's praise.''

At least three of these oldest hymn-tunes should
be examined: *St. Michael, Dundee,* and *Windsor.*
The first is taken from the Genevan Psalter, 1543.
The last two are by Sir Christopher Tye, 1553.*
They are characteristic of their age.   All are written
in common time, in radical chords, and without flour-

---

* As we give no account of these composers, the student who
desires to be informed concerning them should consult some
cyclopedia of music and musicians, or any similar work.

ishes of any kind.   There is but one note to each syllable and but one syllable to each note, and they are
therefore known as *"syllabic"* tunes.   Their form is
the simplest possible, and in many respects the best.
The movement is dignified and the effect impressive.
Beyond all else they are singable by any congregation,
and so popular, in the best sense of the word.

The New Hymn-Tunes

The period of these old syllabic tunes continued
for more than a hundred and fifty years, during which
no advance was made.   Occasionally we find in our
present books a tune like *St. Ann's* (also called St.
Anne) composed near the close of the period.   St.
Ann's was written by William Croft, 1708.   But
even such additions were few.

With the first half of the eighteenth century, however, came the beginnings of English hymnody, and
with it came the new departure in hymn-tune music.
The two must be associated in our minds.   The old
tunes, as we have already remarked, were *psalm*-
tunes; the new ones will be *hymn*-tunes.   Hymns
and hymn-tunes appear together.

The modification of the old syllabic tune commenced soon after Watts began to publish his hymns
and was in full career during the life of Charles Wesley.   Although most of the best hymn-tunes now in
use were not the product of Methodism, yet Methodism did more to promote them than any other religious
movement except the Lutheran Reformation in Germany.   Methodism created the demand.   It furnished

the hymns; and the tunes were forthcoming. As Professor Dickinson well remarks: "It was like a sunburst, opening a brighter era. The enthusiastic welcome accorded by the Wesleys to popular music and the latitude permitted to free invention and adoption of hymns and tunes gave an impulse to a purer and nobler style of congregational song which has never been lost."

The new departure from the old forms was really a retrograde movement, though it did not so appear at first. A little later, as we shall see, it became apparent; still later was recognized and corrected and the perfection of the modern hymn-tune was reached.

It has often been so in the progress of reform; the advance has been achieved, not in successive uniform improvements, but in a strange alternation of mistakes and master-strokes in which men have learned as much from their failures as from their successes.

The change in form first appears in such tunes as *Wareham*, by William Knapp, 1738; *Arlington*, by Thomas A. Arne, 1762; *Rockingham, Old*, by Edward Miller, 1790; and *Duke Street*, by John Hatton, 1793.

The student should not fail to compare these tunes with those which preceded them, in the illustrations given above. It will be seen that the ruggedness of the old tunes has been much softened. The new tunes are more flowing and melodious. Three of them are written in triple time, which often produces lighter effects, but which is seldom as easily sung by the average worshiper. All of them introduce sliding or "passing" notes, which were unknown to the syllabic tunes, and are marked by more elaborate harmony.

Let us observe that this is indicative of both advance and decline. The movement already bears some resemblance to that which we observed in the generation preceding Palestrina, when the very excesses of counterpoint contributed to the development of harmony. Even so this shall contribute to the perfecting of the hymn-tune. This will appear more emphatically in the next step.

The hymn-tune now passes into a third form and what we know as the *fugue* appears, in which there is an alternation of part with part, one or more voices being silent for a time—each taking up a line and repeating it in succession, generally with increasing force, and massed together in the closing strains. The best examples of these tunes to be found in our collections are *Lenox*, by Lewis Edson, 1782; and *Geneva*, by John Cole, 1800. An illustration will also be found in *Antioch*, arranged by Lowell Mason from Handel (1742) 1836.

These, however, are scarcely examples of the form, since they are almost the only examples which the church has been willing to retain, and therefore they represent the form at its best. The fugue was often indefinitely extended until the tune became a little anthem. The temptation to practice the art became the more enticing the more it was employed, until musicians introduced marvelous involutions, requiring the utmost dexterity in the singers who attempted them. For this reason these tunes became immensely popular and for a time were generally cultivated and sung. We have the suspicion that the old-fashioned singing-schools of our grandfathers' days were supported chiefly in consequence of their devotion to this style of tunes and the pleasure which they afforded the pupils in the practice of vocal gymnastics.

These tunes were not wholly bad, either in character or influence, as some musicians would have us believe. Most of them were, of course, bad art, as we have already indicated. The movement was retrograde. But they expressed the popular demand for a larger variety in congregational song, and indicated a real and commendable religious aspiration.

A certain repetition is an invaluable aid to the power of all art, whether it be painting, oratory, architecture, or poetry. It has been recognized in music from the beginning. The Psalms of David are full of it. It is often the very secret of lyrical beauty and effect, and when it is associated with some sort of antiphony it is specially pleasing and impressive. But it must be kept within reverential bounds; it must be in accord with sacred subjects; and it must not exceed the limits of congregational capacity. While the worshiper should be furnished with a variety sufficient to express his different religious moods, there should be no concession to feelings or sentiments that are merely artistic or superficial. All this has an application to the revival of the fugue in our modern Gospel Songs, which will be noted in another chapter.

The trouble with the old form of the fugue-tune was that it went too far. This fault appeared in two forms: it was so extended that it became inapplicable to consecutive verses of a given hymn; and what was much worse, it served to express merely the ingenuity of the composer and the contortions of the singer's voice. It degenerated into very musical rant. It was the "canon cancrizans" over again; with all its faults, but also with all its possibilities. And so the fugue-tune was abandoned—it was not suited to congregational worship. Yet, as in the days of the old canons, there was a loud cry for some master-musician who should resolve these elements into a new and nobler form, some modern Palestrina who should do for the hymn-tune what the great Italian did for the music of his own age.

We cannot say that another Palestrina did really appear. The service which corresponded to his was rendered by a number of musicians who contributed to the reform and made it effective. Yet among them there was one who beyond all others deserves to be called the Modern Palestrina, an American composer, whose splendid and permanent work and whose vast influence we have not yet learned to estimate at their full value, and with whom the perfected hymn-tune is at last introduced.

LOWELL MASON

The modern school, which began with Lowell Mason (if indeed he may not be called its founder), was the successful creator of a style in which the dignity of the old psalm-tunes is modified and beautified by the color of the period which followed them. The breadth is reinstated and warmth is added. There is a wider range and more liberty; there is a judicious selection of melodies from secular sources; but all with the most worshipful intent. The harmony is more varied, and while it is sometimes more difficult than in the old psalm-tunes, it is within the reach of the members of any congregation whose leaders are willing to make a little effort in their instruction. In order that we may understand this we begin with a particular notice of the work of the man to whom its inauguration is principally due.

Lowell Mason was born at Medfield, Massachusetts, January 8, 1792, and died at Orange, New Jersey, August 11, 1872. He taught himself the rudiments of music and was in charge of the church choir at Medfield when he was only sixteen years old.

In 1812, at the age of twenty, he removed to Savannah, Georgia, where he was engaged as a clerk in a bank; but continuing to teach and conduct. In 1827 he returned to the North and resided in Boston. Here he became president of the Handel and Haydn Society, and soon after (1832), in connection with George James Webb, established the Boston Academy of Music. In 1835 New York University conferred upon him the title of Doctor of Music. He visited Europe in 1837, prosecuting his studies and adding to his reputation. Upon his return he engaged largely in musical publication, putting forth many

volumes in the interest of better sacred music, not
only for the congregation, but for the choir, the Sabbath school, and church societies.   In this work he
continued until within a few years of his death.

The influence of Lowell Mason on congregational
music may be inferred from the fact that more than
seventy tunes of which he was the author may be
found in modern collections.   The new Presbyterian
Hymnal, one of the latest and most severely critical
in its selections, contains thirty-three of his tunes,
besides eight repetitions—this number being exceeded
only by Dykes with forty-three and Barnby with
thirty-five.   The wide range of his work appears in
that of these thirty-three tunes twenty-three are
original, and the others are arrangements of melodies
derived from various sources.   The best known of
his original tunes, with their dates of composition in
historical order are as follows: *Missionary Hymn,
1823; Hebron, Uxbridge, Laban, Wesley, Cowper,
1830; Boylston, Olivet, 1832; Harwell, 1840; Bethany, 1859.*   Arrangements of German melodies are *Naomi, 1836; Azmon, Mendebras, 1839;
Lischer, 1841; Dennis, 1845.*   Gregorian, *Hamburg,
Olmutz, 1824.*   Scotch air, *Ward, 1830.*   From
Mozart, *Ariel, 1836.*   From Handel, *Antioch, 1836.*

It will be observed that the *Missionary Hymn* is
his earliest production.   The story of its composition
is told on page 170.

A study of Lowell Mason's hymns, in the light of
preceding history, and as indicating the transition
from the fugue-tune to the modern form and as con-

necting all periods in the one final production, will amply repay the careful student. The dignity, solemnity, and breadth of the old Gregorian music is well reproduced in *Hamburg*, most appropriately set to that greatest of all hymns, "When I survey the wondrous cross." The utmost permissible use of the fugue, according to present standards, in conjunction with the "authentic" mode, is found in *Antioch*. The best element of the "rapport" is heard in *Cowper* and *Bethany*. Other similar illustrations of the change which is being effected will be found upon examination of other tunes.

The Perfected Hymn-Tune

It will be recognized that the change which was inaugurated in hymn-tune music with Lowell Mason was great and momentous, but it will also be seen that it was not fully effected. A brief study of the tunes whose titles are given above, in connection with the dates of their composition, makes it very clear that their composer had not formulated any positive principle. He has no uniform style. On the contrary, he alternates between one form and another, and there is no steady progress. His influence therefore depends upon the general direction in which he is moving rather than upon any goal which he has reached. Nevertheless his influence was most profound. Direction is much, though not everything. Being once established, the goal is sure to be reached. Lowell Mason broke away from current forms, supplied the corrective of many abuses, and started upon a path in which others, following his leadership, soon achieved the best results. He was immediately followed by five great composers, whose names are the greatest in hymn-tune music, and between whom and all others there is a manifest if not indeed a mighty gulf. These are Sir John Goss, 1800–1880; Henry Smart, 1813–1879; Rev. John B. Dykes, Mus. Doc., 1823–1876; William Henry Monk, Mus. Doc., 1823–1889; and Sir Joseph Barnby, 1838–1896.

It will be observed that these men were contemporaries; the oldest of them was only eight years younger than Lowell Mason, and the youngest was thirty-four years old when Mason died.

These men established a certain form of hymn-tune music in which all that is best in sacred song is reverently cherished and employed; in which the blemishes of the experimental stage are removed; in which all needful variety is introduced; and in which the very best in art is made to serve the highest in religion, so that the demands of the most cultivated musician and those of the most devout worshiper are alike supplied.

It is not necessary to refer to the works of these great composers in detail. Let the student examine them in any modern hymnal. He will find in some cases tunes by two or more of them set to one hymn; for example, number 623 of the Presbyterian Hymnal is set to tunes by Barnby, Smart, and Dykes.

JOHN B. DYKES

While we accord to these five composers a place in the first rank, there is one who, by common consent, is at least *primus inter pares*. This is the Rev. John B. Dykes. It is not that his music is so superior to that of the others as that it is more generally representative of the perfected hymn-tune. We may take anything which he has contributed to modern collections and set it up as a standard, saying, "This is what a tune ought to be for such a hymn as this." Dr. Dykes was born at Hull, March 10, 1823. He could play well by ear upon the organ before he learned to play by note. His musical career began as conductor of the Cambridge University Musical Society, and was never interrupted. Though employed in a number of places as a priest of the English Church, and with rare fidelity and success, he continued to devote much time and effort to sacred music. From 1849 to 1862 he served both as dean and precentor in Durham Cathedral, and during these years most of his most important musical compositions were published.

In 1862 he took charge of St. Oswald's, a parish church in Durham, and continued as its vicar until his death. And then the extent to which he had touched the heart of the English people is indicated in the fact that they contributed ten thousand pounds for his memorial.

One thing is to be noted concerning Dr. Dykes' tunes, which gives them special prominence and value.

His deep religious instincts and superb literary taste led him to select for his compositions the finest of modern hymns, so that we have in his productions the union of the best in hymnody with the best in music. For example, Bishop Heber's "Holy, Holy, Holy," is the finest hymn of adoration in the language. It is set to *Nicæa*, one of Dykes's finest tunes. It thus becomes in its twofold aspect a positive standard of the perfected hymn-tune in time, pitch, movement, range, and harmony. Again, Bonar's "I heard the voice of Jesus say" is a sweet, persuasive evangelistic hymn. Dykes has united it to *Vox Delicti*, a remarkable composition, in which the Saviour's quest and the soul's joyful answer as set forth in each verse are very beautifully expressed in the music in the change from the minor to the major. These and other tunes by Dr. Dykes should be carefully examined. Then let the student review the history which has been given and survey the road by which he has been led to this splendid height of popular praise. Let him recall the many mistakes committed, the many experiments tried, the many improvements made. The road has not been unlike that by which the mountain top is reached—now up steep ascents, now across broad plains, now down through deep gorges; but ever tending upward and on towards the glorious summit. We know not what may be the surprises of the future, but whatever may be in store for us, let us thank God for the present and rejoice in the treasures of praise which we possess.

CHAPTER XIX

THE BEST TUNES

[NOTE. —From the large number of excellent hymnals recently published, the author has selected the *Presbyterian Hymnal* and *In Excelsis* for his chief illustrations in this chapter. The student should procure and make use of them.]

No one has yet done for our tunes what King and Benson have done for our hymns in the *Anglican Hymnology* and *The Best Church Hymns*, but no doubt the same general principles will apply to both words and music. The best tunes may be determined by usage, but usage must be defined in this case, as it has been in the case of our hymns, by reference to those hymnals which have been compiled by competent authority, indorsed by leading denominations, and used in the stated worship of regularly organized congregations. When a large number of such hymnals shall have been collated, we shall be furnished with a standard by which to determine our best hymn-tunes. For the present, however, we may note the drift of sentiment as indicated in the kinds of tunes which are the more and more discountenanced and in the kinds which are the more and more indorsed by accredited compilers. Take, for example, the successive editions of the Robinson series. Wherein is the advance from the *Laudes Domini* to the *New Laudes Domini*, and thence to the *In Excelsis?* Or take the old and the new *Presbyterian Hymnal*, and what are the differences?   Then compare these books with those in use a generation ago.   A superficial examination will supply a fairly satisfactory answer; a careful study will reveal a wealth of suggestion, into which we may not enter, but which will prove exceedingly profitable to him who undertakes it.   We must content ourselves with a few illustrations:

1. *The fugue-tune has almost disappeared.*

The older hymnals contained a considerable number, the newer ones contain only two or three.   Some that were once great favorites have disappeared. *Northfield*, for example, a stirring tune, usually set to "Lo! what a glorious sight appears," and sung by our fathers with great zest, is missing from the later publications.   Even *Geneva*, still retained in the Presbyterian Hymnal, is cast out of the *New Laudes Domini* and *In Excelsis*.   Some tunes, once written as fugues, have been modified and the fugue eliminated.   So it is with *Lenox*—our sires would scarcely recognize it.

This would indicate that few if any fugue-tunes are suitable for congregational purposes; the consensus of the best judgment is against them, and for reasons given before.

2. *New tunes are offered for hymns to which old familiar tunes are wedded.*

This is hazardous business for the compiler, and frequently his very best efforts are ignored, or even indignantly condemned.

The writer was recently engaged in teaching a choir one of these new tunes when an old minister who was present, rudely shocked by the displacement of his favorite melody, shook his finger in my face and solemnly said, "What God hath joined together let not man put asunder"; a zeal for the antique which might remind one of "Daavit's Psaams to Daavit's tunes!"

We may be very sure that when, in a serious collection, an alternate tune is offered for a given hymn, there is good reason for it; and much more so when a new tune is offered in lieu of an old one. It is because competent judges believe it to be better—usually it *is* better—it marks some distinct advance.

This is not to advocate the hurried substitution of new tunes for old ones. There is sometimes a world of holy associations connected with an old tune which it were almost a crime to sunder. Sometimes old words have been fused together with old music and a sort of "one flesh" has been created in the holy wedlock. In such a case divorce is not permissible. If the tune is not positively bad, let it alone.

We are not to encourage mere novelties in sacred music. The passion for such things is too intense as it is. Certain irresponsible publishing houses thrive upon it and succeed all too well in imposing a lot of periodical trash upon credulous congregations. But we are not to stand in the way of genuine reform, honestly attempted; and the hymnals that are published with this in view should be welcomed.

When old associations are not emphatic, when certain hymns have been sung to more than one tune, or more especially, when even the tune which we have been accustomed to sing, however much we are attached to it, is manifestly unsuitable, we ought not to resist the adoption of the new tune.   It ought at least to be examined and considered.

The later hymnals furnish many illustrations of the changes indicated above.   Let us select those that are associated with the most familiar hymns.

[1.] "All hail the power of Jesus' name" is generally sung in the United States to *Coronation*, but there is no positive wedlock in this case.   It is sung in England and Canada to *Miles Lane*, a tune much admired by our British cousins.   It has one remarkably fine feature—the thrice-repeated acclaim, "crown him!" in the last line.   *In Excelsis* gives the first place to this tune, follows it with *Coronation*, and then adds a third tune, *Southwich*.   This is as much as to say that *Coronation* is not satisfactory. The Presbyterian hymnal does not contain *Miles Lane*, but gives the first place to Smart's *St. Leonard* and follows with *Coronation*.

What is the student to conclude?   Whatever may be his pious prejudices he cannot fail to note that competent judges agree that *Coronation* is not one of our best tunes.   If he asks Why not? he will find his answer in the principles already revealed.   The "rapport" is not good form; the repetition does not add to the effect—it is an anti-climax.   The movement does not accord with the sentiment and the passing notes—particularly those of the last bar—are weak almost to insipidity.

There is a question still as to which is the best tune for this hymn; but either of those preferred by the compilers is better than *Coronation*. Let the student test them for himself.

[2.] There are cases in which the composer of an older tune has himself added a newer tune to the same hymn—testimony of the strongest possible kind. *Merrial* (called *Twilight* in *In Excelsis*), formerly known as *Emmelar*, is a very beautiful tune by Barnby. No alternate tune was formerly given for it, but *In Excelsis* adds *Bard* and the *Presbyterian Hymnal* adds *Repose*, also by Barnby. (This is not the *Repose* of *In Excelsis*.) The reason for this is at once apparent; the counterpoint of the older tune is too involved for the average worshiper. The singing of the tune is limited to the choir.

Illustrations similar to the above might be multiplied. "Just as I am, without one plea" has been commonly sung to *Woodworth*. Barnby's *Just as I am* (Presbyterian Hymnal) is so much better every way that it should be substituted. Even Dykes is not equal to himself in *Lux Benigna* to "Lead Kindly Light." The hymn is hard to sing to any tune, but *Lux Beata* by Peace, or more particularly *Sandon* by Purday is more singable. Other examples will appear upon examination of the hymnals.

3. *Changes have been made in the tunes themselves in order to their improvement.*

Sometimes these changes are in notation, harmony, or rhythm, as already observed in the case of *Lenox*. Sometimes the notes themselves are altered. Our English friends complain that Sir Arthur Sullivan's *St. Gertrude* has been mutilated by its Ameri-

can arrangement.   Perhaps, however, it was only a
wise surgical operation.   It appears in two forms in
In Excelsis and the *Presbyterian Hymnal*, the former·
containing a little fugue imitation in the last line,
eliminated in the latter.   It will be well to compare
the two forms.

Sometimes the time in which a tune is written is
changed.   In the older books *Serenity* is written in
three-four time.   In nearly all the recent ones it is
written in six-eight time, though *In Excelsis* restores
it to three-four.   This is so important a matter that
the tune, written in the two forms, is herewith given.

SERENITY—(Older form).

SERENITY—(Later form).

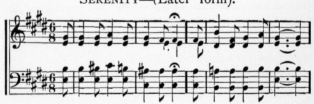

The older form of the tune is the more pleasing, and judged by the standard of the mere musician, the more artistic; but the simplest test will show that the later form is more suitable for congregational worship, because the average worshiper can follow it much more easily.

4. *Tunes containing unusual intervals are discouraged and others of a more simple structure are substituted.*

For example, Bishop Phillips Brooks' sweet song "O little town of Bethlehem" was formerly sung almost exclusively to Redner's *St. Louis*. It is a beautiful tune, but not easily mastered, especially by the children, who are the most generally interested. Other tunes have been suggested—two of them by Burnap, of which that in the *Presbyterian Hymnal*, *Ephratah* should be carefully compared with *St. Louis*. It is none the less beautiful without the same difficulties. Similar substitutions are presented in other cases.

5. *Tunes with too great a range for the average voice have been discarded.*

This rule has been severely followed. Some tunes found in former collections which went above

F in the treble, or to a corresponding low note in the bass, have been rejected by later compilers.   No illustrations are necessary.

From such an examination as the foregoing they that conduct the service of praise may be aided in determining the best tunes, and may formulate certain rules for their proper guidance.   The fundamental form of the best tune embraces the following features: common time, one syllable to each note, simple melody, and radical chords.   When there is a departure from these fundamental features great care must be exercised.   While it is neither wise nor desirable to limit our congregations to one class of tunes we owe it to our religion to be dignified and worshipful.   We do not wish to return to the monotony of the old psalm-tunes on the one hand, neither do we wish to encourage a collection of glees upon the other.   Some such simple rules, therefore, as the following may be adopted:

1.   *Tunes must be singable.*

Some little training ought to be expected in every congregation.   The best tunes are seldom mastered by hearing them a couple of times.   Both the pleasure and the profit of worship are enhanced in the attempt to render a worthy composition.   But tunes that can never be sung except by trained musicians ought not to be announced from the pulpit.   If they are embraced in a collection let them be relegated to the use of the choir.

2.   *Tunes should be selected.*

Our collections all embrace too many—both hymns

and tunes. It is almost as vicious to propose five hundred to a congregation as it was forlorn in the old Scotch days to be reduced to six. Every wise leader —in pulpit and choir—should have an idea of what constitutes a suitable *repertoire*. It should be large enough to avoid too frequent repetitions of the same tune in public worship and to give needed variety, and it should be small enough to be thoroughly familiarized by a congregation.

3. *Tunes should be adapted to the hymns.*

Sometimes the minister will need expert advice in this matter. Oftentimes the accent of the hymn and tune do not coincide—the beat comes in the wrong place. Thus a tune, excellent in itself, may seem wretched, because of its lack of adaptation. Sometimes also a good tune for one hymn is a poor tune for another. It is no sure sign that it suits the hymn that the compiler has placed it on the same page. Upon a certain occasion Doddridge's hymn beginning "Ye servants of the Lord" was announced. It is set in the Presbyterian Hymnal to *Laban*, on the opposite page. On the same page, however, is found a new copyright tune *Soldiers of Christ*, written for Wesley's hymn beginning with these words. Both tunes are short meter tunes; both are written in common time. They might seem to be interchangeable. Yet when the leader rejected *Laban* and started *Soldiers of Christ*, the effect was simply horrible. When asked why he selected this tune, he answered, "Because it is a better tune." There is no questioning his judgment—it *is* the better tune; but it is not better for this hymn, as a glance at the illustrations will show.

Laban

Ye   servants of   the Lord

Soldiers of Christ

Soldiers   of   Christ   arise

In the hymn "Ye servants of the Lord," the accent is on the second syllable (*Ser*); in "Soldiers of Christ, arise," the accent is on the first syllable, (*Sol*). In *Laban* the beat is right for the hymn; in *Soldiers* it is wrong. When, therefore, "Ye servants of the Lord" is sung to *Soldiers* the whole performance is out of joint. These hymns and their tunes cannot be transposed without confusion. Such cases are not infrequent, and when they occur it is a serious bar to good congregational music.

It is equally important also to adapt the tune to the sentiment of the hymn. Is the hymn joyful? Why sing it to a slow tune in a minor key? Is it serious and penitential? Why sing it to a glee?

For like reasons new tunes that are offered for old hymns deserve careful examination. They often give to the words new force and beauty.

4. *Tunes should be sung at the rate in which they are written.*

Some congregations have the bad habit of dragging; some habitually sing too rapidly. "Do you never sing a tune slowly?" asked the officiating minister in a series of Y. M. C. A. services. "Not often," was the reply, in substance, "the boys like to keep the thing hot!" But undue speed in sacred song is more reprehensible than undue slowness. Yet many congregations do not seem to know the difference between singing promptly and singing fast.

Some organists are to blame in this matter. They do not seem to understand that they should lead— they only follow. The chief reason why the organ should play the tune before it is sung is found in its interpretation. It shows the worshiper not only what the tune is, but how it is to be rendered. It sets the pace for the entire hymn and gives the shading at least for the first verse, and virtually says to the people, "Sing it in this way." This prelude ought to be such that, sung in any other way, even the best tune is injured—often well nigh ruined.

Other rules are already embodied in our notes concerning the changes which have been made in tunes; but they may be briefly added by way of recapitulation.

5. *Avoid tunes of florid counterpoint.*

6. *Avoid tunes containing difficult melodic intervals.*

7. *Avoid tunes of too great range.*

The staff indicates all the notes which can be sung by the average voice, and even such tunes as continue for several notes on the extremes should be barred.

In order to the determining of the best tunes something should be said in addition to the above with regard to the proper treatment of tunes.

What is it that makes a tune sacred or secular? This question is much in dispute. There may be some intrinsic differences, some characteristic elements whereby the two are differentiated, *but they have never been actually defined*. Critics have been very free in declaring "this is sacred" and "that is secular"; but so far they have not been able to give satisfactory reasons. We have many excellent hymn-tunes derived from old folk-songs, ballad-tunes, and operas; and so long as they do not suggest improper scenes and associations they are unobjectionable. Yet we all believe that there is a difference between sacred and secular music and every devout worshiper will insist upon maintaining it. What rule, then, can be given in this matter?

Without entering into the details of the controversy, it is enough for our purposes to show that very much—indeed almost everything—depends upon *treatment*. Into this a number of elements may enter, such as the key, the time, and the like. A tune which has a sacred character in one key may sometimes have a distinctly secular character in another; and therefore the leader should be cautious in transposing, as he is sometimes tempted to do. In like manner, a tune sung or played in fast time may be a jig, which in slow time is a serious melody.

There are certain tunes in some books which make excellent dance music by such easy manipulation. The reverse also may be accomplished and dance music be transformed into the serious.

A striking illustration is given in the following tune. Let it be played as written, without attempting to analyze it.

Probably not one person in ten will recognize this nor will any one object to it. It seems like dignified church music. Yet it is "Yankee Doodle!" Let it now be played rapidly in the ordinary key and mode, and the lesson of the illustration will be self-evident.

A similar illustration of the opposite tendency is given by Curwen in his *Studies in Worship Music* (first series), showing what may be done in the degradation of an eminently sacred tune, so that it may become emphatically secular.

Old Hundred in its original form is written as follows:

It is usually written to-day as follows:

There is no question that the present form is an improvement upon the past. But Dr. Curwen suggests that it may yet be written thus:

"This," he says, "is the *reductio ad absurdum* of the extreme chromatic style. The piece is intended as a caricature and the contrast of the harmonies with the old melody is ridiculous; but passages may be found in recent hymn-tunes every bit as bad."

There is a world of suggestion in these illustrations for him who would determine the best tunes. No arbitrary rules can be given. After all, a sanctified taste is the only arbiter—a *taste* which sets the spirit of pure worship above all else; a *sanctification* in which the sense of the truly beautiful is normally developed.

CHAPTER XX

GOSPEL SONGS AND SINGERS

The term "Gospel Songs" is applied to a certain class of sacred lyrics, chiefly of an evangelistic character, composed for use in popular gatherings of a heterogeneous character. The term is distinctly associated with the work of Mr. Moody, but is not confined to the music which he and his associates were chief in promoting. There has always been more or less music of this character, though in its modern form it was the distinct outgrowth and concomitant of that lay evangelism which came in with Mr. Moody. It must therefore be understood and interpreted in this connection. What lay evangelism was to the ordained ministry, the Gospel Song is to regular church music. If the right relations of the former be determined, so also will the right relations of the latter. If lay evangelism is a proper, permanent system, so also is the Gospel Song. If it is exceptional and temporary, so also is all that which necessarily goes with it as part and parcel of the same general movement.

The Gospel Song was born in Newcastle, England, in 1873, during the Moody and Sankey campaign.*

The evangelists had been using Philip Phillips' book, "Hallowed Songs," supplemented by such

* See W. R. Moody's *Life* of his father.

331

original compositions as Mr. Sankey supplied. Before long a demand was created for the publication of these original pieces and on the personal guarantee of Mr. Moody, Morgan & Scott published a pamphlet of sixteen pages, entitled "Sacred Songs and Solos," September 18, 1873. From time to time additions were made to the volume until the pamphlets were discontinued and their combined contents printed in a single book.

Meanwhile Mr. Moody's friend and lieutenant, Major D. W. Whittle, was conducting evangelistic meetings in America. Following Mr. Moody's example he, too, had associated with himself a musician much beloved by all who knew him—the lamented P. P. Bliss. These evangelists, still copying their leader, issued for Americans a book similar to that which Mr. Moody had prepared for the English, entitled "Gospel Songs"—the name by which such compositions were thereafter to be known. When Moody and Sankey returned in 1875 the double set of partners decided to combine their compositions in one book, which was accordingly published. Its title-page reads, "Gospel Hymns and Sacred Songs, by P. P. Bliss and Ira D. Sankey, as used by them in Gospel Meetings." This title has been maintained ever since. The book became immensely popular; many writers and composers joined together to extend its circulation, edition followed edition, and addition followed addition, until a No. 6 was finally reached. It was a series of hymn and tune books whose extent and popularity was unparalleled in the history of sacred song, and furnished a market for many other books of a similar kind by various authors.

There has been much debate concerning the character and place of these Gospel Songs. Some hold that they have done great mischief in vitiating the taste and corrupting the manners of worshiping congregations. Others insist as strenuously that they have been mightily influential in promoting true praise and positive devotion. The best judges seem to take a middle ground. Humphreys, in his *Evolution of Church Music*, says: "The character of piety they cultivate is somewhat superficial, not to say hysterical; but it cannot be denied that they stir the heart of the common throng. The refrains which are generally attached to them are readily caught by the ear; and that wave of emotional sympathy, easily started in large audiences, soon sweeps over the meeting, and choir and congregation are at once drawn into close accord. . . . . No doubt the participants are moved by profound and genuine feeling, yet we are unable to approve of the introduction of such melodies into church services." Curwen says, in his *Studies in Worship Music* (second series): "After the musician has vented his spleen upon this degenerate psalmody, an important fact remains: music in worship is a means, not an end, and we are bound to consider how far these tunes serve their end in mission work, which, after all, has not musical training for its object, so much as the kindling of the divine spark in the hearts of the worshipers. Without doubt these songs touch the common throng; they match the words to which they are sung and carry them.'' Professor Dickinson, in his *Music in the History of the Western Church*, takes somewhat different ground. He says: ''Those churches which rely mainly upon the Gospel Songs should soberly consider if it is profitable in the long run to maintain a standard of religious melody and verse far below that which prevails in secular music and literature. . . . . The church cannot afford to keep its spiritual culture out of harmony with the higher intellectual movements of the age. One whose taste is fed by the poetry of such masters as Milton and Tennyson, by the music of such as Handel and Beethoven, and whose appreciations are sharpened by the best examples of performance in the modern concert-hall, cannot drop his taste and critical habit when he enters the church door. The same is true in a modified degree in respect to those who have had less educational advantages. It is a fallacy to assert that the masses of the people are responsive only to that which is trivial and sensational.'' Yet he adds: ''In all this discussion I have had in mind the steady and more normal work of the church. Forms of song which, to the musician, lie outside the pale of art may have a legitimate place in seasons of special religious quickening. . . . . The revival hymn may be effective in soul-winning; it is inadequate when treated as an element in the larger task of spiritual development.''

These opinions of eminent experts should receive most respectful consideration; but as they furnish no adequate basis for mature judgment we may give attention to certain considerations which may help us to our own decisions.

1. As to the poetic material of these songs this much is certain—*they are not hymns.* If the definitions upon which we have already fixed, after the most careful study in hymnology, be accepted, we are compelled to deny them this quality. They are exactly what they are generally called, "Gospel Songs," and it was a mistake to change the title to "Gospel Hymns." This was probably done because in the first edition of the Bliss and Sankey book—as in subsequent ones, certain hymns of the church were added. But still the addition of the words "Sacred Songs" indicated their character.

This is not to say that there are no hymns among them. There are a few that we may call such. Yet even those that rank as hymns do not fully conform to the standard. They are such as Mrs. Hawks' "I need thee every hour" and Fannie Crosby's "Jesus, keep me near the cross." But the characteristic Gospel Song, like "There were ninety and nine," "Hold the fort," "Tell me the old, old story," and "What shall the harvest be?" is not a hymn in any proper sense of the word.

Some of these poems are very beautiful and effective, like "Almost persuaded," "Safe in the arms of Jesus," and "Rescue the perishing"; but a poem does not become a hymn by virtue either of its beauty or its effectiveness, any more than a drama becomes a sermon or a meditation a prayer for like reasons.

If we do not confine our words to certain meanings we open the way to endless confusion; and if we do not limit, even with some severity, the proper agency to its proper sphere, we invite abuses which it will be very hard to correct.   A hymn is one thing; a sacred song is another thing.   Each has its distinct character and uses.   Sometimes they overlap, but they never lose their distinct character and their appropriate purpose.   A true hymn is worship; a sacred song is not.   The ultimate objective point contemplated in a hymn is God himself; in a sacred song it is the hearer.   A hymn co-ordinates with prayer.   A sacred song co-ordinates with exhortation.   This consideration goes far in fixing the quality of the Gospel Song.   It also serves to determine its proper use.

2.   As to the quality of the music, so far as known to the author, *no one has ever claimed that it is up to the standard of our best hymn-tunes.*

Curwen reports that Mr. Sankey said to him in London, "I am no musician; indeed, I am no singer," and there was no reason for Curwen to disagree with him.   Mr. Sankey well knew his abilities and his limitations.   He claimed to be no more than he was.   Indeed, we may claim for him even more than he claimed for himself.   He was a great artist in his peculiar line—as much so as the technical virtuoso. He was an expert musical elocutionist, and communicated his skill to vast audiences whom he taught to sing simple melodies with unusual power.   He and his companions are sometimes called "singing evangelists.'' The term accurately describes them. Musicians they were not.

Take the four leading Gospel singers who were associated in the publication of the series of *Gospel Hymns*—Bliss, Sankey, McGranahan, and Stebbins— and judge their work by the only competent standard to which we are at liberty at present to appeal—the authoritative permanent collections. *In Excelsis* does not contain a single tune by any of them. The *Presbyterian Hymnal* selects but one out of the vast number which they have published — ''Evening Prayer,'' by George C. Stebbins. If this is any reflection upon their attainments it is to be laid at the door of these compilers. But really it is no reflection upon them in the line of their special work. It is only that their gifts and their compositions were abnormal; that is, aside from the permanent purposes and required grade of congregational worship. As the songs to which they set their music were not as a class hymns, so their melodies were not as a class hymn-tunes. Some particulars may be mentioned in which they are defective.

[1.] *The solo and chorus feature is objectionable.* Let us carefully guard this remark. Remember we are dealing with congregational music in stated worship. Our choirs render music in this form; but the Gospel Hymns are surely not intended for the use of the choir; and just as surely this style of music cannot be employed in the services of congregations that gather only once a week.

Moreover, many of these pieces are such simply

because of the musical incapacity of their authors.   It
requires much less skill to write a solo with a simple
refrain than to write a good hymn-tune.   The Gospel
singers were not masters of counterpoint and harmony.   They did the best they could.

[2.] *The imitation of the fugue-tune which prevails in these tunes is objectionable.*

It was a revival of the style of music which the
church had, by common consent, abandoned.   But it
was a very weak imitation.   The same limitations
which compelled the frequent use of solo and chorus
restricted the composers to that which was little else
that simple antiphony—mere repetition without real
accord.

These Gospel fugue-tunes were used with great
effect.   ''Deep answered unto deep'' in the emotions
which stirred the gathered multitudes.   The occasion
justified the means.   But sung in the times of ordinary religious feeling, and by smaller congregations,
these tunes are weak and meaningless.

[3.] *The structure of these tunes*—even when
the above features do not appear—*is loose and
prosaic.*

The better hymn-tunes introduce a fundamental
harmony with every beat; they move with stately
steps and majestic strength.   But the very simple
harmony of these Gospel tunes generally changes but
once in a bar.   The lower parts are little else than an
accompaniment to the soprano.   This gives a very
attenuated effect and renders them exceeding cheap
and common.

[4.] *But the most objectionable of all features has been the dissociation of old standard hymns from the stately tunes to which congregations have been accustomed to sing them, connecting them with trifling melodies.*

This has been done in some cases in which unwarranted liberties have not only been taken with the hymn, but the tune which has been joined to it is altogether out of keeping with the words.

So it has been with two of Watts' most serious hymns, "Alas, and did my Saviour bleed" and "Come we that love the Lord." In both cases a chorus has been added that we hesitate to characterize. The words of the chorus are a deep and pitiable decline and the music is almost sacrilege. This is a serious charge; but let the tunes be examined. How can any devout worshiper, before the cross of his crucified Saviour, take up such a strain as that which this Gospel chorus furnishes. It is inexplicable. The other chorus is simply tawdry, picnic music—unworthy of pilgrims to the heavenly city.

[5.] *The fact that a number of the standard hymns of the Church are always added to the editions of Gospel Songs is sufficient criticism.*

The exceptional and temporary are thus made to pass current; an imprimatur is attached to them. Frequently in Gospel meetings, at the very climax of interest the standard hymns were used. They compelled their own adoption. The audience had reached a spiritual frame to which they alone could give expression.

[6.] *The multiplication of these Gospel tunes settled into a mannerism.*

This would have been an evil, even if the mannerism itself was not specially obnoxious. The old
Scotch tunes, as we have seen, were good tunes; but
their inflexible style was disheartening. The error in
the case of the Gospel tunes was more serious. They
created a musical idiom which was undesirable. They
degenerated into a kind of musical "slang," which
while it was eminently sincere and pious, yet operated
to deprave the purity of praise as its counterpart in
language operates to deprave purity in speech. Many
a worshiper has been misled with regard to the qualities of a true hymn and the nature of sacred music.
Reverence degenerates into familiarity, and solemn
worship is displaced by musical harangue. The best
effects of these songs were therefore local and temporary.

And yet the Gospel Songs have had this permanent influence; they have served to suggest a better
use of the better tunes. Our congregational singing
has been much improved by observing their methods.
It might be still more improved, would we only heed
the lessons we have been taught. There is by far
too much sameness in our praise. We sing most of
our tunes at the same rate and with the same degree
of force. The minister and the choir care all too little
whether any attempt is made to interpret the sentiment of the hymn or to express the meaning of the
tune to which it is set. The great congregations

which sang the Gospel Songs were taught to "shade" them. There was always an interacting sympathy between choir and congregation, which we might continue to cultivate as well as not; and the variety introduced in the method of singing the same song might often be introduced in our church services—particularly at evening worship—to the greater pleasure and profit of the worshipers. If the same interest were taken in the proper rendering of our solid church tunes as was shown in the Gospel Songs their great and manifest superiority to the Gospel Songs would quickly and emphatically appear.

Notwithstanding what has been written above, the student ought not entirely to neglect the study of the Gospel Songs. After all, the proportion of good hymns and good tunes to the whole number does not reveal a great disparity to that displayed in those of the church at large. When we consider that some four hundred thousand hymns have been published, of which not more than five hundred are in common use, and not more than one hundred and fifty attain to the first rank, we should be somewhat sparing of our criticisms.

Still further, there are, and ever will be, occasions when the best Gospel Songs may be wisely and effectively employed, and the student should seek, by careful examination, an intelligent judgment of their respective merits. He is already sufficiently familiar with them. They have been so generally sung that we need not attempt a detailed notice of the authors, either of hymns or tunes. His judgment will be materially assisted by inquiring which have been received into permanent collections, and it should be matured by a review of the material, which his studies now render him more competent to pursue.

CHAPTER XXI

THE CO-ORDINATION OF PUBLIC PRAISE

We have been concerned, in this volume, with the acquisition of the best possible in Sacred Song. We have traced the history of the words and music in which it has been expressed. We have endeavored to reach some standard by which hymns and their tunes may be tried. We have sought to realize that the best words and the best music must be united, in order to the highest praise. And now we reach our final question: what relation should sacred song bear to all those other exercises which are conducted in the sanctuary? What is its proper co-ordination?

We assume that it will be admitted that the chief function of the congregation is worship. The service is properly called, "public worship"; the place in which it is held is a "house of worship." God, then, is the one supreme factor, and all acts of worship take character from their relation to him.

Omitting certain special acts of worship which are performed occasionally, the three chief features are the following: God speaks to us; we speak to God; and one speaks to us in the name of God. God speaks to us through his holy Word; we speak to God in prayer and praise; and the ordained minister speaks to us in God's name, in the sermon. Each of these

343

elements should receive its due proportion of attention, else the character of the service is impaired; none of them should be performed carelessly or hurriedly.

What attention, then, should public praise receive? Shall it be relegated to a select number of hired musicians? Shall it be introduced for mere relief or mere variety? Shall it be rendered in cheap and meaningless phrases?

The tendency of some modern congregations has been toward the exaltation of one single element of worship—the sermon. They have insisted that this be of the highest possible order, whatever the others might be. They have sought for men of eloquence and wit, who, before all else, should interest and please them. They have scarcely given a thought as to whether their preachers could lead them in prayer and praise. And so worship has suffered, and those elements of worship which are the most worshipful have suffered the most.

All this is wrong—sadly, terribly wrong. Let us do what we can to right it. Let us seek to install public praise in its proper place and to give it the attention which it demands. Therefore, let us determine its co-ordination.

1. *We first inquire what is the proper order of precedence in public worship.*

We answer as follows: (1) The reading of the Scriptures is first; (2) Sacred Song is second; (3) Prayer is third; (4) The Sermon is fourth.

Be it understood that this does not indicate the *amount* of attention that should be given to each; but

the *kind*.   Much more time may be given to the sermon than to any one of the other three; but its dignity
is not determined by the time consumed.   We will
never get the best outcome from our services until
we establish the correct order of precedence and
govern ourselves accordingly.

We cannot enter into any extended argument with
regard to the above.   We simply appeal to the Scriptures and to our best Christian sentiment and best
sense of truth and beauty.

The Scriptures are first.   They are the source of
all else—knowledge, authority, service, and salvation.
They demand for themselves, in repeated passages,
the first place.   They always held it in synagogue
days.   They ought to hold it still.   However brief
may be the passages read, the enunciation should be
distinct, the emphasis correct, and the manner serious.   The most important thing for the minister to
cultivate is Scripture reading; its judicious selection,
and proper interpretation; sacred elocution.   In the
long run, too, it is the most impressive feature of public worship.   "Thus saith the Lord" has an almight-
iness behind it.

*But next to the reading of the Scriptures is
public praise.*   The Scriptures themselves give it
second place.   They are full of it.   They indicate
very plainly that we are to praise before we pray;
that praise is to outlive prayer; and that we are
always to praise, even if prayer be intermittent.   The
book of Psalms contains much prayer; but more
praise.   "Praise ye the Lord!" may be called its

keynote. The worship of the heavenly hosts is praise; and the redeemed in heaven are represented in the book of Revelation as praising God in such lofty strains and mighty volume as ear hath never heard. Such being the case, how sadly has public praise been neglected and abused.

2. *Public praise is the most characteristic feature of the worship of the true God.*

Judaism of old, and now Christianity, is more particularly distinguished from the worship of all other religions by its praise than by any other element. We say "*the worship*" of other religions. We do not mean that this is its chief distinguishing feature in general; but that its public exercises are absolutely unique in this particular. In the public exercises of other religions there are sacrifices, forms of prayer, recitation from sacred books, and rude forms of the chant; but no such praise as ours. Judaism, as we have seen, was peculiar in this—its music was all religious. Even Pliny took particular note of the hymns of the early Christians. Christian song has always come like a heavenly message and with heavenly power to those who were unfamiliar with it. Savages have been disarmed by it; tumult quelled; enemies conciliated. Luther conquered through his songs. Wesley's hymns prevailed as effectively as the other Wesley's preaching. Confucius asked, "Desire ye to know whether a land is well governed and its people have good morals? "Hear its music." John Harrington Edwards* writes,

* "God and Music."

with great suggestiveness, "Infidelity has no hymnology"; and again, "Atheism, as a rule, is musically barren.   Unbelief does not praise."

The fundamental difficulty is that we do not realize how much sacred song is to us—what it means; what it expresses, and what it is capable of accomplishing.   And therefore it is pitiably neglected. We need to ponder such a message concerning music as this, from John Sebastian Bach, himself the greatest master of its structure: "Its final cause is none other than this, that it ministers solely to the honor of God and refreshment of the spirit; whereof, if one take not heed, it is no proper music, but devilish din and discord."

3. *The relation of public praise to preaching.*

Some ministers pay no attention to this matter, and most congregations have never been taught its need. To such the sermon is one thing, the music another thing, without inter-relation or inter-dependence. And so, some say they come to church for the sermon and some say they come for the music; whereas it ought to be that they could not possibly come for one without coming for the other.   Many ministers select their hymns with considerable care, that they may be in keeping with the sermon theme, but give no thought to the anthems.   The few that look after both have little concern beyond the unity of the service.

But there is a much closer and more important connection between public praise and preaching than is comprised in mere unity.   The congregation itself needs to be unified as well as the exercises in which it engages. It needs more than this—it needs to be stirred, uplifted, moved toward God. It is not a mere aggregation of individuals, each of whom imparts nothing to the others and receives nothing from them. It constitutes, or should constitute, a vitalized whole. When this is accomplished preaching exercises its greatest power, and even poor preaching is effective. The lay evangelists understood this. What would their services have been without their songs? How much easier it is to touch and move those souls already vibrant with holy emotion! What minister does not know the peculiar power he enjoys when he rises to address an audience that has just poured forth its voice in an inspiring hymn? And what minister does not know the added power of a hymn, following the sermon, in which its best lessons are repeated?

After all, why do we preach? What do we seek in a sermon? Are we intent upon anything that is not often sought and secured in a suitable sacred song?

What, then, if preaching and praise were properly co-ordinated, as they are not in these days! What if our preachers were better trained in sacred song? Would they not preach more persuasively? What if our congregation were taught to exalt worship? and praise, as its most important element? Would not their spiritual state be much more favorable to the reception of the message which the preacher brings to them from their God?

We need not prolong this discussion. The relation of praise to prayer, and of praise to the public reading of the Scriptures, has been suggested, and the reader can readily pursue the suggestions for himself. When once the proper co-ordination of public praise is established, recognized and acted upon, a brighter and more beautiful day will dawn upon the church, and heaven will be brought nearer to earth than ever it has been.

"The real function of music is spiritual." Its first and fundamental relations are to divine worship. Its highest ministry is to man's highest nature. Modern music is the creation of the Christian religion. Harmony is the peculiar property of the church. Herein is expressed the most distinctive and vital elements of our creed—the sovereignty of God, the brotherhood of man, the indissoluble union of the beautiful and the true, the elevation of mankind from sin to holiness through the Redeemer.

God speed the day when this shall be better understood and our worship maintain the right proportion between the spiritual, the practical, and the æsthetic.

"LET THE PEOPLE PRAISE THEE, O! GOD:
LET ALL THE PEOPLE PRAISE THEE."

Finis.

I. INDEX OF FIRST LINES

Of Hymns Quoted at Length

351

II. INDEX OF TUNES

III. GENERAL INDEX

Abbreviations, L. and W.—Life and Work

ABELARD, 31.

ADAMS, SARAH F., L. and W., 209.

ADDISON, JOSEPH, L. and W., 97.

AINSWORTH PSALTER, 64; example from, 69.

ALEXANDER, CECIL F., L. and W., 243.

ALEXANDER, REV. DR. J. W., translation of, 34.

ALFORD HENRY, L. and W., 227.

ALTENBURG, REV. J. M., "Battle hymn" of, 44.

AMBROSE, work in hymody, 25; in music, 258.

AMERICAN BOARD OF MISSIONS, 79.

ANATOLIUS, Bishop of Constantinople, 24.

ANATOLIUS, the hymn-writer, 24.

ANDREW, ST., OF JERUSALEM, 24.

"ANGLICAN HYMNOLOGY," quoted, 83, 95, 116, 124, 162, 180, 197.

ANGLICAN CHURCH MUSIC, 295.

ANGLO-GENEVAN PSALTER, 58.

ANTHEM, THE, 295.

ARIANS, hymns of the, 21.

ARMINIAN HYMNODY, 117, 144, 147.

ARNE, THOMAS A., 305.

ASAPH, 14.

AUBER, HARRIET, L. and W., 161.

AUGUSTINE, ST., 259.

BACH, JOHN SEBASTIAN, 273, 286, 292, quoted, 347.

BAPTIST MISSIONARY SOCIETY OF ENGLAND, 79, 149.

BARNBY, SIR JOSEPH, 312.

BAXTER, 75.

"BAY PSALMIST," 63.

BEDDOME, BENJAMIN, L. and W., 149.

"BELGIAN SCHOOL, THE," 278, 281.

"BENEDICITE, THE," 18.